Horse Trails

A relaxing trail ride

Horse Trails

The Traveler's Guide to Great Riding Getaways

By
Vicki Hogue-Davies

Irvine, California
A Division of BowTie, Inc.

Karla Austin, *Business Operations Manager*
Nick Clemente, *Special Consultant*
Barbara Kimmel, *Editor*
Allyn A. Salmond, *Interior Design*
Curtis Boyer, *Cover Design Concept*
Melody Englund, *Indexer*

Library of Congress Cataloging-in-Publication Data

Hogue-Davies, Vicki.
  Horse trails coast to coast : the traveler's guide to great riding getaways /
by Vicki Hogue-Davies.
      p. cm. — (Coast to coast)
  Includes bibliographical references and index.
  ISBN 1-931993-75-0 (alk. paper)
  1. Trail riding—United States—Guidebooks. 2. Trails—United States—
Guidebooks. 3. United States—Guidebooks. I. Title. II. Series.

  SF309.255H64 2006
  798.2'30973—dc22

2006001019

BowTie Press®
A Division of BowTie, Inc.
3 Burroughs
Irvine, California 92618

Printed and bound in Singapore
10 9 8 7 6 5 4 3 2 1

TABLE OF CONTENTS

Traversing the meadow

ACKNOWLEDGMENTS

*T*his book would not have been possible without the help of the national and state park and forest services; state and local horse councils, horse camps, and trail organizations; state and local tourism organizations and chambers of commerce throughout the country; and other groups and individuals associated with the locales featured in these pages. Thank you for patiently answering questions and graciously providing photographs.

Thanks also go to Barbara Kimmel, BowTie Press editor, for her diligent managing and editing of the book; April Balotro, BowTie Press editorial assistant, for helping check facts and fill in some of the blanks; Cindy Hale, *Horse Illustrated* columnist, for providing the appendix as well as a thoughtful critique of the book; and Moira Harris, *Horse Illustrated* editor, for her support and friendship. In addition, many of the images in the book came from professional horse, wildlife, and nature photographers. Their talent is impressive and use of their photographs is appreciated.

Researching and writing a book is a long and time-consuming process, and I owe many thanks to my good friend Mary Bestgen for her research assistance. Mostly, this book couldn't have been completed without the support and understanding of my husband, Tom, and son, Trevor. Thank you for being there.

Finally, it is the horses I have known who most inspired my interest in writing this book. From Velvet, the bay mare I spent many hours on the trail with as a child, to Roxy, the gray mare I ride today. Thank you.

Stopping to take in the majestic scene

INTRODUCTION

*D*oes life feel a whole lot sweeter to you when you're heading down the trail on the back of a horse? You're not alone. Recreational riding is the fastest growing sector of the horse industry. More and more people are packing up the truck or the RV, loading up the horses, and setting out to find that perfect trail-riding location. From taking daylong rides in local settings to weeklong trips in the backcountry—and everything in between—men, women, and children are saddling up in record numbers to hit the sometimes dusty, sometimes sandy, sometimes rocky, sometimes grassy, sometimes snow-covered, and always enjoyable trail.

This book introduces you to some of the best places to ride throughout the country. You'll find trails in state and national parks, forests, recreation areas, seashores, and more. It is not all inclusive, as it would take many massive volumes to discuss all the great horse trails available from coast to coast. Rather, the book will give you a snapshot into the wonderful and diverse places across America that are available for riding. If you're a seasoned trail rider, it may introduce you to a new riding location. If most of your riding takes place in the arena, perhaps it will inspire you to get out onto the open trail. If you're a horseless rider or planning to take a trip without your horse, you'll find horse rentals at or near many of these riding locales.

Before you visit any of these places, call ahead to make sure the riding venues, trails, and camps are still open to horses, as availability can fluctuate, especially in an era of budget cuts to state and federal recreation areas and increasing pressure on open spaces. Similarly, there are many Web sites, fees, and prices given in the book; remember that they are always subject to change. And don't forget to ask about the types of horse health paperwork that is required to enter the state, the venue you are visiting, or the camp or other accommodation where you will be staying. A negative Coggins is standard, but overall health certificates may also be required, especially for out-of-state horses.

If you're new to horse camping or would like tips on renting horses for trail rides, consult appendix 1. If you're looking for even more great places to ride, take a look at appendix 2; it lists agencies and Web sites that can help you find other horse trails throughout the country.

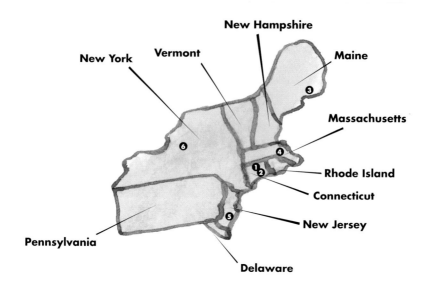

Northeast Map Legend

Connecticut
① Natchaug State Forest

② Pachaug State Forest

Maine
③ Acadia National Park

Massachusetts
④ Boston Area Trails

New Jersey
⑤ Allaire State Park

New York
⑥ Otter Creek Horse Trails

THE NORTHEAST

I n 1614, well-known British explorer Captain John Smith gave the name New England to the area that includes Maine, Rhode Island, Vermont, Massachusetts, New Hampshire, and Connecticut. In less than two hundred years, a new nation would be born, and most of these future states would be among its original colonies. Although the New England of today is much different from the New England of Smith's time, riders on the area's wilderness trails can still witness much of the original beauty that Smith found nearly four hundred years ago and can experience a taste of what this new land felt like to its early visitors.

When marveling at the majesty of Maine's rocky coast from horseback or enjoying the changing autumn leaves near Boston, it is easy to feel a sense of communion with the early explorers, British colonists, and other inhabitants who traveled via the horse. This feeling extends throughout the Northeast to the equestrian-friendly trails of New York's Adirondack and Catskill mountains and New Jersey's state parks and to the picturesque rail trails of Pennsylvania and Delaware. So pack up the truck or the RV, hitch up the trailer, load the horses, and hit the road to some great riding throughout the Northeast.

CONNECTICUT

NATCHAUG STATE FOREST

The Natchaug and Pachaug state forests are both located in eastern Connecticut. Pachaug borders Rhode Island, and Natchaug sits in the northeastern area of the state. Being the only two horse campgrounds in the state of Connecticut, Natchaug and Pachaug are the places to go for all serious trail riders.

The more than 12,900-acre Natchaug State Forest is covered with a variety of terrain, including woods, marshes, and river shores. *Natchaug* is a Native American word meaning "land between the rivers." It refers to the land at the junction of the Bigelow and Still rivers, which join to form the Natchaug River.

Civil War history buffs will find Natchaug State Forest of special interest. General Nathaniel Lyon, the first Union general killed in the Civil War, was born on what are now park grounds. Lyon is credited with saving Missouri for the Union at the battle of

Northeastern fall

Wilson's Creek, in 1861. A large stone fireplace and chimney from his birthplace still remains and is located less than a mile from the main entrance to the forest.

The extensive trail and dirt road system in the forest is used by equestrians, hikers, and mountain bikers. All trails are multiuse and open to horses except for the 5.6-mile Natchaug Trail, which is part of the 600-mile Blue-Blazed Hiking Trail System that runs through the state. It is open to foot traffic only.

Resting in Natchaug State Forest

Enjoying the day

PACHAUG STATE FOREST

At more than 24,000 acres, Pachaug State Forest is the largest state forest in Connecticut, spreading into six towns. The area that now makes up the state forest was once home to several Native American tribes, including the Pequot and Mohegan. The Pequot were virtually wiped out of the state during the Pequot War in 1637 in which British colonists and the Mohegans aligned in battle against the Pequots. This war was the first in the Northeast between Native Americans and British settlers and set the stage for European domination of the region.

The word *Pachaug* is derived from a Native American term for "bend or turn in the river." Rolling through the

Eastern Connecticut

forest's center is the Pachaug River, which runs from Beach Pond to the Quinebaug River.

With its abundant water supply, the area was once covered with farms, pasturelands, and mills. Miles of stone

SNAPSHOT - NATCHAUG STATE FOREST

Description: Natchaug State Forest is popular with equestrians for its miles of trails and horse camping. Equestrians share the trails with hikers and mountain bikers. The Silvermine Horse Camp, which marks the trailhead for several trails, is offered for overnight stays. Alcoholic beverages are allowed in the forest, and leashed pets are permitted. There are no other overnight stabling accommodations for horses in the area, so expect to camp or to visit for the day.

Open: Forest recreation areas are open year-round, 8:00 a.m. to sunset; other forest areas are open one-half hour before sunrise to one-half hour after sunset; the Silvermine Horse Camp is open mid-April through Columbus Day

Address: c/o Mashamoquet Brook State Park, RFD #1, Wolf Den Road, Pomfret Center, CT 06259

Phone: 860-928-6121

Web site: http://www.dep.state.ct.us/stateparks/forests/natchaug.htm

Getting there: From the east: Route 6 West to Route 198 in Chaplin, right on Route 198 North for approximately 5.4 miles. From the west: I-84 East to Exit 69, right on Route 74 East, at the end of Route 74, take Route 44 East to Route 198 South for 2.6 miles. From the north: Route 198 South, cross Route 44 and continue approximately 2.6 miles. From the south: Route 6 East to Route 198 North, continue north approximately 5.4 miles

Fees/permits: None

Horse rentals: None

Horse camping: Available in the forest

Trail conditions/level of difficulty: Easy to moderate

Northeastern vista

fencing, cellar holes, dams, and old mill sites remain as evidence of the land's early usage. Riders share forest trails with mountain bikers, and the forest has marked hiking trails. Fishing and boating are also popular in Pachaug's seven lakes. There are two areas to the forest: the Green Falls area and the Chapman area. Horse camping is available in the Chapman area.

MAINE

ACADIA NATIONAL PARK

Acadia National Park is located primarily on the shore of Mount Desert Island,

near the resort town of Bar Harbor, Maine. The park consists of more than 47,000 acres of rocky coastline, granite cliffs, marshes, glacier-carved lakes, dense woodlands, meadows, ocean shoreline, streams, lakes, and waterfalls. Its natural beauty and diversity have attracted people throughout the centuries, beginning with native peoples who called the area home at least 6,000 years ago. Over the years, explor-

Otter Cliffs at Acadia

ers, early settlers, artists, writers, conservationists, and tourists have all been inspired by the park's majesty.

For horse lovers, the park offers 45 miles of easy to moderate riding and carriage roads. The integrated carriage road system, listed on the National Register of Historic Places, was built by

SNAPSHOT - PACHAUG STATE FOREST

Description: Pachaug is popular for horseback riding, hiking, biking, fishing, and boating. Equestrians enjoy miles of riding trails and can camp overnight at the Frog Hollow Horse Camp in the Chapman area. Pick up a map of horse trails and of the camp at forest headquarters on Headquarters Road at the entrance to the forest. Leashed pets are permitted. There are no other overnight stabling accommodations for horses in the area, so expect to visit for the day or to camp at Frog Hollow.

Open: Campgrounds are open from mid-April to Thanksgiving; forest recreation areas are open 8:00 a.m. to sunset; other forest areas open one-half hour before sunrise to one-half hour after sunset

Address: Route 49, PO Box 5, Voluntown, CT 06384

Phone: 860-376-4075

Web site: http://www.dep.state.ct.us/stateparks/forests/pachaug.htm

Getting there: To Chapman area, from the south: I-395 North to Exit 85, right onto Route 138 East, continue 9 miles, then left onto Route 49 North; the forest entrance is 1 mile on the right. From the north: I-395 South to Exit 85, left onto Route 138 East, continue 9 miles then left onto Route 49 North; the forest entrance is 1 mile on the left.

Fees/permits: $11 per night campsite fee

Horse rentals: None

Horse camping: Available in the forest

Trail conditions/level of difficulty: Easy

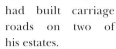

John D. Rockefeller Jr. specifically for use by horses and horse-drawn carriages. An avid horseman and recreational carriage driver himself, Rockefeller recognized that one day automobiles would replace horse-drawn carriages in America's national parks. He desired a place where carriages could continue to travel undisturbed by honking horns and speeding cars. Rockefeller worked with the National Park Service from 1913 to 1940 to create the original 57-mile interconnecting system of horse and carriage roads. Following completion of the roads, he donated them to Acadia National Park, although he continued to pay workers to ensure that the roads were well maintained.

Stone bridge at Acadia

In building the roads, Rockefeller integrated them with existing hiking paths in the area, and he kept the roads separate from the shorter auto road that he also built in the park. The approximately 16-foot-wide carriage roads are broken stone roads, which were common to the time. Rockefeller's design also took into account the existing landscape. Rather than change the landscape to accommodate the roads, he aligned the roads to follow the land's contours and to take optimum advantage of the views. He used retaining walls to preserve hillsides and to save trees. He planted native vegetation on the sides of roads to help blend the roads into their surroundings. Many of the road-building techniques he used came from his own father, Standard Oil founder John D. Rockefeller Sr., who had built carriage roads on two of his estates.

In recent years, the roads have undergone extensive rehabilitation, ensuring that Rockefeller's beautiful legacy is maintained. New surface materials were applied to replace surfaces washed away over the years, woody vegetation was removed, and drainage systems were restored. Once-closed areas of the roads have been reopened, again greeting horseback and carriage riders with sweeping views as in years past.

Today, equestrians share the roads with bicyclists and pedestrians. The wide roads wind throughout the park, bounded by large granite stones serving as guardrails and connected by sixteen stone bridges that span streams, waterfalls, roads, and cliffs. Road intersections feature signposts that help trail users find their way through the park.

Wildwood wagon ride

Acadia National Park

Horseless camping is permitted at two designated campgrounds on the island: Seawall and Blackwoods. Horse owners who enjoy camping shouldn't be disappointed, though, as Wildwood Stables, located inside the park, offers overnight camping and stabling as well as carriage rides. Horse owners not wishing to camp can stay at local hotels. Another stable in the area, Eochaidh Stables (pronounced "yawk-hee"), provides overnight horse boarding. That stable, which currently does not have ride-on access to the park, is a short trailer ride away. If you are leaving your horse behind or are a horseless rider, Eochaidh also rents horses for use on the stable's private trails.

Horseback riding is allowed as long as weather permits, although in-

park stabling facilities close in October. Many of the roads are closed in winter, when the average annual snowfall is approximately 60 inches. Other outdoor activities at the park include kayaking, hiking, and bird watching. The Thompson Island Information Center, located on the causeway at the head of Mount Desert Island on Route 3, is open mid-May to mid-October;

Acadia's rocky shoreline

SnapShot - Acadia National Park

Description: The mountains meet the sea at Acadia National Park, on Mount Desert Island in Maine. Bring your own horse for riding on approximately 43 miles of well-marked carriage trails, or take a carriage tour. Horse boarding facilities and owner camping are available inside the park.

Open: Year-round

Address: PO Box 177, Eagle Lake Road, Bar Harbor, ME 04609

Phone: 207-288-3338

Web site: http://www.nps.gov/acad

Getting there: Six hours from Boston: I-95 North to Augusta, Maine, then Route 3 East to Ellsworth and on to Mount Desert Island. From Bangor, Maine: Route 1A East to Ellsworth, then Route 3 to Mount Desert Island

Fees/permits: Admission is $20 for a seven-day pass

Horse rentals: Available locally for guided rides on private trails

Horse camping: None; camping available at Wildwood Stables

Trail conditions/level of difficulty: Easy to moderate

Hulls Cove Visitor Center, off Route 3 in Hulls Cove, is open from mid-April through October; the Park Headquarters and Winter Visitor Center, on Route 233 near Eagle Lake, are open all year except Thanksgiving Day, Christmas Eve, Christmas Day, and New Year's Day. Acadia Visitor Online (http://www.acadia-national-park.com) provides more information on lodging, restaurants, and activities in the park.

MASSACHUSETTS

BOSTON AREA TRAILS

Paul Revere's famous midnight ride, immortalized in verse by Henry Wadsworth Longfellow, took him through miles of beautiful and lush Boston countryside. Employed by the Boston Committee of Correspondence and the Massachusetts Committee of Safety as an express rider, Revere was called upon on April 18, 1775, to warn Samuel Adams and John Hancock that

Statue of Paul Revere

British troops were marching to arrest them. On a horse he borrowed from his friend Deacon John Larkin, Revere galloped through the night, alerting each house along his route that the British were coming, finally arriving in Lexington at midnight and successfully warning the two men. Although the great patriot wouldn't recognize the Boston area of today, horse enthusiasts can still capture the flavor of the countryside of Revere's time when visiting the city that played such a significant part in this country's battle for independence.

No trail riding is available in the city itself—only park rangers and mounted city police travel via horseback in Boston—but guided western-

Crossing a meadow

style trail rides on 2,000 scenic acres are offered nearby. Horse owners can access these trails and park their rigs at Bobby's Ranch in Acton, forty minutes northwest of Boston (6 Durkee Lane, Acton, MA 01720;978-263-7165;http://www.bobbysranch.com. The ranch offers guided ridgetop trail rides throughout the year for beginning through advanced riders. Much of the land—1,500 acres—is accessible to riders without ever having to cross a road. The ranch, surrounded by rolling hills, ponds, streams, and forest, was incorporated in 1972 by owner Bob Haigh. It is a family ranch, with three generations involved in its operation. In addition to providing rental horses, Bobby's Ranch allows horse owners wishing to bring in their own horses to ride the trails to park horse trailers on the property. Open year-round, trail rides leave on the hour from 9:00 a.m. to one hour before dusk every day except Tuesday. There is no overnight stabling available at the ranch, however; it's for day use only.

Bobby's Ranch has 2,000 acres to ride on and thirty rental horses, most of

Horse and carriage sign

them quarter horses or quarter horse crosses, chosen for their willingness to please and their quiet temperaments. Riders are matched with horses suitable to their stated riding experience. Once on the trail, licensed riding instructors acting as guides assess riding ability and split riders into two groups: beginners and experienced equestrians looking for a faster pace for hour-long rides.

Heading home

Horse rentals are $25 per hour on weekdays and $30 per hour on weekends and holidays.

Bobby's Ranch also offers wagon and sleigh rides and western riding lessons. It is the headquarters for the Massachusetts Association of Stable Owners, Operators and Instructors and, according to Haigh, is the only stable in the state to have its own mounted search and rescue team. Reservations are highly recommended and are especially important during the scenic fall months.

Additionally, approximately 20 miles west of Boston is The Arabian Horse Inn (see Where to Stay & Stable), an 1880 Queen Anne Victorian farmhouse. The bed-and-breakfast inn is located on 9 wooded acres and, as suggested by the name, is home to several Arabian horses. Guests can bring their own horses and stable them on the property. The inn has its own trails for riding and offers both trail and carriage rides to guests. Other "horsepower" that visitors to Boston can partake of includes horse carriages that travel the city's streets and are available for hire.

Scenic Northeast

SNAPSHOT - BOSTON AREA TRAILS

Description: Although no riding is allowed in the city itself, there are plenty of trails in the vicinity to enjoy, especially from Bobby's Ranch. And there are many historic inns and hotel chains offering lodgings in Boston and its environs. Area towns such as Concord, Lexington, and Sudbury also have places to eat that offer a variety of fare.

Open: Area trails are open year-round

Address: Greater Boston Convention and Visitors Bureau, Two Copley Place, Suite 105, Boston, MA 02116

Phone: 888-SEE-BOSTON

Web site: http://www.bostonusa.com

Getting there: Located in eastern Massachusetts, 4 miles southwest of Boston's Logan International Airport (BOS)

Fees/permits: None; riding is not allowed in the city

Horse rentals: Available nearby

Horse camping: None

Trail conditions/level of difficulty: Rides at Bobby's Ranch are geared to match each rider's ability; easy trails at Arabian Horse Inn are due to be complete in fall 2006

GEORGE WASHINGTON—AMERICAN PATRIOT AND HORSEMAN

As a gentleman farmer from Virginia, George Washington felt exploited by the British and hampered by their regulations. A member of the Virginia House of Burgesses, he firmly yet calmly voiced his resistance to British rule; and as a delegate from Virginia, he was elected commander in chief of the Continental Army when the Second Continental Congress assembled in Philadelphia in May 1775. A couple of months later, he took command of his troops and embarked on a war that would last six years and would come to be known as the American Revolution. In peacetime and wartime, the patriot who would later be nicknamed father of his country depended on his horses.

Washington, who was known as one of the finest horsemen of his time, maintained a large stable at his home in Mount Vernon, Virginia. His horses included Arabians, some having bloodlines from the famed Godolphin Arabians, as well as Andalusians and Chincoteague ponies. However, because few formal breeds were established at the time, most of Washington's horses were listed in his records as simply "carriage horse" or "plow horse" with the gender, age, and color noted. He participated in horse breeding, racing, training, trading, hunting, and carriage driving, and he also used his horses to tread wheat and do other work on his plantation. (Today, visitors to Mount Vernon can still see horses treading wheat as part of the George Washington: Pioneer Farmer exhibit.) Some of his stallions were named Samson, Steady, Leonidas, and Magnolia. He also had a horse named Traveller, just as the famous Civil War General Robert E. Lee did. In fact, Light Horse Harry Lee, Robert E. Lee's father, was a close friend of Washington's, and Washington traded his prized Arabian, Magnolia, to the elder Lee for 5,000 acres of land in the Kentucky territory.

Although Washington was extremely fond of horses, he was also a pragmatist when it came to farming. Following the Revolutionary War, he began breeding mules for their strength, sure-footedness, and endurance to replace the horses in his fields. After fifteen years of breeding mules, he had fifty-eight of them. He is credited with helping promote the widespread use of the mule in the United States.

During the Revolutionary War, Washington rode several horses, but two of the most well known were Blueskin and Nelson, who were with him throughout the war. Although he is often depicted astride a light gray horse during the war, as in the painting *The Prayer at Valley Forge*, created for the country's bicentennial, his favorite mount while in action was Nelson, a sorrel. Blueskin is thought to have been light gray.

Washington's concern for his horses was exemplified by his care of them. John Hunter, a visitor to Mount Vernon, noted that following dinner they visited Washington's stables, where they saw the two old warhorses, Blueskin and Nelson, then twenty-two. "The General makes no manner of use of them now," Hunter wrote. "He keeps them in a nice stable, where they feed away at their ease for their past services." Another story claims that Washington ordered that the teeth of his horses be brushed every morning. Perhaps the nation's first president, who had only one tooth left when he was inaugurated, did not want to repeat his own dental mistakes with his beloved horses.

Reenactment at Valley Forge

NEW JERSEY

ALLAIRE STATE PARK

Allaire State Park is located in Monmouth County off the Jersey Shore. The 3,086-acre park and the historic village in the park are named for James P. Allaire, who owned and operated the bog-iron foundry there in the nineteenth century. Bog iron, believed to be the earliest iron ore mined by humans, comes from ore nodules that form within peat soils.

The foundry, which developed into a complete and self-contained village, was originally known as the Howell Works after Benjamin B. Howell, who founded it in 1821. Allaire, a well-known steam engine manufacturer in his time, purchased the approximately 5,000-acre property a year later and rapidly expanded the business, which employed five hundred people in its heyday. It was economically sustaining—producing cauldrons, pots and pans, screws, pipes, and more—until the middle of the nineteenth century, when the production of superior grade iron from Pennsylvania rendered bog iron obsolete. Several buildings remain, however, to give present-day visitors a little taste of what life was like in an early nineteenth-century manufacturing town. Some of the original buildings still standing are the blacksmith

Allaire State Park

shop, the general store, the carpenter's shop, the manager's house, the foreman's house, and a church. A row house where workers lived is now the Visitor Center and Museum.

Of special interest to horse lovers are the carriage house and the stables. The present carriage house was erected in 1833 to house company vehicles and to be used as a stagecoach depot. By this time, the village was a major transportation center with several stage lines running through it. Today's stable is a re-creation built on the foundation of the original mule barn. The original stables housed draft horses and carriage horses, mules, and oxen belonging to the Howell Works Company, the Allaire family, and the workers who could afford the animals. It also served as a boarding stable for visitors to the town.

Although equestrians will be fascinated by the history of the village, they'll most appreciate the park for its

Gazebo at Allaire

Allaire's Carpenter's Shop

Canoeing, kayaking, and fishing are popular pursuits on the Manasquan River, which winds through Allaire Park and flows east to the Atlantic Ocean. The river's floodplain provides habitat for birds and other wildlife as well as more than two hundred species of trees, plants, and wildflowers, so nature lovers will find much to see. The Nature Interpretive Center conducts tours daily during summer. Other items of interest at the park include the Pine Creek Railroad.

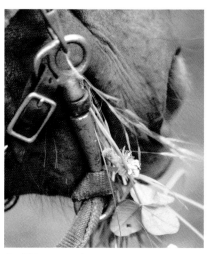

miles of looping trails that pass through thick pine and oak forest. Equestrians need only share the park's trails with hikers, mountain bikers, and the occasional deer or other animal. The multiuse orange trail is 16.5 miles long. Riders bringing their own horses will find trailheads off of Route 524 and off of Hospital Road. Open gravel lots at the two locations allow trailer parking.

Grabbing a snack

SNAPSHOT - ALLAIRE STATE PARK

Description: Here you can experience day riding on miles of multiuse trails in a 3,000-plus-acre park. Although there are more than fifty campsites in the park for overnight stays, camping with horses is not permitted. Overnight stabling is available within an hour's drive of the park. If you've left your horse at home, head to Circle A Riding Stables (116 Herbertsville Road, Howell, NJ 07731; 908-938-2004) for guided trail rides.

Open: Year-round; park hours are from 8:00 a.m. to 8:00 p.m. in summer, 8:00 a.m. to 6:00 p.m. in spring and fall, and 8:00 a.m. to 4:00 p.m. in winter

Address: Box 220, Route 524, Farmingdale, NJ 07727

Phone: 732-938-2371

Web site: http://www.state.nj.us/dep/parksandforests/parks/allaire.html

Getting there: Take Exit 98 from the Garden State Parkway or Exit 31B off of I-195.

Fees/permits: Admission is $5 on weekends for autos entering through the park's main entrance; no fee for horse trailer parking at trailheads

Horse rentals: Available locally

Horse camping: None; stabling is available locally

Trail conditions/level of difficulty: Moderate

A cool drink

NEW JERSEY LOVES HORSES

There is no doubt horses are held in high esteem in New Jersey. The horse adorns the state seal and flag, it is the official state animal, and it is recognized by the state with its own official month. The United States Equestrian Team, which is the nonprofit organization supporting equestrian sports in the United States, has its headquarters in New Jersey.

New Jersey's founding fathers included the horse on the state seal and flag because of their high regard for the noble animals. One of the five symbols in the seal, a knight's helmet and horse-head crest, represents New Jersey's independence as a state. The forward-facing knight's helmet, topped by the horse's head, denotes sovereignty for a state that governs itself. The horse also represents speed and strength. In 1977, two hundred years after the state seal was designed, Governor Brendan Byrne named the horse the state's animal, signing the horse's official place into law at the Sussex County Farm and Horse Show. Two New Jersey boys, in the fifth and eighth grades, had helped drive the effort to make the horse the state's official animal. The horse's placement in the role acknowledges its importance to the agriculture and economy of the state. Slightly more than twenty years later, in 1998, Governor Christine Todd Whitman proclaimed June the Month of the Horse. She noted that the annual observance would give residents a chance to focus on the state animal and the recreational, economic, and scenic benefits provided by the horse industry throughout the state.

Visitors will quickly recognize the horse's high status in New Jersey once they exit the infamous Jersey Turnpike and travel the aptly named Garden State's bucolic back roads. According to recent figures (http://www.horsecouncil.org/statistics.htm), there are approximately eighty-three thousand horses in the state, and several thousand horse-related facilities. The national horse industry has a $1.1 billion annual impact on the New Jersey economy. And Monmouth County, where Allaire State Park is located, ranks number one in New Jersey in the number of horses and the amount of land devoted to them.

English riders on trail

NEW YORK

OTTER CREEK HORSE TRAILS

Made just for horsemen and horsewomen and their trusty steeds, the Otter Creek Horse Trails—managed by the New York Department of Environmental Conservation—are located about 50 miles north of Utica, New York. This premier horseback riding location in New York State is made up of approximately 65 miles of interlocking trails located on the Independence River Wild Forest Unit of the Adirondack Forest Preserve and on the Independence

Otter Creek trails

River and Otter Creek State parks on the western border of Adirondack Park. Avid riders with time to spare can easily spend a week here to explore the area's many well-marked trails.

Winding through forests and flatlands, well-maintained, mostly sandy trails access, follow, or cross several bodies of water, including Adirondack ponds; Independence River; and Otter, Little Otter, Beaver Meadow, Chase, Burnt, and Crooked creeks. The bridges for water crossings are sturdy and safe for horses. Riding is easy to moderate, although the sandy composition of the trails can tire your horse after a long day's ride, so it's wise to ensure that your mount is used to riding in sandy soil or to take it slowly, gradually building up to longer rides. Be sure to stay on the trails and not wander onto private roads, as many private landowners in the area do not appreciate horses and riders on their properties. You don't want to have a run-in with an irate property owner, who can be angrier and scarier than the occasional black bears also found in the area.

And speaking of wildlife, it is abundant on this picturesque trail system. Bears, deer, foxes, coyotes, wild turkeys, grouse, and wild fowl highlight the natural beauty of this trail system. For visitors wishing to catch their fresh fish dinners, the aforementioned creeks—Otter, Little Otter, Beaver Meadow, and Crooked—as well as Payne Lake and Pitcher Pond contain brook trout. Catspaw Lake and Upper Chases Lake have pickerel, brown bullhead, and pumpkinseeds swimming in their depths. And Little Otter Lake offers a variety of choices to the fishing enthusiast, with brown and brook trout, pumpkinseeds, and brown bullheads.

A view of the water

At the hitching rail

Otter Creek provides a horse assembly area with trailhead parking and camping. The primitive campground has one hundred covered tie stalls, water, toilet facilities, and mounting platforms. There is no electricity at the campsite, and water is shut off after Columbus Day and turned back on in April. Campsites are available on a first-come, first-served basis. Visitors must self-register when entering the park; parking is not available at all locations.

White-tailed deer

SnapShot - Otter Creek Horse Trails

Description: The Otter Creek Horse Trails system in northern New York State offers days of riding on 65 miles of interlocking trails designed and marked specifically for horses. There are no horse rentals available, but horse camping is allowed. Lodging facilities (see Where to Stay & Stable) that can accommodate both riders and horses are nearby, with direct access to the trails.

Open: Year-round, but services such as water are available only from April through Columbus Day because of freezing weather

Address: 7327 State Route 812, Lowville, NY 13367

Phone: 315-376-3521

Web site: http://www.dec.state.ny.us/website/dlf/publands/stateforests/reg6/ottercreek.html

Getting there: Located approximately 48 miles north of Utica, New York, and 7 miles east of Route 12: Take NYS Route 12 to the hamlet of Glenfield, take Greig Road East, turn left onto Pine Grove Road, proceed 1.2 miles to Chases Lake Road, turn right, and continue 3.4 miles to the trailhead parking lot on the right.

Fees/permits: No fees to camp or ride trails

Horse rentals: None

Horse camping: Available along the trails and at trailheads; stabling is available locally

Trail conditions/level of difficulty: Easy to moderate; sandy

OTHER GREAT PLACES TO RIDE

Delaware

Lums Pond State Park
1068 Howell School Road, Bear, DE 19701
302-368-6989
http://www.destateparks.com/lpsp/lpsp.asp
The 1,790-acre park is built around the largest freshwater pond in Delaware. It allows horses on its trails and has an equestrian center on site. Horse rentals are available at the center.

New Hampshire

Bear Brook State Park
Route 28, Allenstown, NH 03275
603-485-9874
http://www.nhstateparks.org/ParksPages/BearBrook/
BearBrk.html
Bear Brook, located in the southeastern area of the state, is the largest developed state park in New Hampshire. Forty miles of shared-used trails meander through the heavily forested park.

New Jersey

Wharton State Forest
4110 Nesco Road, Hammonton, NJ 08037
609-268-0444 or 609-561-0024
http://www.state.nj.us/dep/parksandforests/parks/
wharton.html
This state forest in southern New Jersey is the largest single tract of land in the New Jersey park system. It measures 114,793 acres and features miles of horse trails and camping.

New York

Brookfield Trail System
2715 State Highway 80, Sherburne, NY 13460
607-674-4036
http://www.dec.state.ny.us/website/dlf/publands/stateforests/reg7/brookfield.html
This trail system in central New York consists of 130 miles of trails over 13,000 acres of state forests. There is an assembly and camping area that accommodates 150 horses and campers.

Pennsylvania

Allegheny National Forest
PO Box 847, Warren, PA 16365
814-723-5150
http://www.fs.fed.us/r9/forests/allegheny/recreation/
horseback_riding
You'll enjoy riding on hundreds of miles of primitive roads as well as blazing your own cross-country trails. There are no developed horse camps here, but dispersed camping is allowed. Guides and outfitters are available for hire.

Ohiopyle State Park

PO Box 105, Ohiopyle, PA 15470
724-329-8591
http://www.dcnr.state.pa.us/stateparks/
parks/ohiopyle.aspx
This gateway to the Laurel Mountains encompasses more than 19,000 acres of rugged beauty. Equestrians share trails with mountain bikes. A fenced paddock and water are available at the parking area. Horse rentals are available.

Rhode Island

Lincoln Woods State Park

2 Manchester Print Works Road, Lincoln, RI 02865
401-723-7892
http://www.riparks.com/lincoln.htm
Enjoy riding on 10 miles of wooded bridle trails at this 627-acre park. Open sunup to sundown. Horse rentals are available.

Vermont

Merck Forest and Farmland Center

PO Box 86, Route 315 Rupert Mountain Rd., Rupert, VT 05768
802-394-7836
http://www.merckforest.com
The mission of the center is to teach and demonstrate the benefits of innovative, sustainable forest and farmland management. There are miles of hiking and riding trails in this 3,000-acre forest.

Otter Creek campground

NORTHEAST TRAVEL SECTION

IF YOU ARE TRAVELING WITHOUT YOUR HORSE, OR IF YOUR HORSE IS BOARDED SAFELY AT A STABLE, ENJOY THE SITES IN THE NEIGHBORING TOWNS. BELOW, YOU'LL FIND A MILEAGE CHART LISTING THE DISTANCES BETWEEN THE TRAILS AND ALL THE AREAS DISCUSSED IN THE FOLLOWING TRAVEL SECTION. THE AREAS CLOSEST TO THE TRAILS ARE INDICATED BY AN **X**. FOR AREAS WHERE NEITHER STABLING NOR HORSE RENTALS ARE AVAILABLE, NO SIGHTSEEING OPTIONS ARE LISTED.

COAST TO COAST	Arcadia Wildlife Management Area, R.I.	Air Line State Park, Conn.	Bar Harbor, Maine	Boston, Mass.	Concord, Mass.	Freehold, N.J.	James L. Goodwin Sate Forest, Conn.	Old Forge, N.Y.	Pachaug State Forest Area, Conn.	Stone Cavern, N.J.	Thendara, N.Y.
Acadia National Park (Maine)	375 miles	370 miles	**X** *	280 miles	280 miles	540 miles	355 miles	585 miles	365 miles	550 miles	585 miles
Allaire State Park (N.J.)	215 miles	205 miles	550 miles	275 miles	275 miles	**X** 15 miles	215 miles	350 miles	210 miles	**X** 25 miles	345 miles
Boston Area Trails (Mass.)	85 miles	95 miles	280 miles	**X** *	**X** 15 miles	260 miles	85 miles	310 miles	95 miles	270 miles	310 miles
Natchaug State Forest (Conn.)	**X** 40 miles	**X** 20 miles	340 miles	70 miles	70 miles	215 miles	**X** *	275 miles	**X** 30 miles	225 miles	275 miles
Otter Creek Horse Trails (N.Y.)	320 miles	290 miles	590 miles	315 miles	310 miles	340 miles	290 miles	**X** 35 miles	310 miles	350 miles	**X** 40 miles
Pachaug State Forest (Conn.)	**X** 15 miles	**X** 20 miles	365 miles	95 miles	90 miles	195 miles	**X** 30 miles	305 miles	**X** *	205 miles	300 miles

*The area to visit is the same as or is within 10 miles of the trails.

MUST SEE / MUST DO

CONNECTICUT

NATCHAUG STATE FOREST AREA

Riders visiting Natchaug State Forest with their horses will find other trails in the area for day riding. The multiuse, linear **Air Line State Park Trail** stretches for 50 miles through the eastern portion of the state from East Hampton to Putnam. A section near Natchaug runs for 8 miles beginning at the Hampton town line east of the forest and ending at the town of Putnam. The trail goes through the small **James L. Goodwin State Forest**, south of Natchaug, which offers additional riding on a marked trail around Goodwin Pond. These trails are open from dawn to dusk, and there are no fees for using them. For more information on horseback trails in Connecticut, contact the Department of Environmental Protection, Mashamoquet Brook State Park, RFD #1, 147 Wolf Den Road, Pomfret Center, Connecticut 06259; 860-928-6121; http://www.dep.state.ct.us/stateparks/recinfo/horseback.htm.

Riding in the woods

PACHAUG STATE FOREST AREA

Another great riding location that is found near Pachaug State Forest, just across the border in Rhode Island, is the **Arcadia Wildlife Management Area** (RI Department of Environmental Management, Division of Forest Environment, Arcadia Headquarters, 260 Arcadia Road, Hope Valley, RI 02832; 401-539-2356;

Arcadia WMA

http://www.dem.ri.gov). The wildlife area has approximately 40 miles of gently rolling trails that cross streams and wind through pine, beech, and oak forests. There is also a horse camp and staging location called the LeGrande Horsemens Area. The area is open year-round; there are no fees, but permits are required to camp.

MAINE

ACADIA NATIONAL PARK AREA

When visiting Acadia National Park, be sure to spend some time in the charming town of **Bar Harbor**, once a playground of the nineteenth-century rich and famous, including the Vanderbilts and Joseph Pulitzer. The town was originally incorporated as Eden in 1796 but was renamed in 1918 for the long sand bar at the head of the harbor.

Today, you can watch the

Lighthouse

boats come into port or take a boat or kayak ride yourself to see the view of Acadia's cliffs from the ocean. There are many different boat tour and kayak companies in this popular town as well as bike and bus tour companies, so contact the **Bar Harbor Chamber of Commerce** or visit its Web site for more information (93 Cottage Street, Bar Harbor, ME 04609; 207-288-5103;

http://www.visitbarharbor.com). When your sea legs are tired and you're yearning for solid ground again, check out Bar Harbor's galleries, boutiques, and other quaint shops. Most of them can be found in the village center, on Main, Cottage, and West streets, and some are located along Mount Desert Street (Route 3).

For a more cultural experience, visit the **Abbe Museum** downtown to learn about the native inhabitants of the area (26 Mount Desert Street, Bar Harbor, ME 04609; 207-288-3519; http://www.abbemuseum.org). The museum is closed from January through April, open daily in summer, and open October 20 through December 23, Thursday through Saturday from 9:00 a.m. to 5:00 p.m.; admission rates are $6 for adults and $2 for children six through fifteen. There is also a **smaller**

Abbe Museum

Abbe Museum inside Acadia National Park at Sieur de Monts Spring off of Route 3. It is open daily in the summer and fall seasons from 9:00 a.m. to 4:00 p.m. and closed in winter and spring. Admission rates are $2 for adults and $1 for children. Another museum you'll enjoy visiting in Bar Harbor is the **Bar Harbor Historical Society Museum** (33 Ledgelawn Avenue, Bar Harbor, ME 04609; 207-288-3807 or 207-288-0000; http://www.barharborhistorical.org). Listed on the National Register of Historic Places, it features a collection of photographs, pamphlets, and other

information about the town's beginnings and background. Admission is free, and it is open from 1:00 p.m. to 4:00 p.m., Monday through Saturday from June through October. During winter and spring, call for an appointment.

MASSACHUSETTS

BOSTON AREA

When you are finished riding the Boston area trails, there are many, many things to see in the area. In addition to colonial sites and places associated with the country's battle for independence, homes of several literary giants are open for touring.

The **Minuteman National Historic Park**, in Concord (174 Liberty Street, Concord, MA 01742; 978-369-6993/Fax: 978-318-7800; http://www.nps.gov/mima), commemorates the earliest battles of the American Revolution through preservation of the sites, lands, and structures associated with the fighting of April 19, 1775. On that day, British soldiers and American

Minuteman National Park

minutemen skirmished along a 22-mile stretch of road running from Boston to Concord. The park, which was created in 1959 and consists of 900 acres, winds along original segments of that road. Educational demonstrations and interpretive programs teach visitors about the Revolution's earliest days.

Additionally, The Wayside, once home at separate times to literary greats Nathaniel Hawthorne and Louisa May Alcott, is located at the park and is open for tours. The park grounds are open daily from sunrise to sunset, with various hours for visitor centers. There is no fee to enter the park, but the Wayside House charges $4 for adults (children 16 and under free).

Walden Pond, also located in Concord (915 Walden Street, Concord, MA 01742; 978-369-3254; http://www.mass .gov/dcr/parks/ northeast/ wldn.htm), is a historic landmark considered to be the birthplace of the conservation movement. It is the place where Henry David Thoreau lived from 1845 to 1847 and was the inspiration

Thoreau's Cabin

for his famous book *Walden*. A replica of Thoreau's house stands on the site. The number of visitors to the **Walden Pond State Reservation**, which encompasses 400 acres, including the 102-foot pond, is limited to no more than one thousand at a time. Visitors are advised to call ahead for parking availability. Day parking is $5; annual passes are good for entrance into all Massachusetts state parks and are available for $35 for residents and $45 for nonresidents. Educational tours and programs are offered. The reservation is open daily from 8:00 a.m. to sunset.

NEW JERSEY

ALLAIRE STATE PARK AREA

The area around Allaire State Park offers many entertainment and recreational options. Antique stores, historic sites, and a wide variety of museums abound. And horse lovers will especially enjoy watching the trotters and pacers at Freehold Raceway, in Freehold, or taking in a show at the Horse Park of New Jersey, located in Stone Tavern.

Freehold Raceway (130 Park Avenue, Freehold, NJ 07728; 732-462-3800; http:// www.freehold raceway.com), established in 1853, features live standardbred harness racing for trotters and pacers from mid-August through late May. The racetrack also features simulcast Thoroughbred and harness racing from tracks throughout North America seven days a week all year-round. Admission is free, and the fee for general parking is $2.

Horse Park of New Jersey, in Stone Tavern (County Route 524, Freehold, NJ 07728; 609-259-0170/908-996-2544; http://www.horseparkofnew jersey.com), is a world-class exhibition facility offering a variety of equine events in various disciplines from March through November. In 2004, the horse park hosted the final mandatory outing for horse and rider teams competing for a place on the U.S. Olympic team for three-day eventing. Contact the facility by mail at Horse Park of New Jersey at Stone Tavern, PO Box 419, Cream Ridge, New Jersey 08514.

NEW YORK

OTTER CREEK HORSE TRAILS AREA
Take a scenic ride on the Adirondack Railroad, leaving from **Thendara Station**, the depot nearest the Otter Creek Horse Trails (Route 28, PO Box 84, Thendara, NY 13472; 315-369-6290; http://www.adirondackrr.com). While on your train trip, you can stop and shop in **Old Forge** (Tourist Information Center, Old Forge, NY 13420; 315-369-6983; http://www.oldforgeny.com). Or you can opt for a boat trip on the

Thendara Station

Adirondack's Fulton Chain of Lakes from **Old Forge Lake Cruises** (Route 28 Main Street, Old Forge, NY 13420; 315-369-6473; http://www.oldforgecruises.com). Schedules and fares for the train and boat tours will vary depending on the route or tour you select. In July or August, you may witness a mock train robbery.

Adirondack train from the air

WHERE TO STAY & STABLE

CONNECTICUT

NATCHAUG STATE FOREST AREA

Horses and Riders:

Silvermine Horse Camp
Located in the forest
860-974-1562
http://www.dep.state.ct.us/stateparks/forests/
natchaug.htm
No fee for campers
Silvermine Horse Camp is the trailhead for several dirt and gravel trails, many of which are closed loop trails. The camp offers fifteen wooded campsites with very basic facilities. Campers must clean the sites and carry out all trash. Open mid-April through Thanksgiving.

PACHAUG STATE FOREST AREA

Horses and Riders:

Frog Hollow Horse Camp
Located in the forest
860-376-4075
http://www.dep.state.ct.us/stateparks/camping/index.htm#natchaug
$11 per night for campsites
Frog Hollow Horse Camp, off of Headquarters Road, accommodates up to eighteen campers and horses in semiwooded sites. The camp has water spigots and compost restrooms. Campsites are available on a first-come, first-served basis. Select a site, and rangers will come around for registration and to collect fees. The camp is open April through Thanksgiving.

MAINE

ACADIA NATIONAL PARK AREA

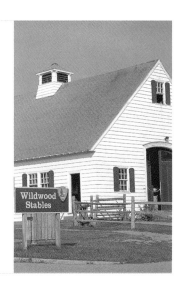

Horses and Riders:

Wildwood Stables
Box 241
Seal Harbor, ME 04675
207-276-3622 (June through October); 859-356-7139 (winter months)
http://www.acadia.net/wildwood
$20 per night for box stalls; $10 per night for campsites
Wildwood Stables is located next to the Park Loop Road inside Acadia National Park. The stable is on park land but is operated as a private concession. Reservations to board horses and camp at the stables are highly recommended. Horse rentals are not provided at the stable, but daily carriage tours are available for horseless visitors who wish to see the park using true horsepower. Open during the summer season from mid-June through Columbus Day.

Riders Only:
Cleftstone Manor
92 Eden Street
Bar Harbor, ME 04609
207-288-8086/Reservations: 888 288 4951
http://www.cleftstone.com
$70–$225 per night (highest rates during summer)

The Cleftstone Manor is a historic inn located a few minutes from Acadia National Park and less than 1 mile from downtown Bar Harbor. Built in 1881, the Cleftstone Manor is one of the few Victorian mansions to have survived a devastating fire that swept through the area in 1947. Guest rooms are decorated with antiques and antique reproductions, upholding the ambience of the period. Rooms feature air-conditioning and private baths, and some have fireplaces, whirlpool bathtubs, and balconies. A full breakfast and afternoon refreshments are included in the room rate. Children ten and older are welcome. Smoking is not allowed in the inn. Open from May through October.

Edgewater Motel and Cottages
Old Bar Harbor Road
Salisbury Cove, ME 04609; send correspondence to PO Box 566, Bar Harbor, ME 04609
207-288-3491/888-310-9920
http://www.edgewaterbarharbor.com
$59–$161 per night (highest rates during summer)

As the name implies, the Edgewater Motel and Cottages are located on the waterfront of Frenchman Bay. The 5-acre establishment, which offers both private cottages and motel rooms, is 2.5 miles from Acadia National Park. All cottages and rooms provide close-up water views and the chance to view migratory waterfowl feeding offshore as well as seals, porpoises, eagles, loons, and ospreys. Cottages have kitchenettes and porch decks, and some have fireplaces. All motel rooms offer balconies for taking in the view, and some have fully equipped kitchens. Open April through October.

Horses Only:
Eochaidh Stables
2 Lakewood Farm Road
Bar Harbor, ME 04609
877-727-8715/207-288-5111/207-288-2519
http://www.northisle.com/stablein.htm
$30 per night, $180 per week for box stalls;
$50 per hour for horse rentals

Eochaidh Stables is located near Bar Harbor, bordering Acadia National Park. It has box stalls, 23 acres of turnout area, and a riding ring. In addition to its proximity to Acadia National Park trails, Eochaidh Stables offers private riding trails. The stable does not have direct access to Acadia, although that could change in the future. Rental horses are available for riding on the private trails. Reservations are required for short-term boarding and horse rentals. There is no camping at Eochaidh, but there are lodging and camping options nearby, and the owners of Eochaidh Stables have a waterfront vacation house and cottage available for rent.

MASSACHUSETTS

BOSTON AREA

Horses and Riders

The Arabian Horse Inn
277 Old Sudbury Road
Sudbury, MA 01776
978-443-7400/800-ARABIAN (272-2426)
http://www.arabianhorseinn.com
$169 per night for rooms, $269 and $319 for suites, full country breakfast included; call for current stabling rates
Guest accommodations include two suites and one room with a king-size bed; each room is named after one of the owner's horses. Reservations are highly recommended.

Riders Only

The Colonial Inn
48 Monument Square
Concord, MA 01742
978-369-9200/800-370-9200/Fax: 978-371-1533
http://www.concordscolonialinn.com
$125–$350 per night (highest rates during foliage season, September 7 through October 25)
The Colonial Inn is on the National Register of Historic Places. Built in 1716, it became a hotel in 1889. Prior to becoming an inn, it served as a home, an arms storage building, a variety store, and a boarding house. President Franklin D. Roosevelt, actor John Wayne, Queen Noor of Jordan, as well as many other famous people have been guests at the inn. The inn consists of several buildings with fifty-six guest rooms, suites, apartments, and private cottages. Two restaurants, serving seafood and other New England fare, and a tavern are located at the inn. Extended stay rates, group rates, and bed-and-breakfast packages are also available.

Maxwell House Bed and Breakfast
9 Laws Brook Road
Acton, MA 01720
978-264-4840
$75–$95 per day, includes continental breakfast and wine/cheese greeting
The Maxwell House Bed and Breakfast is a small Cape Cod–style country home. It boasts of two comfortable guest rooms, a fireplace in the living room, and a sunny breakfast porch for enjoying morning scones and coffee. (Note: The accommodations are not suitable for children.)

NEW JERSEY

ALLAIRE STATE PARK AREA

Horses and Riders

Cricket Hill Bed and Breakfast
228 Betsy Scull Road
Egg Harbor Township, NJ 08234
609-653-8697
http://www.crickethillbandb.com
$125 per night, breakfast included; $10–$15 per night for overnight horse boarding
Cricket Hill Bed and Breakfast, located approximately one hour south of Allaire State Park, is part of a 20-acre horse farm. It can accommodate both people and horses. The two guest rooms overlook horses grazing in their pasture. A pool and pond help keep riders cool while horses relax in box stalls, a corral, or the pasture. A small park

with riding trails is accessible. Cricket Hill is also within a short driving distance to other trail-riding venues, including Belleplain State Forest, west of Atlantic City; and Atsion Lake, within Wharton State Forest.

Riders Only:

Hepburn House Bed and Breakfast Inn
15 Monument Street
Freehold, NJ 07728
732-462-7696
http://www.hepburnhouse.com
$100–$150 per night, breakfast included
The inn is close to Freehold Raceway's harness-racing track, and the Battle of Monmouth Monument Park can be seen from the inn. Horse farms dot the area, and downtown is a short walk away. Beautifully decorated rooms feature king- or queen-size beds and private baths.

The White Lilac Inn
414 Central Avenue
Spring Lake, NJ 07762
732-449-0211
http://www.whitelilac.com
$139–$349 per night
Built in the late 1800s, this charming inn reflects the ambiance of the bygone Victorian era. It is located approximately fifteen minutes from Allaire State Park and less than five blocks from the lapping waves of the Atlantic Ocean. Various amenities are offered in the eclectically decorated rooms, including fireplaces, whirlpool tubs, and porches. Children over fourteen are welcome.

Horses Only:

Good Times Training Stable
278 Jackson Mills Road
Freehold, NJ 07728
732-409-2882
http://www.mywebpages.comcast.net/eczarnecki/gtts.htm
Call for current prices
Good Times Training Stable is located minutes from Allaire State Park. This training and boarding facility, owned by Arabian trainer and exhibitor Guilene Mallard, has forty stalls on its premises. It offers overnight stabling based on available space in the barn, so be sure to call well in advance of your trip. In addition to its proximity to the riding trails at Allaire, it is also a short distance from Manasquan Reservoir and Colliers Mills trails. An added plus: the stable has ride-on access to Turkey Swamp Park, a not-so-well-known equestrian jewel in the New Jersey park system.

NEW YORK

OTTER CREEK HORSE TRAILS AREA

Horses and Riders:

Camp Manestay
6255 Erie Canal Road
Glenfield, NY 13343
315-376-7924

http://www.manestay.com

$55 per night for cabin for two, $75 per night for cabin for four, $20 per night for each extra person in the cabins; $200 per night for house for four with DirecTV, air conditioning and more, price includes four horse stalls or paddocks, $50 each additional person in the house; $10 per day for covered box stall or paddock, $5 additional to provide hay; camping with hookups $20 per night; truck and trailer camping without hookups $10 per night; parking for truck and trailer $10 if not renting overnight accommodations; tent camping $10 per night.

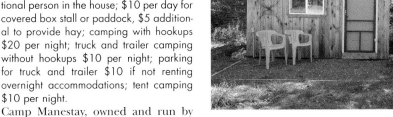

Camp Manestay, owned and run by Jerry and Debbie Van Zile, has direct access to the trails of the Otter Creek Horse Trail system. The facility offers camping and cabin rentals as well as accommodations for horses. Hot showers are $3.50 extra for campers and free for cabin renters. Riders can stay here with their horses or stay elsewhere and board their horse here. Turnout paddocks and a round pen are available for use with both basic and full-care packages. Hay and baled shavings are available for sale. Horse transportation and a farrier are available upon request, and there is also a veterinarian on call for emergencies twenty-four hours a day. Seminars on trail safety, horse conditioning, horse behavior management, and saddle fitting and other courses are offered on site.

Otter Creek Lodge

285 Benson Road
Victor, NY 14564
585-377-7913
http://www.ottercreeklodge.com

$1,000 per night, two-night minimum stay; no extra charge for horses

The Otter Creek Lodge is located in a tall pine forest on 115 acres overlooking a spring-fed glacial lake. It is a vacation rental offering group accommodations for up to twenty-four people and their horses. The lodge does not rent single rooms and does not serve food. There are twelve bedrooms, nine and a half baths, ample public space, and a large commercially equipped kitchen. The lodge also includes overnight stalls for up to eighteen horses and a small pasture. It has direct access to the Otter Creek Horse Trails.

Riders Only

Haffs Adirondack Cabin Rentals

445 Lewistown Road (mailing address)
Columbus, NJ 08022
609-894-9522
http://www.adirondacksrentals.com
Call for current rates

Located on Brantingham Lake, Haffs has three fully furnished cabins available that sleep up to ten people. Guests who board their horses at Camp Manestay receive a discount on lodging. The facility has tennis courts, a basketball court, paddle boats, and rowboats for use by guests and a playground area for young equestrians when they're not riding the trails.

WHERE TO WINE & DINE

MAINE

ACADIA NATIONAL PARK AREA

Atlantic Brewing Company
15 Knox Road
Bar Harbor, ME 04609
800-475-5417/207-288-2337
http://www.atlanticbrewing.com
$9.00 and under for meals; $3.75 for pints of beer
The Atlantic Brewing Company, built in 1991, occupies the site of an old farm. It features The Knox Road Tavern & Bistro, which serves burgers, sandwiches, salads, and other casual fare and handcrafted ales. Visitors can taste ale in the gift shop and witness the brewing process through a brewery tour. The Atlantic Brewing Company produces six ales and brews at the rate of thirty barrels of ale a day, the majority of which is sold within a 15-mile radius of the facility. Beer tastings and brew house tours are free. The brewery also offers its own wines. Children and visitors who don't imbibe can try the brewery's own root beer. Reservations are required for groups of ten or more. Open from Memorial Day to Columbus Day.

Jordan Pond House
Park Loop Road
Bar Harbor, ME 04605
207-276-3316
http://www.jordanpond.com
$9–$25
The Jordan Pond House is located inside Acadia National Park. The Jordan family built the original farm house in 1847, and the restaurant was founded in the 1870s. In 1979, fire destroyed the original structure, which was rebuilt through private donors. Afternoon tea has been served at the Jordan Pond House since the late 1800s, and the tradition is still carried on today as visitors partake of popovers and strawberry jam on the lawn. Lunch and dinner are also available, offering salads, soups, stews, sandwiches, seafood, chicken, and steaks. Reservations are recommended. Open May through October.

MASSACHUSETTS

BOSTON AREA

Atlantic Sea Grill and Fish Market
77 Great Road
Acton, MA 01720

978-263-3162
http://www.atlanticseagrill.com
$6–$20 and up

The Atlantic Sea Grill serves fresh seafood, steaks, chicken, pastas, salads, and burgers in an informal setting. Inspect the day's catch in the adjoining fish market before enjoying lunch or dinner from the extensive menu. The restaurant offers a children's menu, and on-the-go diners can order takeout.

Scupper Jack's Restaurant and Bar

3 Nagog Park, Route 2A
Acton, MA 01720
978-263-8327
http://www.scupperjacks.com
$7–$28

Enjoy a water view at Scupper Jack's, located on Nagog Pond. This family-friendly restaurant serves lunch and dinner and offers a children's menu. Lunch and dinner takeout is also available. Menu items include salads, sandwiches, fresh fish, and other seafood dishes such as lobster pie, seafood crepes, and stuffed shrimp. Dine in the enclosed porch or outdoors on the deck in fair weather. Listen to live music in the lounge on Friday and Saturday evenings. A full bar is available.

Union Oyster House

41 Union Street
Boston, MA 02108
617-227-2750
http://www.unionoysterhouse.com
$10.00–$21.95 for lunch; $18.95 to market prices for dinner

Located on Boston's Freedom Trail, the historic Union Oyster House has been serving hungry diners since 1826. When the restaurant first opened, as the Atwood and Bacon Oyster House, an oyster craze was overtaking the country. The restaurant's semicircular oyster bar, which dates back to its opening, has been visited by many of Boston's most prominent people. The Kennedy family has patronized the Union Oyster House for years, and the favorite booth of JFK bears a plaque in his honor. In addition to oysters, you'll enjoy a wide range of seafood here, including Boston scrod, sole, swordfish, lobster, scallops, mussels, and salmon. Meat and poultry, including filet mignon, are also on the menu. The Union Bar is open until midnight.

NEW JERSEY

Allaire State Park Area

Our House Restaurant

420 Adelphia Road
Farmingdale, NJ 07727
732-938-5159
http://www.ourhouserestaurant.net

$15.00–$24.00 for dinner; $16.95 for adults, $8.95 for children twelve years and under for brunch
Our House Restaurant offers steaks, seafood, pastas, and other fine continental cuisine. Built in 1747 as Marriner's Tavern, it was a gathering place for the colonial community, including a band of outlaws called the Fagen Gang. One of the unlucky members of the gang, Lewis Fenton, was hanged in front of the tavern in 1779, according to local lore.

Spring Meadow Inn
Route 524, 4185 Atlantic Avenue
Wall Township, NJ 07727
732-974-7717
$7–$9 for lunch; $11–$20 for dinner
The Spring Meadow Inn offers American fare in a country club setting. It is located on the east side of the Spring Meadow Golf Course, which is owned by the state and open to the public. Open for lunch and dinner.

NEW YORK

OTTER CREEK HORSE TRAILS AREA

Central Hotel
Main Street
Glenfield, NY 13343
315-376-3475
http://www.centralhotel.freeservers.com
$9–$18
The look and feel of the Central Hotel takes you back to the days of the Old West. A large front porch, country decor, and locals hunkered up to the bar telling tall tales make for comfortable and pleasant surroundings. Enjoy the ambience as you dine on home-style meals of soups, steaks, sandwiches, and roasted foods.

Coachlight Inn
5555 Partridgeville Road
Brantingham Lake, NY 13312
315-348-8960
http://www.coachlightinn.com
$9–$20
The Coachlight Inn is located near Haffs Adirondack Cabins. It features prime rib and other delectable meals. Lunch and dinner are served daily; happy hour from 3:00 to 6:00 p.m.

Hacking in the fall woods

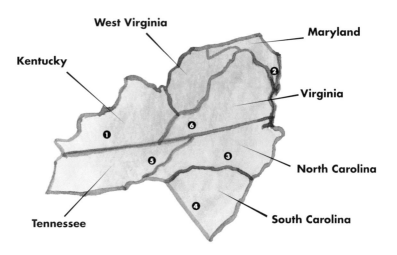

West Virginia

Maryland

Kentucky

Virginia

North Carolina

South Carolina

Tennessee

SOUTHEAST MAP LEGEND

Kentucky
❶ Mammoth Cave National Park

Maryland (and Virginia)
❷ Assateague Island

North Carolina
❸ Uwharrie National Forest

South Carolina
❹ The Hitchcock Woods

Tennessee (and North Carolina)
❺ Great Smoky Mountains National Park

Virginia
❻ Mount Rogers National Recreation Area

THE SOUTHEAST

Mild weather in the southeastern United States and diverse places for riding that vary from rugged, densely treed mountains and gentle bridle paths to fragile white beaches make the Southeast a special place to visit and ride. The often mild weather (except for late summer and early fall, when hurricanes might be brewing) also adds to the enjoyment of year-round riding. Horses are welcome on many trails in the Southeast, and that attitude is reflected in the well-maintained trails, horse camping, and relatively numerous accommodations accepting horses. There is also the possibility of catching a glimpse of wild horse herds.

Some particularly interesting aspects of the Southeast include the opportunity to explore the bluegrass and caves of Kentucky; to ride in an area that is branded in the memory of many horse lovers, as is Assateague Island with its ponies, immortalized in Marguerite Henry's book *Misty of Chincoteague*; to enjoy gentle bridle trails in the middle of an urban area that evolved into what it is today expressly because of horses; and to travel the trails in the mountains of Tennessee.

Wherever you ride in the Southeast, whether at one of the locations discussed here or anywhere else in the Southeast, you can bet it will have its own intriguing story to tell.

KENTUCKY

MAMMOTH CAVE NATIONAL PARK

All horse people, and even most "non-horsey" people, will naturally think of horses when they think of Kentucky. What you might not know is that in addition to having a reputation as horse country, the state is also cave country. The 52,830-acre Mammoth Cave National Park in south central Kentucky features the longest cave system in the world. It is three times longer than any other cave yet discovered. Cave explorers have mapped 365 miles of caves in the system and are still discovering more passages, with no end in sight to this phenomenal natural wonder.

The park was established in 1941 to preserve this majestic cave system as well as the nearby river valleys of the Green and Nolin rivers, and part of

Mammoth Cave entrance

south central Kentucky's hill country. The cave first got its name back in the early 1800s when it was described as mammoth because of its chambers and passages. The name has nothing to do with the woolly prehistoric mammals who lived on earth at the time the massive cave began forming, approximately ten million years ago.

SnapShot - Mammoth Cave National Park

Description: This national park is home to the most extensive cave system in the world at more than 360 miles long and still counting. You can enjoy riding your own horse or a rented horse on 60 miles of trails at Mammoth Cave National Park. Horse camps are available inside and outside of the park, and day-use riders will find trailer parking across the road from the Maple Springs Group Campground at the Lincoln Trailhead, at the Maple Springs trailhead located .25 mile north of the campground, and at the Good Springs Church. Horseless riders can rent horses from the Double J Stables, the local livery (see Where to Stay & Stable).

Open: Year-round; visitor center is closed on Christmas Day; tour times and dates vary

Address: PO Box 7, Mammoth Cave, KY 42259

Phone: 270-758-2180

Web site: http://www.nps.gov/maca/

Getting there: From Louisville: Take I-65 south to Exit 53 at Cave City, continue fifteen minutes to the park's visitor center. From Nashville, TN: Take I-65 north to Exit 48 at Park City, drive ten minutes to the park's visitor center (Nashville and the park are both in the central time zone; Louisville is in the eastern time zone, one hour ahead of the park.)

Fees/permits: Admission is free; park camping with horses is $15 per night; cave tours are from $4 to $45, lower prices for children and seniors

Horse rentals: Available locally

Horse camping: Available in the park

Trail conditions/level of difficulty: Easy to moderate; none very steep, but trails can get muddy during rainy season

Fall leaves at Mammoth Cave

Long before that time, a shallow sea covered most of the southeastern United States. Over the eons, tiny organisms with shells made of calcium carbonate lived and died in the water, leaving their shells to accumulate on the sea floor. This material built up for millions of years until 700 feet of limestone and shale was deposited. Then, a large river system deposited a thick layer of sandstone over much of the area. Eventually, the sea level dropped and the continent rose, exposing the layers of limestone and sandstone. Erosion went to work, and tiny cracks and holes appeared across the sandstone and limestone. Rainwater began working its way underground, dissolving limestone and creating caverns. Cave passages continue being formed today.

This force of erosion not only shaped the Mammoth Cave system but also worked to influence the aboveground landscape, shaping the look of the entire region and consequently influencing the types of plants and wildlife that make their homes here. Rivers, bluffs, sinkholes, cave entrances,

Green River

and ridgetops provide different habitats in which distinct animal and plant communities are found. Maple, beech, hickory, and poplar trees are found on different levels of forest slope, and wildlife in the park ranges from frequently seen white-tailed deer to the gravely endangered freshwater mussels, which make their home in the Green River, the base-level stream in the region. Surprisingly, within the cave system itself, biologists have found more than two hundred species of animals. Some of these are aboveground animals who have wandered into the cave by accident, but many others are creatures who are designed to live only in the darkness and cannot adapt to conditions outside the caves.

Although equestrians will certainly appreciate the cave and its passages, they may enjoy the park even more for the aboveground trails both they and their horses can enjoy. All 60 miles of connecting trails (2 to 10 miles long) north of the Green River (except Ganter Cave Trail) are open for horseback riding. The well-marked trails offer hills, streams, and plenty of bubbling brooks to stop beside for a snack or some rest.

MARYLAND (AND VIRGINIA)

ASSATEAGUE ISLAND

Assateague Island, a 37-mile-long barrier island off the coasts of southern Maryland and northern Virginia, is bounded by the Atlantic Ocean on one side and Chincoteague Bay on the other. The island is made up of sandy beaches, dunes, salt marshlands, and inland pine forests. It is home to the wild ponies made famous by Marguerite Henry's children's book *Misty of Chincoteague*, as many a once horse-crazy child will remember, and the annual pony swim and penning. With the island's prime location along the Atlantic Flyway, it is also an important spot for many types of birds, including waterfowl, shorebirds, wading birds, and songbirds. Peregrine falcons and two pairs of bald eagles also can be seen on the island. Elk and deer populations make their homes here as well.

When you visit Assateague Island today and revel in its raw, wild beauty, it's hard to believe that this national treasure almost went under the developer's bulldozer. In the 1950s, investors in the island planned to turn it into a summer beach resort. The island was subdivided and new homes, vacation villas, and condominiums were planned. In fact, some of the new abodes had already started going up. Then, in 1962, nature added her two cents' worth to the idea in the form of a powerful Atlantic storm—one of the well-known northeasters—that leveled the island and many of its new developments. Like the homes they were building, the developers scattered into the wind, leaving the island to the wild

Birds in flight

horses and the seagulls. The federal government later bought the land, and on September 21, 1965, President Lyndon Johnson signed the act that declared this precious stretch of shoreline a national seashore.

Three government agencies manage Assateague Island. The Maryland side of the island, known as Assateague Island National Seashore, is managed by the National Park Service. Within the Assateague Island National Seashore is Assateague State Park, which is administered by the state of Maryland. The Virginia district is overseen by the U.S. Fish and Wildlife Service as the Chincoteague National Wildlife Refuge.

You can ride your horse on the beach and camp in the off-road vehicle zones from early fall through spring at Assateague Island National

Chincoteague National Wildlife Refuge

Chincoteague pony at the refuge

Seashore. Assateague State Park provides 350 campsites open from April through October. (Call 410-641-2120

for more information.) Riding is not permitted during the summer and early fall months because of the presence of biting insects and the risk of insect-borne diseases such as West Nile virus, equine infectious anemia, and equine encephalitis. In the Virginia district, horseback riding is permitted in the off-road vehicle area and along Beach Road. Some areas are open year-round, whereas others are available seasonally to horses and riders. There is no camping allowed in the Virginia district.

SNAPSHOT - ASSATEAGUE ISLAND

Description: Horse camping is available at Assateague Island National Seashore, on the Maryland side of the island. In addition to horse campgrounds, there are year-round ocean-side and bay-side campgrounds available as well as backcountry camping. Contact the Maryland district of the island for more information. No camping of any kind is allowed in the Virginia district. Other options for accommodations for both horse and rider are available nearby (see Where to Stay & Stable). Horseless riders wishing to experience riding near Assateague should contact the local recreational riding stable and therapeutic riding center, Hoof Prints in the Sand (410-835-8814). Hoof Prints in the Sand rents horses for guided rides into the 5,000 acres of trails in Maryland's Wicomico State Forest.

Open: Year-round riding in some areas of Chincoteague National Wildlife Refuge; riding in Assateague Island National Seashore from October 9 through May 14 (horse camping allowed through April 14)

Addresses: Maryland District: 7206 National Seashore Lane, Berlin, MD 21811; Virginia District: PO Box 38, 8586 Beach Road, Chincoteague, VA 23336

Phone: Maryland District: 410-641-1441; Virginia District: 757-336-6577; National Seashore Camping: 410-641-3030

Web site: http://www.nps.gov/asis

Getting there: To Assateague, MD: From Washington, DC: Take US 50 East from the Bay Bridge, follow signs for Ocean City, turn right on Route 611 to Assateague Island. From Virginia Beach: Take the Bay Bridge Tunnel, stay on US 13 North, then go north on US 113 toward Snow Hill/Ocean City, turn right on MD 376, then right on MD 611 to Assateague Island. To Assateague and Chincoteague, VA: From Washington, DC: Take US 50 East across the Bay Bridge and on to Salisbury, Maryland. At Salisbury, take US 13 South to Route 175 East to Chincoteague Island. From Chincoteague Island: Turn left onto Main Street, then right on Maddox Boulevard to Assateague Island. From Virginia Beach: Take the Bay Bridge Tunnel, stay on US 13 North, then go right on Route 175 East to Chincoteague Island. From Chincoteague: Turn left onto Main Street, then right on Maddox Boulevard to Assateague Island.

Fees/permits: Admission is $10 for a seven-day vehicle pass valid at both the National Seashore and the National Wildlife Refuge; $3 for visitors on foot or bicycles; separate $4 entrance fee to Assateague State Park from Memorial Day to Labor Day; camping fees are additional

Horse rentals: Available locally
Horse camping: Available on the Maryland side only
Trail conditions/level of difficulty: Easy

RUNNING FREE ON ASSATEAGUE

Local lore says that the feral horses roaming Assateague Island descended from stock that swam ashore from a ship-wrecked Spanish galleon in the seventeenth century. Another story claims they came from horses put ashore by Spanish pirates. Although these explanations for the horses' presence on the island make for romantic and colorful tales, no one really knows how they came to be here. The most plausible expla-

Chincoteague pony

nation, historians believe, is that they are descendants of horses brought to the area by early colonists from England. The colonists grazed the animals on the island to avoid mainland fencing laws and livestock taxes.

However the horses arrived on the island, the hardy animals managed to survive by adapting to the island's tough conditions. The island's harsh environment and the poor diet it offers the horses—mostly consisting of salt marsh cordgrass, American beach grass, and occasionally leaves and twigs—probably account for the small size of today's animals. They are actually the size of ponies, averaging 12 to 13 hands. Horses who have been taken off the island as foals and fed a higher-protein diet have grown to horse size.

The Chincoteague pony is now a recognized breed. Two main herds of the horses live on the island: one on the Maryland side and the other on the Virginia side. They are separated by a fence at the border of the two states. The horses have further divided themselves into bands of two to twelve horses who occupy various home ranges. The number of animals in each of the two main herds is kept to approximately 150 to lessen the negative impact of overgrazing.

In Maryland, the National Park Service manages the herd. To control the population, the park service administers nonhormonal contraceptive vaccines with dart guns. The method has proven 95 percent effective, and the horses haven't exhibited any harmful side effects. Horses in the Maryland district live their entire lives on the island.

Bonding on Assateague

The Virginia herd is cared for by the Chincoteague Volunteer Fire Company. The herd undergoes veterinary checks twice a year, and its size is managed through the famous Chincoteague Pony Penning. The event, which began in 1924 to raise money for the fire department, takes place each year on the last Wednesday and Thursday of July. The herd is rounded up on Wednesday for a ten-minute swim across the channel to Chincoteague Island, where many of the foals are auctioned on Thursday; the remaining foals and adult horses swim back to their home on Assateague the following day. In 2001, an auction record was set when one foal, a pinto filly, brought $10,305. One note: if you see the horses when visiting the island, be aware that they sometimes approach visitors for food. Although you may be tempted to feed them or pet them, it is not safe for you or for them. Feeding can make this normally gentle creature behave aggressively toward you, and the horses have been known to chase the hand that feeds them right into the ocean, as well as bite and kick. Feeding also encourages the horses to hang around roads on the island, and a number of them are hit and killed by cars each year because of it.

If you are visiting the National Seashore and don't wish to camp, a popular place to stay is Ocean City, Maryland, where lodging is plentiful and you are only 8 miles north of Assateague Island's north entrance. The Virginia side of the island does not allow camping, but commercial campgrounds and plenty of other lodgings are available on the small neighboring island of Chincoteague, Virginia. Assateague's south entrance is .25 mile east of Chincoteague. Call the Chincoteague Chamber of Commerce at 757-336-6161 for information. You must have reservations in advance if you are planning to visit the area for pony penning in July.

NORTH CAROLINA

UWHARRIE NATIONAL FOREST

Uwharrie National Forest is located in North Carolina's *Piedmont* region, in the central part of the state. Piedmont means "at the base of the mountains," and this national forest, the smallest in the state (though packed with recreation opportunities), gets its name from the Uwharrie Mountains. The forest is 60 miles northeast of Charlotte and approximately 90 miles southwest of Raleigh, the state capitol. The 50,189-acre forest is one of the more recent additions to the national U.S. forest system. Then President John F. Kennedy declared the area, which spreads into Montgomery, Randolph, and Davidson coun-

Looking up in the forest

Uwharrie National Forest

ties, a national forest in 1961. Uwharrie provides a variety of natural resources, including abundant wildlife habitat; clean water in its rivers, streams, and lakes; scenic and diverse vegetation; and timber.

Prior to attaining national forest status, Uwharrie was known as the Uwharrie Reservation. Logging and farming had stripped the forest of its trees prior to the 1930s, when the land was purchased by the federal government, so most of today's Uwharrie is young second- and third-growth forest.

The ancient Uwharrie Mountains are really gently rolling 1,000-foot hills today. Geologists believe that the 500 million-year-old mountains, some of the oldest in the country, were once towering 20,000-foot peaks that were part of a chain of volcanoes. In keeping with its ancient heritage, the forest is full of archaeological history, and it has one of the greatest concentrations of archeological sites in the southeast, with seven hundred known archaeological sites with remnants of many prehistoric peoples,

Multiuse trail

European settlers attracted by its gentle hills, and miners hoping to get rich after gold was discovered here in the early 1800s. Old graveyards and homesites as well as remnants from miners are found throughout the forest.

More than 40 miles of trails are marked for equestrian use only, and riding is allowed on forest roads and in off-road vehicle areas. Horse trails are rated easy to moderate, and a color-coded horse trail map is available on the Forest Service Web site. Horseless riders will find rental horses at Uwharrie Stables (4084 Highway 109 North, Troy, NC 27371; 910-572-1614; http://www.uwharriestables.com) or at End of the Trail Stables (2661 NC Highway 24/27, Mount Gilead, NC 27306; 910-439-5459).

Other recreational opportunities abound in Uwharrie. Hiking, biking, fishing, and hunting are popular activities. Trails are marked for different usages and wind through hardwood forest and past meandering streams.

Cantering a wooded trail

SNAPSHOT - UWHARRIE NATIONAL FOREST

Description: Ride in Uwharrie National Forest located in central North Carolina. Miles of dedicated equestrian trails and four areas for horse camping make this a horse-friendly place to visit, and horse rentals are available in the forest. In addition to horse camps, there is an overflow lot with more camping across the street from Canebrake Horse Camp (see Where to Stay & Stable). Another option, but only for serious wilderness buffs, is the very primitive Deep Water Horse Camp at the end of the 6-mile-long Moccasin Creek Forest Service road. No fee is charged there. The town of Troy, which is surrounded by the Uwharrie National Forest, has several grocery stores for picking up food and other supplies for camping or picnicking.

Open: Year-round
Address: Uwharrie Ranger District, 789 NC Highway 24/27 East, Troy, NC 27371
Phone: 910-576-6391
Web site: http://www.cs.unca.edu/nfsnc
Getting there: From Greensboro: US 220 South (changes to I-73)
Fees/permits: Admission is free; camping fees vary
Horse rentals: Available in the forest
Horse camping: Available in the forest
Trail conditions/level of difficulty: Easy to moderate

SOUTH CAROLINA

THE HITCHCOCK WOODS

To truly appreciate riding in The Hitchcock Woods of Aiken, South Carolina, first you must understand the surrounding area. The city of Aiken and greater Aiken County, located approximately 16 miles northeast of Augusta, Georgia, are all about horses and horse activities. The Chamber of Commerce for Aiken touts the county as a place where horses are kings, and indeed they are royalty here. The county has a steeplechase association, several hunt clubs, and multiple polo clubs, with more than thirty polo professionals who make their homes in Aiken. Thoroughbred training farms abound, and there is a mile-long training track as well as shorter tracks. Aiken hosts its own Triple Crown races each March, which include three consecutive weekends of flat racing, steeplechases, and polo matches. Dressage, jumping, carriage driving, and western riding are popular here, and events in all these disciplines are also held in the area.

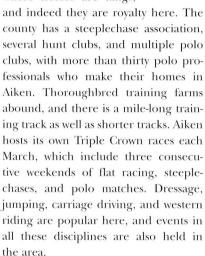

Hitchcock Woods

How did Aiken gain its wonderful equine culture? In the late nineteenth century, wealthy northerners from the United States and Canada flocked here to escape the bitter northern cold, turning the area into their winter playground. It became known as the Winter Colony. Once people discovered that the sandy soil was perfect for conditioning their horses, horse sports such as polo, hunting, racing, and driving became the order of the day. Over the

ensuing years, other horse sports gained in popularity.

A very influential person in the area's horsey evolution was trainer Thomas Hitchcock, who helped found the Aiken Steeplechase Association in 1930. In a steeplechase, thoroughbred horses are raced over fences. The first official steeplechase sponsored by the association was raced here in what is now known as The Hitchcock Woods. The woods are a 2,100-acre tract of land—the largest urban forest in America—in the middle of Aiken used for riding and hiking. Thomas Hitchcock and his daughter Helen Clark

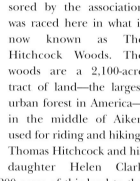

donated 1,200 acres of this land to the city of Aiken for public use in 1939, establishing The Hitchcock Foundation. The foundation manages the land as a reserve, although it is open to public use. Later purchases by The Hitchcock Foundation, as well as donations by other organizations, brought the total amount of land to approximately 2,000 acres.

These quiet, peaceful trails are open for day use. Only horses, horse carriages, and foot traffic are allowed. No bicycles or motorized vehicles mar the stillness found in this urban forest. Equestrians will find a network of

Thoroughbred foal in Aiken

Hitchcock Woods carriages

65 miles of marked trails, including old sandy roads and hunt trails with fences for jumping. Trail maps are at the entrances. There are several points of special interest here, including the Ridge Mile Track, built by Thomas Hitchcock for training his racehorses; the Gamekeeper's Lodge, which is the location of the house where the head woodsman for the Hitchcock family, Monroe Heath, lived; and the Tea Cottage site, which is the site of a cottage built by Celestine Eustis, the aunt of Thomas Hitchcock's wife. The cottage itself burned down during the 1970s.

There are no horse rentals in the Hitchcock Woods, but horseless riders will be able to enjoy the area's horsey culture at Almost Heaven Stables (220 Golf Course Road, Warrenville, SC 29851;803-663-3001;http://www.almost

Enjoying a drink

heavenstables.com) in the nearby town of Warrenville, which is just 5 miles west of Aiken. Guided trail rides are $30 per hour.

SNAPSHOT - THE HITCHCOCK WOODS

Description: Ride in an urban forest in equestrian-centered Aiken, South Carolina, owned and managed by the private Hitchcock Foundation. The trails are open only to horses. No hunting (except organized fox hunts), fishing, firearms, smoking, fires, audio equipment, or metal detectors are allowed. Horse rentals are available in nearby Warrenville.

Open: Year-round, dawn to dusk

Address: The Hitchcock Foundation, PO Box 1702, South Boundary and Laurens Street, Aiken, SC 29802

Phone: 803-642-0528

Web site: http://www.hitchcockwoods.com

Getting there: From U.S. 1 in Aiken: Drive south on York Street and turn right onto South Boundary Street, and continue downhill and look for the parking area at a gated road.

Fees/permits: Admission is free

Horse rentals: Available locally

Horse camping: None

Trail conditions/level of difficulty: Easy to moderate

TENNESSEE (AND NORTH CAROLINA)

GREAT SMOKY MOUNTAINS NATIONAL PARK

More than nine million people visit Great Smoky Mountains National Park annually, making it the most popular

Great Smoky Mountains National Park

national park in the country. There are many good reasons this park holds such an attraction for so many people; one of the reasons is its proximity to civilization. The 520,976-acre park, which straddles the border of Tennessee and North Carolina in the Southern Appalachian Mountains, is easily accessible to residents of several states in

under a few hours. Of course, proximity alone isn't what makes this park so attractive. Its intriguing history, beautiful mountains, plant and animal diversity, and miles of trails to explore explain why people come here in spite of so many other people coming here.

The park was once part of the Cherokee Nation homeland. In the early 1800s, the Cherokees, who had lived here long before European settlers arrived, tried to assimilate to the lifestyles of the settlers. They built log cabins, attended school, developed a written language, and published their own newspaper. Although they strived to fit in, the new Americans did not want them, and the Cherokees were driven from their homeland to be relocated west of the Mississippi, becoming part of the tragedy known as The Trail of Tears. Some of them refused to leave, though, hiding in the mountains. Later in the century, they reclaimed some of their land in western North Carolina.

The settlers, who had taken over, farmed the fertile land, sent their children to school, attended church, and lived here in relative isolation. Their way of life changed with the arrival of

Historic building in Great Smoky Mountains National Park

the lumber industry in the early 1900s. Twenty years later, the forest was rapidly being stripped of its trees—more than 67 percent of what is the park today was clear-cut—and the once largely self-sufficient rural population was dependent on store-bought food and manufactured goods. When forward-thinking people worked to establish the area as a national park, which was authorized by Congress in 1926, the people living in the new park's boundaries moved out, leaving their farm buildings, churches, and mills behind. Many buildings are still standing today and help teach visitors about the area's history.

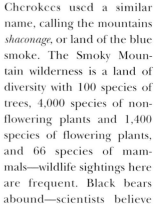

A stately bobcat

The mountains, and thus the park, were named by European explorers for the perpetual blue mist that hovers around their peaks and valleys. The Cherokees used a similar name, calling the mountains *shaconage*, or land of the blue smoke. The Smoky Mountain wilderness is a land of diversity with 100 species of trees, 4,000 species of non-flowering plants and 1,400 species of flowering plants, and 66 species of mammals—wildlife sightings here are frequent. Black bears abound—scientists believe there are 1,800 in the park—and should be admired from afar, but not approached. Cades Cove, the most popular location for visitors to the

SnapShot - Great Smoky Mountains National Park

Description: This park is the most visited national park in the country, so be sure to plan ahead. Don't let the crowds deter you, however, as riding here is a horse person's dream. Horse camping, nearby horse stabling, and horse rentals are all available. If camping at any of the campgrounds, plan to bring your own food; there are no dining facilities in the park. There is a small camp store with limited groceries near the Cades Cove campground, but there are no restaurants and no food and drink concessions on the loop road that circles the valley. Several rental stables offer guided trail rides within the park: Cades Cove (865-448-6286), near Townsend; Smoky Mountain (365-436-5634) and Sugarlands (865-430-5020), both near Gatlinburg; and Smokemont (828-497-2373), near Cherokee, North Carolina (http://www.smokymountains.org/attractions/horseback-riding.html).

Open: Year-round; visitor centers are open all year except Christmas Day

Address: 107 Park Headquarters Road, Gatlinburg, TN 37738

Phone: 865-436-1200

Web site: http://www.nps.gov/grsm/index.htm

Getting there: The following routes provide access to the park's three main entrances. In Tennessee: From I-40, take Exit 407 (Sevierville) to TN Route 66 South, continue to US 441 South, and follow US 441 to the park. From I-40 in Knoxville: Exit at 386B US Highway 129 South to Alcoa/Maryville, proceed on US 321 North through Townsend, continue straight on TN Highway 73 into the park. In North Carolina: From I-40, take US Route 19 West through Maggie Valley, proceed to US 441 North at Cherokee into the park. From Atlanta and points south: Follow US 441 and 23 North. US 441 leads to the park.

Fees/permits: Admission is free

Horse rentals: Available locally

Horse camping: Available in the park

Trail conditions/level of difficulty: Easy to moderate

Two riders making tracks

Cataloochee, which is harder to reach and also less crowded.

There are several backcountry camps in the park for equestrians. The locations of these camps can be seen on the park service trail map, downloadable from the park service Web site or by mail for $1. There are also five drive-in horse camps, open from April through October, providing access to the park's backcountry trails. Additionally, cozy private cabins near the park offer accommodations and horse boarding (see Where to Stay & Stable). For more facilities that board horses or offer accommodations to riders or to both riders and horses, go to http://www.smokymountains.org/attractions/horseback-riding.html.

park, is one of the best places for spotting bears. Deer, raccoons, red and gray foxes, skunks, and bats are frequently seen.

With its mountain trails, beautiful flora and fauna, and opportunities for wildlife spotting, Great Smoky Mountains National Park is a trail rider's mecca. It has more than 550 miles of trails open to horse use. Trails cross mountain streams, wind past historic buildings, and pass under dense trees. There are several drive-in horse camps as well as backcountry campsites, where you can sleep under the stars with your horse. This park is well worth the visit, but in summer and early fall, when the leaves turn dramatic shades of orange, red, yellow, and scarlet, it is extremely crowded, so plan ahead if visiting during those seasons. Spring is less crowded; although early spring brings frequent rain, late spring is awash in wildflowers. The most crowded area is Cades Cove (during summer and fall it can take two to four hours to drive the 11-mile loop road to Cades Cove). At the opposite end of the park is

Rest stop

VIRGINIA

MOUNT ROGERS NATIONAL RECREATION AREA

The Mount Rogers National Recreation Area is located in southwestern Virginia within the 690,106-acre Jefferson

Mount Rogers NRA

National Forest. The National Recreation Area (NRA) covers more than 117,000 acres and has nearly 300 miles of trails, including many miles for riding and several horse camps. The 5,729-foot Mount Rogers, with its summit completely ensconced in Fraser fir, is the highest point in the state. Mount Rogers was named for the state's first geologist, William Barton Rogers, who later went on to found the Massachusetts Institute of Technology. There are three regions to the NRA: the High Country, West End, and East End.

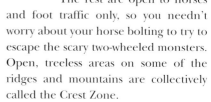

Casual Western rider

The 25,000-acre High Country is a big draw for people to the National Recreation Area. The majority of the High Country is managed by the Mount Rogers National Recreation Area, but 5,000 acres is administered by the adjoining Grayson Highlands State Park. About half of the High Country is federally designated as wilderness land.

Approximately two hundred thousand people visit each year, among them hikers, sightseers, backpackers, cyclists, berry pickers, hunters, anglers, and, of course, equestrians. With spectacular views and more than 66 miles of trails open to horses, equestrians will enjoy riding in this wild and sometimes rugged area. Of the trails allowing horses, only a few also allow bicycles. The rest are open to horses and foot traffic only, so you needn't worry about your horse bolting to try to escape the scary two-wheeled monsters. Open, treeless areas on some of the ridges and mountains are collectively called the Crest Zone.

Horse lovers will enjoy the frequently seen wild ponies who live in the High Country. There are two herds: one lives within the Crest Zone, and the other lives in Grayson Highlands State Park. They originated from fifty ponies

Mount Rogers's ponies

who were placed in the High Country in 1975 as part of a Forest Service experiment to keep the grass down after the use of goats and sheep failed. The ponies have thrived in the area. They

Eating in camp

are kept at an average population of one hundred. The herd population is managed by the Wilburn Ridge Pony Association, which rounds up and auctions off ponies at the Grayson Highlands Fall Festival held annually in the last week of September. As many as fifty ponies are sold each year. Each year, all the ponies who can be caught are given veterinary checks, including vaccinations and worming. A few of the more wily ponies, though, manage to evade the roundup by hiding out in the High Country's swamplands. In winter, hay is brought up to the area in case the ponies cannot find food during their foraging. Grass is so abundant, however, that the hay is rarely distributed.

In the West End of Mount Rogers, riders can pick up the popular shared-use Virginia Creeper Trail. This picturesque rail trail, stretching for more than 33 miles to the state's border with North Carolina, allows horses, foot traffic, and bicycles. The East End offers access to the most popular riding trail in the NRA, the 67-mile-long Virginia Highlands Horse Trail, which traverses into the high country and the fragile beauty of the wilderness areas. Both well-known trails can be crowded on weekends and holidays, though, so to fully enjoy the experience of riding them, you might consider visiting at an off-peak time. Detailed, segment-by-segment information on these trails is available at the Mount Rogers NRA Web site at http://www.fs.fed.us/r8.

SNAPSHOT - MOUNT ROGERS NATIONAL RECREATION AREA

Description: Visit the High Country to see 5,729-foot Mount Rogers, the highest point in Virginia. Enjoy trotting through wilderness areas and seeing the view from the open ridges and mountains of the NRA's Crest Zone. There are four horse camps within the Mount Rogers National Recreation Area, camps and stables in the adjoining Grayson Highlands State Park, and private horse camps nearby. Backcountry camping, a minimum of 200 feet off the trail, is allowed in the High Country. The nearby town of Marion has fast-food chains and stores for picking up food and supplies. There are no horse rentals in the Mount Rogers area.

Open: Year-round; some roads are not cleared during winter

Address: 3714 Highway 16, Marion, VA 24354

Phone: 276-783-5196/800-628-7202

Web site: http://www.fs.fed.us/r8/gwj/mr

Getting there: From the Roanoke area: Take I-81 to exit 50, right onto ramp toward US 11/Atkins, left on SR-622 (Nicks Creek Road), right on SR-16 (Sugar Grove Highway). From Winston-Salem: Take US 52 to I-74 (changes to I-77 in Virginia), exit 32 left toward Wytheville/Bluefield, at exit 50 turn right onto ramp toward US 11/Atkins, left onto SR-622, right on SR-16.

Fees/permits: None for parking or riding trails

Horse rentals: None

Horse camping: Available in the NRA and locally

Trail conditions/level of difficulty: Easy to moderate

OTHER GREAT PLACES TO RIDE

Kentucky

Daniel Boone National Forest
1700 Bypass Road, Winchester, KY 40391
859-745-3100
http://www.fs.fed.us/r8/boone
Hundreds of miles of horse trails with designated horse camps are found in this Kentucky national forest. Trails and camps are available in the Morehead, Somerset, and Stearns ranger districts.

Taylorsville Lake State Park
PO Box 205, Taylorsville, KY 40071
502-477-8713
http://www.parks.ky.gov/stateparks/tl/index.htm
This 1,200-acre state park near Louisville enthusiastically welcomes horseback riders. It features a 16-mile multiuse trail system (horses, hikers, and mountain bikers) and a horseman's camp with water and electricity.

Maryland

Fair Hill National Resources Management Area
1401 National Park Drive, Manteo, NC 27954
410-398-1246
http://www.dnr.state.md.us/publiclands/central/fairhill.html
This 5,600-acre area was original owned by William duPont Jr., an avid equestrian. Purchased by the state in 1975, it features a racetrack, shared-use riding trails, and overnight stabling and rental horses at Fair Hills Stables (410-620-3883).

North Carolina

Cape Hatteras National Seashore
1401 National Park Drive
Manteo, NC 27954
252-473-2111
http://www.nps.gov/caha/
index.htm
Ride your horse on the beach or rent a horse from Equine Adventures, in Frisco (252-995-4897), or Buxton Stables, in Buxton (252-995-4659).

South Carolina

Croft State Natural Area
450 Croft State Park Road, Spartanburg, SC 29302
864-585-1283
http://www.discoversouthcarolina.com/stateparks/index.asp
Ride through dense forests on 21 miles of equestrian trails. Overnight stabling is available in the park's equestrian center, where horse shows are sometimes held.

Lakeview Plantation

875 Cedar Knoll Road, Fairfax, SC 29827

803-584-0689

http://www.lakeviewplantation.com

Explore the 2,600 acres of this private riding facility. Designed specifically for horses and horse people, Lakeview Plantation offers well-marked trails, horse camps, a lodge, and more.

Tennessee

Big South Fork National River and Recreation Area

4564 Leatherwood Road, Oneida, TN 37841

423-569-9778

http://www.nps.gov/biso/index.htm

This recreation area offers hundreds of miles of horse trails and several horse camps. Bandy Creek Stables (423-286-7433; http://www.nps.gov/biso/bsf_stab.htm), a National Park Service concession, provides overnight stabling and rental horses.

Virginia

George Washington National Forest

5162 Valleypointe Parkway, Roanoke, VA 24019

540-265-5100

http://www.fs.fed.us/r8/gwj/index.shtml

Ride various trails throughout this large forest that encompasses several ranger districts. Horse camping and other facilities are available.

West Virginia

Watoga State Park

HC 82, Box 252, Marlinton, WV 24954

304-799-4087

http://www.watoga.com

Rent a horse for a guided ride at Windy Hill Quarter Horse Stables (304-799-5455/304-799-2324) inside the park, open Memorial Day to Labor Day. Please contact the stable for availability of overnight boarding for private horses visiting the park.

Getting there

SOUTHEAST TRAVEL SECTION

IF YOU ARE TRAVELING WITHOUT YOUR HORSE, OR IF YOUR HORSE IS BOARDED SAFELY AT A STABLE, ENJOY THE SITES IN THE NEIGHBORING TOWNS. BELOW, YOU'LL FIND A MILEAGE CHART LISTING THE DISTANCES BETWEEN THE TRAILS AND ALL THE AREAS DISCUSSED IN THE FOLLOWING TRAVEL SECTION. THE AREAS CLOSEST TO THE TRAILS ARE INDICATED BY AN **X**. FOR AREAS WHERE NEITHER STABLING NOR HORSE RENTALS ARE AVAILABLE, NO SIGHTSEEING OPTIONS ARE LISTED.

COAST TO COAST	Aiken, S.C.	Chincoteague National Wildlife Refuge, Va.	Gatlinburg, Tenn.	Hodgenville, Ky.	Midland, N.C.	Mt. Gilead, N.C.
Assateague Island (Md. and Va.)	580 miles	**X** 60 miles	635 miles	755 miles	465 miles	425 miles
Great Smoky Mountains National Park (Tenn. and N.C.)	275 miles	600 miles	**X** * miles	280 miles	240 miles	275 miles
The Hitchcock Woods (S.C.)	**X** * miles	555 miles	280 miles	540 miles	165 miles	205 miles
Mammoth Cave National Park (Ky.)	505 miles	830 miles	270 miles	**X** 50 miles	500 miles	535 miles
Mount Rogers National Recreation Area (Va.)	305 miles	490 miles	**X** 165 miles	385 miles	190 miles	210 miles
Uwharrie National Forest (N.C.)	210 miles	390 miles	280 miles	555 miles	**X** 45 miles	**X** * miles

*The area to visit is the same as or is within 10 miles of the trails.

MUST SEE / MUST DO

KENTUCKY

MAMMOTH CAVE NATIONAL PARK AREA

Visitors to Mammoth Cave National park can experience the wonder of the park's **caves** and its animals by taking one of several cave tours. The tours range in difficulty and time underground and emphasize different things, such as the cave animals, natural cave environment, dripstone formations, geologic development, and much more.

Cave tour

Prices range from $4 for the self-guided .75-mile Mammoth Cave Discovery Tour to $46 for the six-hour 5.5-mile Wild Cave Tour. Tours vary by season. Contact Mammoth Cave National Park (PO Box 7, Mammoth Cave, KY 42259; 270-758-22180; http://www.nps.gov/maca/Tours.html) for more information about the various cave tours.

While you are in the area, you can also visit Abraham Lincoln's birthplace, approximately 40 miles from the park. On February 12, 1809, Lincoln was born in a one-room log cabin on the 348-acre Sinking Spring Farm.

Lincoln birthplace

Abraham Lincoln Birthplace National Historic Site (2995 Lincoln Farm Road, Hodgenville, KY 42748; 270-358-3137; http://www.nps.gov/abli) is open from Memorial Day through Labor Day, from 8:00 a.m. to 6:45 p.m.; for the rest of the year, it is open from 8:00 a.m. to 4:45 p.m. You can visit **Lincoln's boyhood home** at Knob Creek, also part of the park, 10 miles northeast of his birthplace on US 31 East. The boyhood home is open during daylight hours. There are no fees to visit either site.

MARYLAND (AND VIRGINIA)

ASSATEAGUE ISLAND AREA

Experience a bit of Assateague Island's history by visiting the **Assateague Lighthouse**, built in 1833 and located in the Chincoteague National Wildlife Refuge (757-336-3696; http://www.assateagueisland.com/lighthouse/lighthouse_info.htm). The lighthouse is one of several operated to warn passing ships of the treacherous shoals that lie off the barrier islands of the East Coast. Its revolving light, which flashes from a height of 154 feet above sea level, can be seen for 19 nautical miles. The current light was installed in 1963, when power lines were extended to Assateague. Earlier, lights included a candle lantern, an oil-burner plunger lamp, and a flashing electric light powered by generators. The lighthouse also reflects the changing nature of barrier islands. When it was first built, it sat at the southern tip of the island, but the sea deposited sand over the years and has added land to Assateague, leaving the lighthouse inland. The lighthouse is open Easter through Thanksgiving, Friday through Sunday from 9:00 a.m. to 3:00 p.m. Admission is $4 for adults and $2 for children (free for children under two).

Assateague lighthouse

If you plan to visit during the last week in July, don't miss the annual Fireman's Carnival **Pony Swim** and **Auction**, when you can experience first-hand the thrill of watching the horses swim across the channel to Chincoteague Island. The swim and auction are always held the last Wednesday and Thursday in July. Stay for the auction, and then watch the horses swim back to their home on Assateague. There is no charge to watch the pony swim or to attend the auction. In the days leading up to the swim and auction, visitors can enjoy the Fireman's Carnival, which is held throughout July and leads up to the swim and auction event. For more information, contact the Chincoteague Chamber of Commerce (PO Box 258, Chincoteague, VA 23336; 757-336-6161; http://www .chincoteague chamber.com).

Chincoteague ponies swimming

NORTH CAROLINA

UWHARRIE NATIONAL FOREST AREA

Attractions near the Uwharrie National Forest include the **Town Creek Indian Mound** (509 Town Creek Mound Road, Mt. Gilead, NC 27306; 910-439-6802; http://www.ah.dcr.state.nc.us/sec tions/hs/town/town.htm). One of the most well-known historic sites in the state, the Town Creek site, which was discovered in the 1930s, features Indian mounds and reconstructed structures of early people in the area, known as the Pee Dee culture. There are no admission fees, but donations are accepted. Hours are 10:00 a.m. to 4:00 p.m., Tuesday through Saturday, and 1:00 p.m. to 4:00 p.m. on Sunday; it's closed Monday.

Town Creek Indian Mound

Another historic site near Uwharrie is **Reed Gold Mine** (9621 Reed Mine Road, Midland, NC 28107; 704-721-4657; http://www.ah.dcr .state.nc.us/sections/hs/reed/reed .htm). The mine is the site of the first documented discovery of gold in the United States in 1799. Visitors can view restored mine tunnels on guided tours, walk the trails through the mining area, and see real gold and historical min-ing equipment at the visitor center. You can pan for gold from April through October and enjoy a picnic at one of the twenty picnic tables.

There is no charge for admission or tours of the mine. Gold panning is $2 per pan. In spring and summer, the mine is open Tuesday through Saturday from 9:00 a.m. to 5:00 p.m., closed Sunday and Monday; in fall and winter, it is open Tuesday through Saturday from 10:00 a.m. to 4:00 p.m., closed Sunday and Monday.

SOUTH CAROLINA

THE HITCHCOCK WOODS AREA

Located in a 1902 carriage house inside Hopelands Gardens on Dupree Place (off of Whiskey Road), the **Aiken Thoroughbred Racing Hall of Fame** (135 Dupree Place, Aiken, SC 29803; 802-642-7631; http://www.aikenracing halloffame.com) pays tribute to the horse industry of Aiken and to thirty-eight famous horses who trained here. One of these famous horses is Kelso, the only horse (to date) to win five Horse of the Year titles, which he did from 1960 to 1964. Photographs, trophies, books, and magazines about the world of horse racing are on display here. The hall

Pete Bostwick on Flaming

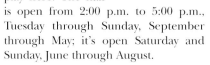

Thoroughbred Racing Hall of Fame

is open from 2:00 p.m. to 5:00 p.m., Tuesday through Sunday, September through May; it's open Saturday and Sunday, June through August.

Depending on when you time your visit to the Hitchcock Woods and Aiken, you can see various equestrian events. In the spring is the **Aiken Triple Crown**, which consists of three consecutive weekends of flat racing, steeplechase races, and polo. Contact the Aiken Chamber of Commerce for dates and details (802-641-1111). The annual **Aiken Horse Show** (http://www.aiken horseshow.com), held in the Hitchcock Woods, occurs over three days in the spring. Polo matches can be seen at one of Aiken's polo clubs. Information for polo in Aiken is listed at http://www.aikenpolo.net. For information on steeplechase events in Aiken, including the Imperial Cup in the spring and Holiday Cup in the fall, contact The Aiken Steeplechase Association (PO Box 360, Aiken, SC 29802; 803-648-9641; http://www.aikensteeple chase.com).

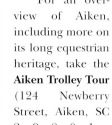

For an overview of Aiken, including more on its long equestrian heritage, take the **Aiken Trolley Tour** (124 Newberry Street, Aiken, SC 29801; http://www.aikenprt.net/Aiken_Tours.html), which leaves at 10:00 a.m. every Saturday. The two-hour guided tour will give you the opportunity to learn more about historic homes and churches, equestrian sites, Civil War battles, and other interesting points in the area. The price is $6 per person, and reservations are strongly recommended.

If you are seeking an equine-themed sculpture or other art piece for your home or that perfect horse-related gift, stop in at **Aiken's Equine Divine** (135 Laurens Street NW, Aiken, SC 29801; 802-642-9772). The store's hours are 10:00 a.m. to 5:00 p.m., Monday through Saturday, and 10:00 a.m. to

6:00 p.m. during polo season. **Jackson Gallery** (300 Park Avenue SE, Aiken, SC 29801; 802-648-7397; http://www.jacksongallery.com) also offers horse sculptures and other art. Jackson Gallery is open by appointment only.

TENNESSEE (AND NORTH CAROLINA)

GREAT SMOKY MOUNTAINS NATIONAL PARK AREA

There is so much to see and do in Great Smoky Mountains National Park that you won't need to go anywhere else. A must when visiting the park is to learn about this beautiful area. To find out more, visit one of the multiple visitor centers that have trail maps and provide backcountry permits.

Visitors to Cades Cove can stop at the **Cades Cove Visitor Center** inside

Great Smoky Mountains National Park

the park near the midpoint of the 11-mile, one-way Cades Cove Loop Road. It is open all year, from 9:00 a.m. to 4:30 p.m. in December and January, from 9:00 a.m. to 5:00 p.m. in February, and from 9:00 a.m. to 5:30 p.m. in March. The center hosts exhibits related to settler life in the area and has a bookstore and gift shop. There is no telephone at this visitor center.

If entering the park from the south, visit the **Oconaluftee Visitor**

Center, 2 miles inside the park north of Cherokee, North Carolina, on US 441. It is open all year, from 8:00 a.m. to 6:00 p.m. in October, from 8:00 a.m. to 4:30 p.m. November through March, and from 8:00 a.m. to 5:00 p.m. in April. There is a bookstore and gift shop at the visitor center. The adjacent **Mountain Farm Museum** (828-497-1904) contains a fascinating collection of log structures that includes a farmhouse, barn, smokehouse, apple house, and corncribs. Demonstrations of farm life are conducted seasonally.

Sugarlands Visitor Center is inside the park on US 441, 2 miles south of Gatlinburg. It is open all year, from 8:00 a.m. to 6:00 p.m. in October, from 8:00 a.m. to 5:00 p.m. in November, and from 8:00 a.m. to 4:30 p.m. December through March. Items of interest there include a short film about the park and exhibits of the park's natural history. There is also a bookstore and gift shop.

Additionally, the town of **Gatlinburg**, Tennessee, which is the main gateway to the park, has two welcome centers that provide information about the town and the area. The downtown welcome center is open all year long from 9:00 a.m. to 5:00 p.m. The other welcome center is 2 miles outside of Gatlinburg on US 441 South and is open all year, from 8:00 a.m. to 5:30 p.m. November through March, and from 8:30 a.m. to 6:00 p.m. April through October.

Spinning wheel demonstration

WHERE TO STAY & STABLE

KENTUCKY

MAMMOTH CAVE NATIONAL PARK AREA

Horses and Riders:

Double J Stables and Campgrounds
542 Lincoln School Road
Mammoth Cave, KY 42259
270-286-8167
http://www.doublejstables.com
$15.00 per night for rustic campsites; $20.00 per night for water and electric sites; $5.00 per night for horse stalls; $3.00 for pens; $2.00 per day for day-use area
Double J Stables and Campgrounds, located off the northeastern corner of Mammoth Cave National Park, offers overnight horse camping, day-use camping, and guided trail rides. Guided rides on rental horses range from $15 for a one-hour ride to $125.00 for an eight-hour ride. The facility has modern restrooms and showers, turnout and picketing area, and some campsites with water and electricity. Park trails are located adjacent to the campground. Reservations are required for camping and rentals but not for day use.

Maple Springs Group Campground
Located in the park
800-967-2283 for reservations
http://www.nps.gov/maca/horses.pdf
$30 per night
This campground allows horses on four of its seven camping sites. Each campsite accommodates up to twenty-four people and eight horses. The campgrounds have fresh water, chemical toilets, picnic tables, grills, and picket areas near the horse campsites. Open March through November.

Riders Only:

Mammoth Cave Hotel
Mammoth Cave National Park, PO Box 27
Mammoth Cave, KY 42259
270-758-2225
http://www.mammothcavehotel.com
$62–$92 per night for rooms; $36–$63 for cottages
The Mammoth Cave Hotel offers lodging in its Heritage Trail rooms and Sunset Terrace rooms. Quaint and cozy historic cottages and lower-priced rustic cottages nestled in the trees are also available. The hotel, three restaurants, and two gift shops are on site and have easy access to cave tours.

MARYLAND (AND VIRGINIA)

ASSATEAGUE ISLAND AREA

Horses and Riders:

Assateague Island National Seashore Camping
7206 National Seashore Lane
Berlin, MD 21811
410-641-3030
http://www.nps.gov/asis/horsebackriding.htm
$25 per night for camping, plus $10 for a vehicle pass

Each of the two horse camps at the Seashore has a capacity for twenty-five horses and riders. These campsites are very popular so reservations are required and may be made as far as five months in advance. Camping is allowed from October 9 through April 14.

Hoof Prints in the Sand
5367 Sixty Foot Road
Parsonburg, MD 21849
410-835-8814
http://hometown.aol.com/sfwinter/myhomepage/business.html
$35 per night for campsites, plus $10 for each horse

Hoof Prints in the Sand is a recreational and therapeutic riding center approximately thirty minutes west of Assateague Island National Seashore. You can camp here with your horse on 20 private acres and ride directly into Wicomico State Forest, or you can trailer your horse to Assateague. Hoof Prints also rents out horses for naturalist-guided trail rides into the forest and leads periodic trail rides on the beach at Assateague Island National Seashore (fall months only); its two-hour ecotour trail ride costs $50.

Riders Only

Assateague Inn
PO Box 1038, 6570 Coach's Lane
Chincoteague Island, VA 23336
757-336-3738
http://www.assateague-inn.com
$50–$150 per night

Assateague Inn offers twenty-seven rooms in its setting overlooking a saltwater creek and a salt marsh. In addition to single rooms, efficiency suites and apartments are available. Close to restaurants, shopping, and recreation.

Dunes Manor Hotel
2800 Baltimore Avenue
Ocean City, MD 21842
410-289-1100/800-523-2888
http://www.dunesmanor.com
$45–$300-plus per night, depending on room and time of year

This Victorian-themed hotel replicates a nineteenth-century seaside resort. Built in 1987, it features all oceanfront rooms and private balconies. The Victorian Room, the Barefoot Bar Beachside, and the Zippy Lewis Lounge offer fine dining, light meals, and snacks.

1848 Island Manor House Bed and Breakfast
4160 Main Street
Chincoteague Island, VA 23336
800-852-1505
http://www.islandmanor.com
$90–$195 per night, breakfast included

This charming bed-and-breakfast, built before the Civil War as the name implies, has eight rooms, all with individual names. Some rooms have channel views, whereas others overlook the courtyard and fountain.

Lighthouse Club Hotel
56th Street at the Bay
201 50th Street (mailing address)
Ocean City, MD 21842

410-524-5400/888-371-5400
http://www.fagers.com/hotel
$79–$349 per night, depending on time of year and location of suite
This all-suite hotel, designed as a replica of the Thomas Point Lighthouse on the Chesapeake Bay, sits at the edge of the Isle of Wight Bay surrounded by natural wet-lands. The rooms are airy and contemporary and have private decks with views of the water. The lowest rates are in the off-season, when riding is allowed at Assateague Island National Seashore.

NORTH CAROLINA

UWHARRIE NATIONAL FOREST AREA

Horses and Riders

Badin Lake Horse Camp
Uwharrie Ranger District, 789 NC Highway 24/27 East
Troy, NC 27371
910-576-6391
http://www.cs.unca.edu/nfsnc/recreation/uwharrie/badin_lake_horse_camp.htm
$5 per night per vehicle
Badin Lake has a grassy field for camping and offers hitching posts and toilets. A stream is nearby. There are no designated equestrian trails in this area, but riders can use forest roads and 20 miles of off-highway vehicle trails for easy to moderate riding. No reservations are accepted; camping is on a first-come, first-served basis.

Canebrake Horse Camp
Located in the forest
877-444-6777 or TDD 877-833-6777 for reservations
http://www.cs.unca.edu/nfsnc/recreation/canebrake_horse_camp.htm
$12 per night single, $24 double
Canebrake Horse Camp offers twenty-four single and five double campsites. All sites have parking spurs for horse trailers and include picnic tables, grills, hitching posts, and lantern posts. There are showers and flush toilets at the camp, water spigots for drinking water, a horse-washing rack, and a sewage dump station. No electricity or water hookups are provided. Equestrian trails are accessible via the Home Trail that skirts the campground. Riders and horses can also camp at an overflow lot across the street from this campground, albeit at a more primitive level.

4B Farm
346 Mullinix Road
Troy, NC 27371
910-572-2267
http://www.fourbfarm.com
$5 annual membership fee per person per night camping; $12 per night for stalls includes shav-ings for two nights; $5 per horse per night for corrals; $2 per horse per night for line tie
Located adjacent to Uwharrie National Forest, 4B Farm features forty campsites with electrical hookups as well as some primitive sites, a heated bathhouse, forty-three cov-ered stalls, thirty-four corrals, a line tie area, and a small tack store. There is also an ice cream stand offering dipped ice cream. Church services are held in the barn on Sunday mornings. Reservations are recommended, especially in spring and fall.

Uwharrie Stables
4084 Highway 109 North
Troy, NC 27371
910-572-1614
http://www.uwharriestables.com

$5 per night per camper for primitive sites; $10–$15 per night for sites with water and electricity; $12 per night for stalls with shavings, one horse per stall

Uwharrie Stables offers camping with horses, rentals, riding lessons, and horse boarding. If you don't have a reservation, all campsites, stalls, and rentals are available on a first-come, first-served basis.

Riders Only:

Blair House Bed and Breakfast
105 Blair Street
Troy, NC 27371
910-572-2100
http://www.blairhousebb.com
$90–$110 per night, breakfast included
Blair House was built in 1893 and has been family owned for more than one hundred years. It features four suites, each with a bedroom, sitting area, and private bath. The recently renovated suites have in-room cable television and DVD players and are climate controlled.

SOUTH CAROLINA

THE HITCHCOCK WOODS AREA

Horses and Riders:

Town and Country Inn Bed and Breakfast
2340 Sizemore Circle
Aiken, SC 29803
803-642-0270
http://www.towncountrybb.com
$80–$95 per night
Charming rooms with private baths and a homey atmosphere make equestrians comfortable after a day of riding in The Hitchcock Woods. Guests can cool off in the swimming pool on warm summer days while equine guests enjoy a five-stall barn, a pasture, and a round pen. Other pets are welcome.

Riders Only:

Annie's Inn
3083 Charleston Highway
Montmorenci, SC 29839
803-649-6836
http://www.anniesinnbnb.com
$90–$125 per night for rooms, breakfast included; $500–$600 per week for cottages, breakfast not included
What is now Annie's Inn used to be the main house of a 2,000-acre plantation. Still surrounded by cotton fields, it features five guest rooms and six guest cottages for longer-term stays.

The Willcox Hotel
100 Colleton Avenue
Aiken, SC 29801
803-648-1898/877-648-2200
http://www.thewillcox.com
$175–$225 per night for rooms; $400–$500 for suites
This white-pillared hotel offers fireplaces in most of its rooms and suites. Each room is unique, and they all feature sitting areas. While staying at the Willcox, you can par-

take in a massage, a facial, or other rejuvenating treatments for an extra fee. Pets are welcome with a deposit.

Horses Only:

Augusta Riding Center
1403 Flowing Wells Road
Augusta, GA 30909
706-863-9044
http://www.augustaridingcenter.com
$20 per night

Approximately thirty-five minutes from Aiken, the Augusta Riding Center offers overnight horse stabling in box stalls. Arrangements for turnout can be made if pasture is available. Bring your own hay. When planning your trip, call ahead for stall availability.

Jumping Branch Farm
179 Fox Pond Road
Aiken, SC 29803
803-642-3484
http://www.jbfarm.com
$20 per night

Jumping Branch Farm offers overnight stabling to visiting horses. Bedding is provided, but visitors are responsible for their own feed. Call ahead for availability of stalls and turnout space.

TENNESSEE (AND NORTH CAROLINA)

GREAT SMOKY MOUNTAINS NATIONAL PARK AREA

Horses and Riders:

Gilbertson's Lazy Horse Retreat
938 Schoolhouse Gap Road
Townsend, TN 37882
865-448-6810
http://www.thesmokies.com/lazy_horse/index.htm
$75–$105 per night for cabins for two people, $10 per night per additional person; $10 per night for stalls; $5 per night for paddocks

These accommodations in the Dry Valley area are near trailheads in the national park. Four cabins are available for guests, and there are twelve box stalls, four paddocks, and three round pens for equine visitors. There is a two-night minimum stay requirement, but people passing through can stay one night. Stalls are cleaned daily, but you must bring your own feed.

Great Smoky Mountains National Park Campgrounds
Located in the park
800-365-2267 for reservations
http://www.nps.gov/grsm/index.htm
$20 per day per site for all camps except Big Creek, $25 per site at Big Creek

Six people and four horses are allowed per campsite: Anthony Creek (at Cades Cove), Big Creek, Cataloochee, Round Bottom, and Towstring. Drive-in horse camps have designated parking, grills, picnic tables, and hitch rails. Big Creek also has flush toilets and cold water. The other camps have portable toilets and no drinking water. Water for horses is available in the camps or from nearby streams.

Rock-n-Horse Stables & Cabins
7818 Berry Williams Road
Townsend, TN 37882

865-448-3957

http://www.rocknhorsestables.com/index.htm

$79–$125 per night for cabins; $10 per night per additional person; $15 per night for stalls; $6 per horse per night for paddock or pasture; $15 per night for trailer hookup with electricity and water

Rock-n-Horse Stables & Cabins has four cabins with kitchens, ranging from one to four bedrooms. Horse facilities include a fifteen-stall stable, a paddock, a round pen, and five pastures. Stalls are cleaned daily. Veterinary and farrier services are available. Daily breakfast and Saturday night cookout are available upon request. There is a two-night minimum stay requirement.

VIRGINIA

MOUNT ROGERS NATIONAL RECREATION AREA

Horses and Riders:

Collins Cove Campground and Hussy Mountain Campgrounds

Located in the NRA in the East End of Wythe County

276-783-5196/800-628-7202

http://www.fs.fed.us/r8/gwj/mr

$3 per night per vehicle

Both of these relatively primitive campgrounds have wooden picnic tables, fire rings, hitch rails, and vault toilets. Hussy Mountain provides potable water, but Collins Cove does not. They both allow easy access to the Virginia Highlands Horse Trail, which connects to the Iron Mountain Trail as well as to other horse trails. They are available on a first-come, first-served basis.

Fox Creek Horse Campground

Located in the NRA in Smyth County in the Fairwood Valley

276-783-5196/800-628-7202

http://www.fs.fed.us/r8/gwj/mr

$5 per night per vehicle

Fox Creek Campground has two open fields for camping, vault toilets, and hitch rails. There is no potable water, but there are designated access points for watering horses along the trail. Availability is on a first-come, first-served basis.

Grayson Highlands State Park Horse Camps

829 Grayson Highlands Lane

Mouth of Wilson, VA 24363

276-579-7092

http://www.dcr.state.va.us/parks/graysonh.htm

$11–$23 for camping per night; $7–$9 for stalls

This state park has campgrounds and overnight stabling for horses. There are 2 miles of bridle trails leading to trails in Mount Rogers National Recreation Area. Contact the state park for details.

High Country Horse Camp

1109 Ravendale Drive (mailing address)

Charlotte, NC 28216

276-388-3992

http://www.highcountryhorsecamp.com

$40 per night for minicabins; $21 per night for camping with hookups and tie line for two horses, $5 per additional horse; $10 per night for box stalls

High Country Horse Camp is a private horse camp located near Mount Rogers National Recreation Area and adjacent to the Virginia Highlands Horse Trail. The camp provides lodging in small cabins that sleep two (bring your own linens) or at fully equipped campsites. Guests are responsible for cleaning the stalls daily; rakes and wheelbarrows are provided. There are showers, a horse-washing rack, laundry facilities, and even live entertainment in the form of bluegrass music. A campground restaurant, which is open dependent on camp occupancy, serves hearty meals in the morning and evening for an additional charge.

Hungry Horse Farm
2079 Brush Creek Road
Ivanhoe, VA 24350
276-744-3210
http://www.hungryhorsefarm.com
From $15 per night for campsites to $150-plus per night for a four-bedroom cabin; $15 per night for stalls
The scenic Hungry Horse Farm offers two fully furnished cabins for rent as well as camping among the trees next to a quiet stream. Cabins include kitchens and bathrooms; camping is available with electrical hookups and water or without for a more primitive experience. A bathhouse is available for campers. Reservations are required.

Iron Mountain Horse Camp
PO Box 555
Cripple Creek, VA 24322
276-744-2056
http://www.ironmountainhorsecamp.com
$3 per person for day use and parking; $15 per night for primitive camping; $20 per night for trailer with water and electrical hookup; $160 per night for up to six people and six horses for a cabin with a barn and pasture, additional people and horses are extra
Located in Jefferson National Forest, you can ride out the gate to the trails of the Mount Rogers National Recreation Area. Campsites are located along a creek near the seventy-eight-stall horse barn. A three-bedroom cabin has its own six-stall barn and a pasture. Parking for riders visiting for the day is allowed as is use of the bathhouse and wash bay for horses for day-use visitors. If you've forgotten something or need additional supplies, a well-stocked tack and supply store is on site at the barn. Reservations are recommended.

Old Virginia Group Horse Camp
Located in the NRA, a couple of miles from Fox Creek, toward Troutdale
276-783-5196/Reservations (required): 877-444-6777
http://www.fs.fed.us/r8/gwj/mr
$40 per night for up to 50 people
This primitive camp is available by reservation only and for groups up to fifty. From either Fox Creek or Old Virginia campgrounds, you must ride on the side of the highway for a short distance to access the Virginia Highlands Horse Trail.

Rocky Hollow Horse Camp
3382 Rocky Hollow Road
Troutdale, VA 24378
888-644-0014/276-677-3900
http://www.rockyhollowhorsecamp.com
$100 per night for cabins; $20 for camping; $10 for stalls
The 40-acre Rocky Hollow Horse Camp, established in 2003, is located on the southern side of Troutdale. A short ride will get you to several popular spots in the NRA, including the top of Mount Rogers and Rhododendron Gap. A secluded cabin with a gas fireplace is available for rent by riders as well as campsites with hookups. There is a bathhouse for cleaning up after a long day on the trails. You can rent a stall for your horse or use a picket line.

WHERE TO WINE & DINE

KENTUCKY

MAMMOTH CAVE NATIONAL PARK AREA

A Little Taste of Texas Cafe
303 South Broadway
Glasgow, KY 42141
270-659-2441
http://www.glasgow-ky.com/littletasteoftexas
$5.50–$16.95
Dine in or carry out at the family-owned Little Taste of Texas. A wide variety of Tex-Mex dishes, steaks, salads, and sandwiches on the menu will have you hankering to come back again. Open for lunch Monday through Friday and for dinner Monday through Saturday; closed Sundays.

Mammoth Cave Hotel
PO Box 27
Mammoth Cave, KY 42259
270-758-2225/Reservations: 270-758-2225
http://www.mammothcavehotel.com
$3.95–$15.75 at Travertine Restaurant; $3–$17 at Crystal Lake Coffee Shop; $5 and under at T017 at TrogloBITES
You can dine inside the park at one of the eateries at the Mammoth Cave Hotel. The hotel's Travertine Restaurant offers "southern hospitality at its finest," and the Crystal Lake Coffee Shop features popular entrées and homemade desserts whipped up by local chefs. TrogloBITES is an on-site fast food restaurant that offers burgers, fries, and sodas. Travertine and the Crystal Lake Coffee shop are open every day from Memorial Day to Labor Day. Travertine hours are 7:00 a.m. to 7:30 p.m. serving breakfast, lunch, and dinner. The coffee shop is open 10:00 a.m. to 4:30 p.m. serving lunch. During the rest of the year, the two restaurants open periodically depending on the number of visitors. TrogloBITES is open from mid-June to Labor Day for lunch items, from 10:00 a.m. to 5:00 p.m.

MARYLAND (AND VIRGINIA)

ASSATEAGUE ISLAND AREA

Bill's Seafood Restaurant
4040 Main Street
Chincoteague Island, VA 23336
757-336-5831
$11.95–$22.95
Bill's, in business since 1960, is wildly popular for its excellent food (large amounts served) and friendly service. Bill's serves breakfast, lunch, and dinner and specializes in seafood, steaks, and chops. In addition to its specialties, pasta and light fare are available as well as homemade desserts. Be sure to make reservations, especially for dinner, as Bill's is always crowded.

The Chincoteague Inn
6262 Marlin Street
Chincoteague Island, VA 23336
757-336-6110
http://www.chincoteague.com/rest/ciptp

$12.95–$25.95 for entrées

At the Chincoteague Inn, you'll find waterfront dining, live entertainment, and a variety of food. The inn serves lunch and dinner and specializes in seafood. Try the fresh fish, crab, or meat in the main restaurant; or sample burgers, sandwiches, pizza, and other lighter fare at the inn's waterfront deck bar, P.T. Pelican's.

The Hobbit
101 81st Street
Ocean City, MD 21842
410-524-8100
http://www.hobbitgifts.com
$20.00 and up for entrées; $9.95–$14.95 for the early bird specials; $4.95–$13.95 for the café fare

Fans of J. R. R. Tolkien are not the only ones who will find the food good and the atmosphere charming at The Hobbit. The bay-side dining room features murals depicting scenes from the classic novel. Table lamps are carved in the shapes of hobbits. There is a deck for outdoor dining on seafood, steaks, chicken, and pasta dinners, and the café and bar serve sandwiches and light meals. The gift shop sells Hobbit-related items.

Phillips Crab House & Seafood Buffet
2004 Philadelphia Avenue
Ocean City, MD 21842
410-289-6821/800-549-2722
http://www.phillipsseafood.com/phillipscrabhouse
$6.99 and up for sandwiches; market price for fresh seafood

This original 1956 restaurant in the family-owned Phillips chain features crab delicacies and fresh seafood. The regular menu is served in the dining room, and the enormously popular seafood buffet is served upstairs. It is open March through October. Or try one of Phillips's other locations: Phillips by the Sea on 1301 Atlantic Avenue and Phillips Seafood House on 14101 Coastal Highway.

NORTH CAROLINA

UWHARRIE NATIONAL FOREST AREA

Better Burger
398 Albermarle Road
Troy, NC 27371
910-572-1244
Up to $2.50 for burgers

Better Burger has been around since the 1950s and is a local favorite. Although the restaurant itself may show its age, you'll find great burgers and other casual food at reasonable prices.

Eldorado Outpost
4021 North Highway 109
Troy, NC 27371
910-572-3474
http://www.eldoradooutpost.com
$5 range

Eldorado Outpost, located directly between the two main entrances to the national forest, is an outdoor outfitter as well as a place to grab a casual meal. It provides everything from charcoal to groceries to horse tack and supplies. The diner in the store serves breakfast, lunch, and dinner. Eldorado Outpost is open year-round from 7:00 a.m. to 8:00 p.m. The only day it closes is Christmas Day.

SOUTH CAROLINA

THE HITCHCOCK WOODS AREA

The Aiken Brewing Company
140 Laurens Street SW
Aiken, SC 29801
803-502-0707
http://www.aikenbrewingcompany.com
$7–$19
The brewery serves sandwiches, steaks, and other pub fare. In addition to good food, The Aiken Brewing Company offers several different home-brewed ales, including the award-winning Thoroughbred Red Ale. Open for lunch and dinner.

Linda's Bistro
210 The Alley
Aiken, SC 29801
803-648-4853
http://www.lindasbistro-aiken.com
$16–$30
Located in the center of downtown Aiken, Linda's Bistro offers steaks, lamb, pork, sea bass, risotto, and other fare. The restaurant also holds periodic wine-tasting dinners. Open for dinner Tuesday through Saturday; reservations recommended.

TENNESSEE (AND NORTH CAROLINA)

GREAT SMOKY MOUNTAINS NATIONAL PARK AREA

Calhoun's
1004 Parkway
Gatlinburg, TN 37738
865-436-4100
http://www.coppercellar.com/cal/loc_gatlinburg.htm
$6.95–$18.95
Dine inside or try the covered patio out back. Calhoun's offers American/Southern fare of barbecued dishes, such as smoked prime rib, as well as steaks, chicken, and fish. Try the fried green tomatoes as an appetizer.

Maxwell's Beef & Seafood
1103 Parkway
Gatlinburg, TN 37738
865-436-3738
http://www.maxwells-inc.com
$12.99–$32.99 for entrées
You'll find a varied menu of American fare at Maxwell's Beef & Seafood, such as pastas, seafood, beef, vegetable, and chicken dishes. House specialties include Smoky Mountain rainbow trout and charbroiled tuna. Reservations are accepted.

VIRGINIA

MOUNT ROGERS NATIONAL RECREATION AREA

Cowboy's
111 Douglas Drive
Damascus, VA 24236

276-475-5444
$1.39–$7.00
Cowboy's, located in the small trail town of Damascus, offers food out of the general store. Cowboy's serves breakfast, sandwiches, hot dogs, hamburgers, and other light fare.

The Creeper Trail Café
37077 Chestnut Mountain Road
Damascus, VA 24236
276-475-3888
http://www.creepertrailcafe.com
$3.95–$10.25
This café is situated along the Virginia Creeper Trail and provides a hitching post for riders wishing to stop for a meal. The café serves hamburgers, hot dogs, submarine sandwiches, ice cream, fish plate specials, and more. It is open for lunch and dinner (11:00 a.m. to 6:00 p.m.) from mid-May through Veteran's Day. The rest of the year it is open periodically based on weather conditions.

Dot's Inn
338 Douglas Drive
Damascus, VA 24236
276-475-3817
$2.35–$14.95
Opened in 1960 by Bob and Pauline Watson, the restaurant is still in the family, now run by their daughter Dot. Dishes include omelets, hamburgers, T-bone and rib eye steaks, and home-cooked meals such as beef stew, chili, and pork barbecue. Don't miss stopping in for a bite at this friendly establishment.

Ona's Country Kitchen
4013 Troutdale Highway
Mouth of Wilson, VA 24363
276-579-4440
http://www.ls.net/~planetva/restaurants/onas
$4.79–$8.99 for dinner; $5 and under for breakfast and lunch
Ona's serves breakfast, lunch, and dinner and offers a wide variety of casual fare. It is at the intersection of Highway 58 and Highway 16.

The Sugar Grove Diner (at the Sugar Grove Bed and Breakfast)
Highway 16 South
Sugar Grove, VA 24375
276-677-3351
$2–5 for breakfast; $5 average lunch and dinner entrées
This diner in Smyth County is worth trying for breakfast, lunch, or dinner. It features pancakes, omelets, and other hearty fare. For lunch and dinner, you can grab a burger or go a little more formal with a rib-eye steak. The diner is open year-round from 5:00 a.m. to 8:00 p.m. Monday through Wednesday and 5:00 a.m. to 8:30 p.m. Thursday through Saturday. It is closed on Sunday. There is also adequate horse trailer parking in the lot. If you are traveling without a horse, the bed and breakfast offers rooms for two people for $55 per night.

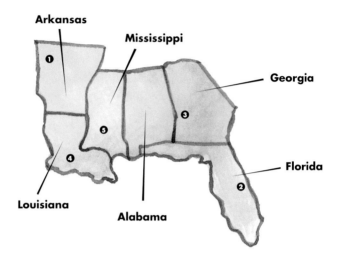

Arkansas

Mississippi

Georgia

Florida

Louisiana

Alabama

SOUTH MAP LEGEND

Arkansas
❶ Devil's Den State Park

Florida
❷ Canaveral National Seashore

Georgia
❸ F. D. Roosevelt State Park

Louisiana
❹ Kisatchie National Forest

Mississippi
❺ Bienville National Forest

THE SOUTH

ou'll find a variety of terrain in which to ride in the South, accompanied by generally mild weather, making for year-round fun. Rain is abundant here, as is high humidity, which means mosquitoes are often out in force, so wear lots of repellent when riding. For the purposes of this book, the South is defined as Alabama, Arkansas, Florida, Georgia, Louisiana, and Mississippi; Virginia and West Virginia are included in the Southeast section.

Within these states, trails are found in national parks and forests, state and county parks, and private recreation facilities. You can canter down a trail in a park that was established because an American president visited the area for polio treatment, meander along a beach with a distant view of massive space vehicles that take people and payloads on a journey to what truly is the final frontier, and wander the bayous of Louisiana.

The region has nearly a dozen areas administered by the National Park Service that allow riding. There are also multiple national forests with miles of trails. Mississippi alone has six national forests encompassing 1.1 million acres of land. Alabama is home to the smallest national forest in the country, the 11,000-acre Tuskegee, and there are also three other national forests in the state. State parks, such as Devil's Den in Arkansas, provide additional riding opportunities.

Wherever you ride, you and your horse are sure to enjoy the unique flavor of the southern United States.

ARKANSAS

DEVIL'S DEN STATE PARK

The 2,500-acre Devil's Den State Park is nestled in the picturesque Lee Creek Valley, in the Ozarks of northwestern Arkansas. In these parts, the deep valleys that characterize the Ozarks are called hollers by old-timers. This term may have originated as a regional pronunciation of *hollow*, which indicates a small valley between mountains. The hollers here developed over hundreds of millions of years. After geological shifts uplifted the Ozark Mountains from an ancient sea, rivers and creeks deeply carved the underlying limestone and sandstone into the steep-sided valleys that are here today. The valley where Devil's Den State Park is located is a place of striking beauty, providing some of the most spectacular Ozark Mountain scenery in Arkansas.

Devil's Den has the largest sandstone crevice cave area in the country, and many visitors come here expressly because of the caves. Visitors can explore all the caves along Devil's Den Trail, including the largest, the 550-foot Devil's Den Cave. Bats are also an

Caving at Devil's Den

attraction in these caves, and each year in June the Bat-O-Rama takes place, which is an entire weekend devoted to educating visitors about these frequently maligned creatures.

Lee Creek, with its clear, mountain waters, runs through the park. Its progress is stopped by a native stone dam, built by the Civilian Conservation Corp (CCC) in the 1930s, when the decision was made that this area would be a park. An 8-acre lake is formed by the dam, which offers fishing and other water activities. The CCC also crafted other hardwood and stone structures in

Devil's Den dam

the park, including cabins that are still used by visitors today. The structures were renovated in the 1970s to preserve them well into the future. The dam itself was heavily damaged by floodwaters in 2004 and underwent additional renovations.

Miles of trails perfect for hiking, biking, and, of course, riding wind into the park's backcountry and the surrounding Ozark National Forest. The Butterfield Hiking Trail, named for the old Butterfield Overland Mail stagecoach line that ran through the area between 1858 and 1861 (until the Civil War shut it down), takes visitors on a 15-mile loop through moderately difficult terrain. A portion of the trail traces a section of the historic stage route that connected the mail stops in Fayetteville and in Fort Smith. There are also campsites along

Riding at Devil's Den

the way for hikers who wish to take their time contemplating the trail's historic significance. The Butterfield trail is not open to equestrians, but other equally enjoyable trails are.

Scenic beauty, 20 miles of riding trails, and a horse camp make the park one of the most popular sites for horseback riding in the state. Its trails lead through oak and hickory forests and past historic sites, scenic vistas, waterfalls, and boulder gardens. The trails vary in length and difficulty, offering enjoyable trail riding opportunities to both novices and experts. There is the easier 5-mile Old Road horse trail, which follows the original route of Highway 170 (be careful on the highway crossings),

Relaxing at camp

SnapShot - Devil's Den State Park

Description: Meandering through the park, located in the steep-walled Lee Creek Valley, are 20 miles of horse trails of varying difficulty. Stay at the horse camp or at private camping facilities, which are within a short drive. A nearby ranch offers overnight lodging and stabling (see Where to Stay & Stable). The park has its own café as well as a store to purchase camping and picnic supplies. There are no horse rentals available in the park.

Open: Year-round

Address: 11333 West Arkansas Highway 74, West Fork, AR 72774

Phone: 479-761-3325

Web site: http://www.arkansasstateparks.com/devilsden

Getting there: From I-540: Drive 8 miles south of Fayetteville, take State Highway 170 at West Fork (Exit #53) 17 miles to the park. (Note: There are no gas stations on Highway 170 or at the park, so gas up prior to getting here. Also, horse trailers should not use Highway 74 from Winslow because of steep and winding roads.)

Fees/permits: Admission is free

Horse rentals: None

Horse camping: Available in the park

Trail conditions/level of difficulty: 5-mile easy trail, 7-mile moderate trail, 8-mile difficult trail (steep climbs and ledge riding)

and the more strenuous, climbing 8-mile Vista Point trail, which has a gorgeous view of the whole valley. The Gorley King Trail is a 7-mile trail, steep in areas, with four creek crossings. (The trails are also known to riders as the Yellow, Green, and Red trails for the colors of the signs they are marked with.) If you finish riding the park's trails, stop at the visitor center for an inexpensive map to many more horse trails in the valley located outside the park.

BATS IN THE DEN

He's no Bruce Wayne, but he's definitely Batman. Harry Harnish, park interpreter at Devil's Den State Park, may not be "the caped crusader" of crime fighting, but he does occasionally don a black cape and bat-wing mask in an effort to educate people about bats and their needed protection. "It gets their attention," he explained.

Harnish has been employed by the Arkansas Parks Department for more than twenty-five years. When he first arrived at Devil's Den more than twenty years ago, he knew nothing of bats or the park's sandstone crevices they call

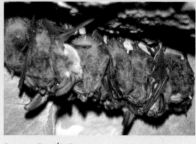

Bats at Devil's Den

home. Interested in the endangered creatures and the geology of the area, Harnish began to study them. His focus has led to the creation of one of the most popular annual events at the park, Bat-O-Rama.

Batman Harry always appears during Bat-O-Rama, an entire weekend of programs dedicated to one of the world's least understood and most maligned creatures. Programs at the Bat-O-Rama include slide presentations and videos, a bat house–building demonstration, exploration of the sandstone crevices at the park, and guest speakers.

During the summer, Harnish also shows a slide program on bats every Saturday night at the park amphitheater. On Monday nights, he demonstrates the bat detector, which enables visitors to hear the ultrahigh frequency sounds the bats make as they fly from their shelters in search of food.

"People help me count them," Harnish said. "They definitely can see bats if they come to Devil's Den in the summer. You can see hundreds of them flying over the lake." On the hottest days of the year, the bats move from the shelter to roost in the rafters of the café pavilion. "So people can go down there anytime in the summer and see the bats hanging out in the open," he added.

Bats can also be found hibernating in the park's crevices and caves, which are some of the most unique elements of the park. "I've plotted about sixty caves," Harnish said. "Most visitors know of only two—the Devil's Den and the Devil's Icebox. But up above that trail are crevices twice as deep. They're not off limits any time, but most people don't know they are there because they're not on the trail maps."

Bats hibernate in the caves at Devil's Den about five or six months out of the year. The eastern pipistrelle, a common bat that is not easily disturbed, can be found in the caves, as can two endangered bats, the Indiana and the Ozark big-eared. The latter is the second rarest species in the country. Because the endangered bats are easily awakened, the cave in which they hibernate is closed to the public. Devil's Den also has a large colony of big brown bats. Pregnant brown bats usually give birth to twins.

"A lot of people are just downright afraid of bats and are surprised to learn they're not going to attack them," Harnish said. "If you leave them alone, you have nothing to worry about. A lot of people also think all bats have rabies. It's possible for them to get rabies, but if they do, they get sick and die and flop on the ground. The only time I'm really careful is when I see one on the ground."

—*Courtesy of Arkansas Department of Parks & Tourism, by Jill M. Rohrbach*

FLORIDA

CANAVERAL NATIONAL SEASHORE

Fifty years ago, the United States was on the brink of the space race with the Soviet Union, which would ultimately culminate with man walking on the moon. The Soviets had launched *Sputnik* in 1957, and a year later the United States launched its first satellite, *Explorer 1*. So the competition to conquer outer space, and prove scientific and military superiority, began. In 1961, the Soviets again "got there first" by putting the first human into space, Cosmonaut Yuri Gagarin. This milestone by the Soviets further embarrassed the United States, and later that year President John F. Kennedy announced to the world that the United States would put men on the moon before the end of the decade. On July 20, 1969, *Apollo 11* Commander Neil Armstrong stepped into the history books with his first step onto the moon's surface. Sadly, President Kennedy did not live to see his dream of going to the moon realized.

Ospreys at Kennedy Space Ctr.

The country's desire to explore space resulted in the area near Canaveral National Seashore being used to test and launch the rockets that would take satellites into the cosmos and men to the moon. As a result, the seashore was protected from development. It received national seashore status in 1975. Managed by the National Park Service and the adjacent Merritt Island National Wildlife Refuge, the majority of the seashore is owned by the National Aeronautics and Space Administration, or NASA. It consists of 57,000 acres and 24 miles of undeveloped beach that is home to more than one thousand plant and animal species, including fourteen threatened and endangered species as well as protected animals such as alligators. Some of the endangered species found here include several varieties of sea turtles, the West Indian manatee, Southern bald eagle, Eastern indigo snake, and Florida scrub jay.

The seashore is divided into north and south districts, both of which allow horseback riding from late fall through

Aerial view of Canaveral National Seashore

early spring during limited daytime hours. Riding is not allowed from May through October because of the sea turtles who nest on the island each year. There is a limit to the number of horses and trailers allowed in each district, and reservations are required at least seven days in advance of visiting. The information center is located at 7611 South Atlantic Avenue, New

Looking to the trails

Smyrna Beach, Florida 32169; 321-867-0677. For North District information, call 386-428-3384.

In the North District, riders can enjoy Klondike Beach. The south end, near Kennedy Space Center, allows rid-

Space shuttle launch

ing south of parking area #1 on Playalinda Beach, although this use is sometimes curtailed because of launches at Kennedy Space Center. (Check the

SnapShot - Canaveral National Seashore

Description: Canaveral National Seashore is in the shadow of America's space program, and space shuttle launch pads are visible from the South District. This area offers riding on beautiful undeveloped beaches that look much the same as they did hundreds of years ago. Bring your own horse or rent one from the local stable for a guided ride. Ace of Hearts Ranch (7400 Bridal Path Lane, Cocoa, FL 32927; 321-638-0104) offers guided rides on the beach. Horse camping is not allowed in Canaveral National Seashore, but there is overnight stabling nearby (see Where to Stay & Stable). There are many hotels and motels in the area, but be aware that accommodations can be hard to come by during space shuttle and rocket launches; make reservations ahead of time if planning to visit during a launch.

Open: Horses are allowed from November 1 through the end of April, reservations are required at least seven days in advance (earliest 8:30 a.m., latest 1:00 p.m.); all horses must leave riding areas no later than 3:00 p.m.

Address: 308 Julia Street, Titusville, FL 32796

Phone: 321-267-1110

Web site: http://www.nps.gov/cana

Getting there: North district: I-95 to State Road 44 (Exit 249), east on SR 44 to A1A, south on A1A 9 miles to park entrance. South district: I-95 to State Road 406 (Exit 220), 406 East to 402 East to Park Entrance Station

Fees/permits: Admission is $5 per day per vehicle

Horse rentals: Available locally

Horse camping: None; stabling available locally

Trail conditions/level of difficulty: Easy; flat and sandy

launch schedule at http://www.nasa
.gov/missions/highlights/schedule
.html.) To access the beaches, horses
use wooden boardwalks and bridges, as
they are not allowed on the dunes.

At Canaveral National Seashore,
the focus is on nature and its beauty,
and the only amenities on the beach
are self-contained chemical toilets. Be
sure to bring enough food and water
for both you and your horse. There are
no concessions stands or running water,
and horses are not allowed to munch
on the vegetation.

Canaveral National Seashore

TURTLE HAVEN

From May through August at Canaveral National Seashore, loggerhead, leatherback, and green sea turtles lumber onto the beach to lay their eggs in the sand. Brevard County, where the southern section of the park is located, is the largest nesting site in the Western Hemisphere for loggerhead sea turtles, and half of all green sea turtle nests in the country are found in the area. Loggerheads are classified as threatened species, and both leatherbacks and greens are endangered. Keeping the turtles and their eggs safe is critical and is the reason horses are not allowed on the beaches during the nesting period.

The loggerheads lay between 3,500 and 4,500 nests each year. Green sea turtles and leatherbacks also nest here, but

Sea turtle

in much smaller numbers. On average, each female turtle nests about three times at two week intervals during the summer nesting season. About one hundred eggs are deposited in each sea turtle nest. Surviving eggs, those not eaten by predators—namely raccoons—or washed away by beach erosion, begin hatching in about sixty days. Until the early 1980s, approximately 98 percent of nests were destroyed by raccoons. Upon recognizing the destruction the wily critters were causing, experiments began on the best way to protect the eggs. Ultimately, park rangers chose wire mesh screens to cover the nests, which prevent raccoons from getting in but allow the tiny turtle hatchlings to get out. Today, more than 80 percent of the nests are protected by screens.

Once the hatchlings leave their nests, they face more perils. Birds, ghost crabs, raccoons, and even the early morning sun's drying heat stand between them and the ocean. After making it to the water, birds and fish prey on them as they swim frantically to the sargassum weed beds several miles offshore. The lucky hatchlings who reach the safety of the weed beds will live in the weeds for anywhere from an estimated ten to twenty years, until reaching a size of 8 to 12 inches and returning to coastal waters. Scientists estimate that sea turtles do not reach reproductive maturity until they are fifteen to fifty years old. Often, female sea turtles return to the beach where they were hatched to lay their own eggs.

GEORGIA

F. D. Roosevelt State Park

The 9,049-acre F. D. Roosevelt State Park is named for the thirty-second president of the United States, Franklin Delano Roosevelt. It is located in Pine Mountain, Georgia, one hour southwest of Atlanta at the foot of the Appalachian Mountains.

The four-term president, who served in the White House from 1933 until he died in office in 1945, came to this area of Georgia during the 1920s seeking treatment for polio. Diagnosed with the disease, otherwise known as infantile paralysis, in 1921 at the age of thirty-nine, the future president believed that the mineral springs at the nearby town of Warm Springs could offer help for

Hats shield sun and rain.

his disease. Eventually, he built the Georgia Warm Springs Foundation for the treatment of polio there. He also built a home for himself known as the Little White House. It was the only home he ever owned. Upon moving in the year he was elected president in 1932, FDR threw a large housewarming party "for the residents of the village of Warm Springs, also the foundation guests, employees, and cottagers," according to the "Little White House Historical Narrative," Franklin D. Roosevelt Little White House State Historic Site. Subsequent parties followed, but the house also had a more serious and far-reaching influence as many of the president's New Deal policies were formed there. Roosevelt died in 1945 at the Little White House of a cerebral hemorrhage

SnapShot - F. D. Roosevelt State Park

Description: Enjoy the legacy of our thirty-second president, Franklin Delano Roosevelt, as you ride 20 miles of trails at Georgia's largest state park. Roosevelt Stables in the park supplies maps to horse owners and guided rides to renters with its twenty-five rental horses. Horses can be boarded overnight here, and riders stay at one of the park camps or cottages or at outside accommodations. The park offers 140 tent, trailer, and RV campsites and twenty-two quaint cottages. There are two lakes, a boat rental, a small store, and picnic spots. Bring in your own food for picnicking under the stars or cooking in your cozy cottage. There are grocery stores in Pine Mountain and a trading post in the park.

Open: Daily, year-round, from 7:00 a.m. to 10:00 p.m.

Address: 2970 Georgia Highway 190, Pine Mountain, GA 31822

Phone: 706-663-4858

Web site: http://www.gastateparks.org/info/fdr

Getting there: Located off I-185 near Callaway Gardens west of Warm Springs on Georgia Route 190 or south of Pine Mountain off US Highway 27

Fees/permits: Parking is $2

Horse rentals: Guided rides range from $30 for a one-hour ride to $200 for an overnight trip; lunch and dinner rides are available for $95

Horse camping: None; stabling is available in the park

Trail conditions/level of difficulty: Easy to difficult; steps, rocks, steep hills, creeks

Following the trail

while posing for his portrait. The unfinished portrait is still on display there.

The F. D. Roosevelt State Park is within thirty minutes of Warm Springs. It is the largest park in the Georgia state park system. In addition to lending the park his name, Roosevelt had an influence that extends into the park itself. During the Great Depression in the 1930s, when millions of people were out of work, FDR put the Civilian Conservation Corp (CCC) in place to employ men and beautify the country. Workers from the CCC, using their hands and mules, built a rock-bottom pool in what is now the park. The Liberty Bell Pool, completed and opened in 1940 and still in use today, holds more than 550,000 gallons of clear spring water and reaches depths of 10 feet. Other structures in the park were also built by Roosevelt's conservation corp. Each year, the CCC gets together and holds a reunion at the park.

Visitors to the park will also experience a bit of Roosevelt heritage at Dowdell's Knob, the former president's favorite picnic spot, which offers beautiful valley vistas. Equestrians will appreciate its 20 miles of horse trails. You can bring your own horse and park your trailer at Roosevelt Stables, located inside the park, or rent one of the stable's horses. Miles of horse trails include the Overlook Trail, which climbs the mountain and offers a beautiful valley view; the Mountain Lake Trail, a scenic ride around Lake Franklin; and the Creek, Coyote, and Cowboy trails.

Taking a walk

LOUISIANA

KISATCHIE NATIONAL FOREST

The 600,000 acre Kisatchie National Forest is the only national forest in Louisiana, and it is a unique one. The Kisatchie is different from many other national forests in that it is not one large connected unit; rather, it is spread across seven parishes in the state and

Tacking up at the trailhead

consists of five ranger districts, all geographically separate from one another. The ranger districts are the Caney Ranger District in the north near the Arkansas border and the Winn, Catahoula, Kisatchie, and Calcasieu districts in central Louisiana.

The name *Kisatchie* was derived from the Kichai Indians (also called Kitsai), a small tribe who lived in Louisiana and Texas. (The Kichai were linguistically related to the Pawnee.) The area was designated national forestland in 1930. Prior to that time,

the land that would become the Kisatchie National Forest helped contribute to Louisiana's rank as one of the top lumber producers in the country. In the late nineteenth century, virgin forests covered 85 percent of the state. The quality and volume of the timber as well as the area's level terrain were a dream for loggers. Within twenty-five years, loggers had turned the once magnificent native longleaf pine stands into wasted stumps, just as the state found itself in the throes of the Great Depression. Sawmills closed their

SNAPSHOT - KISATCHIE NATIONAL FOREST

Description: Ride in the only national forest in Louisiana. Four of its five separate ranger districts, located in the central part of the state, allow horses. Miles of horse trails take you into pine forestland, dark bayous, and even sandy beaches. There are horse camps, and backcountry camping is allowed, so pick your spot along the trail. Be sure to stock up on food that you can enjoy at the campsite or along the trail. Groceries and supplies are available in Pineville, Natchitoches, and other communities surrounding the forest. There are also fast-food and chain restaurants available in these towns if you want to catch a quick meal. Horse rentals are available in the park from 4B Dude Ranch (30 Squyres Lane, Melder, LA 71433; 318-659-3332).

Open: Forest trails are open year-round, unless closed for weather or repair

Address: Kisatchie National Forest Headquarters, 500 Shreveport Highway, Pineville, LA 71360

Phone: 318-473-7160

Web site: http://www.fs.fed.us/r8/kisatchie/index.html

Getting there: The forest is spread through the following parishes in northern and central Louisiana: Vernon, Rapides, Grant, Natchitoches, Webster, Claiborne, and Winn. It can be reached via Interstate Highway 49, north or south.

Fees/permits: Fees to use forest trails vary, from free to a nominal charge

Horse rentals: Available in the park

Horse camping: Available in the park

Trail conditions/level of difficulty: Easy to moderate; flat and hilly, sandy

doors, including one of the largest in the region, the Gulf Lumber Company. As good fortune would have it, though, the U.S. Forest Service acquired some of Gulf's land as well as land in other areas, which eventually became Kisatchie National Forest. Workers restored the forest, planting thousands of seedlings of loblolly pine—a prolific grower—yellow pine, and others. Efforts to restore the native longleaf pine were more difficult, but today the Forest Service is having more

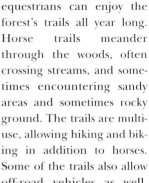

Riding among the trees

success, and the potential for restoring the native pine to sites where it was once predominant have increased.

In addition to its open stands of tall pines, which present an almost parklike atmosphere, the forest is also characterized by dark bayous and rocky bluffs. These rich lands offer habitat for a variety of wildlife, including many bird species, otters, wild boar, alligators, and even feral horses. (Horses sometimes stray into the forest or are abandoned here; visitors might see small bands of them.) Recreation opportunities abound in the various ranger districts, including camping, fishing, hunt-

ing, and hiking as well as mountain biking, off-road vehicle riding, and horseback riding.

With its relatively mild climate, equestrians can enjoy the forest's trails all year long. Horse trails meander through the woods, often crossing streams, and sometimes encountering sandy areas and sometimes rocky ground. The trails are multiuse, allowing hiking and biking in addition to horses. Some of the trails also allow off-road vehicles as well. Four of the five ranger districts have multiuse trails that allow horses: the Calcasieu, the Catahoula, the Kisatchie, and the Winn districts.

MISSISSIPPI

BIENVILLE NATIONAL FOREST
Named for Jean Baptiste Bienville, a French governor of Louisiana and founder of New Orleans and Mobile, Alabama, this national forest in south central Mississippi encompasses 178,000 acres of flat and gently rolling land. Established in 1934 with land pur-

Following the leader

On forest trails

chased from four large lumber companies, Bienville National Forest stretches into four Mississippi counties: Scott, Smith, Jasper, and Newton.

Timber is harvested here, although following the U.S. Forest Service's acquisition of the land more than seventy years ago, much work went into successfully turning it back into a healthy ecosystem. The Forest Service, with help from the Civilian Conservation Corps and other programs, replanted the land, which had been badly in need of reforestation, soil conservation, and protection from wildfire following its early use for timberland. Today, the forest is managed for the use and protection of its natural resources and for a continuing supply of its timber, water, and wildlife. Fish and wildlife in Bienville are overseen cooperatively by the Forest Service and the Mississippi Department of Wildlife, Fisheries, and Parks. There are three designated wildlife management areas in the forest.

This land is truly one of many uses. It offers horseback riding, hiking, fishing, camping, hunting, swiming, boating, picnicking, mountain biking, wildlife viewing, and more. The

Preparing to ride

Shockaloe Equestrian and Hiking Trail allows riders to view firsthand the forest's multiuse management practices. Along this nationally recognized trail, which is listed in the National Register of Trails, you'll see watering holes for wildlife, prescribed burn areas, and, if you're really lucky, the endangered red-cockaded woodpecker, or at least hear his insistent tapping as he goes about his daily business.

Horse crossing

Horses tied at camp

The winding but well-marked 23-mile trail allows horses, pedestrians, and bicycles but no motorized vehicles. It crosses several local roads (be careful when crossing) and offers rides in varying lengths from 1.5 to 23 miles. A note of interest to more adventurous riders: there are several challenging jumps located at various places along the trail. The jumps are marked with signs showing a horse and rider jumping. If you prefer that your horse keep his hooves on the ground, there is an alternate route you can take around the jumps.

One caution when riding the Shockaloe trail: hunting is very popular in Mississippi's national forests. Hunters here pursue deer, wild turkey, duck, quail, and more, so it is a good idea to call ahead and find out about the various hunting seasons. If you do ride during hunting season, wear orange, red, or other brightly colored clothing.

Be seen by hunters.

SNAPSHOT - BIENVILLE NATIONAL FOREST

Description: Ride the 23-mile Shockaloe Equestrian and Hiking Trail in Bienville National Forest. Two camps set up for equestrians are located along this nationally recognized trail. If you don't want to camp, overnight accommodations for you and your horse can be found nearby (see Where to Stay & Stable). *Note to readers: At this printing, the campground has been temporarily closed as a result of damage from Hurricane Katrina in 2005.*

Open: Year-round

Address: 3473 Highway 35 South, Forest, MS 39074

Phone: 601-469-3811

Web site: http://www.fs.fed.us/r8/mississippi/bienville

Getting there: Bienville National Forest is just east of Jackson, Mississippi. Take I-20 from the east or west; Shockaloe Trail is located between the towns of Forest and Morton just north of US Highway 80.

Fees/permits: $3 for day use of the trail

Horse rentals: None

Horse camping: Available in the forest; stabling is available locally

Trail conditions/level of difficulty: Easy to moderate

OTHER GREAT PLACES TO RIDE

Alabama

Talladega National Forest
Shoal Creek Ranger District, 450 Highway 46, Heflin, AL 36264
256-463-2272
http://www.800alabama.com/alabama-attractions/details.cfm?id=1050
Ride in the Talladega National Forest on the Shoal Creek Horse Trail system. Trails are well marked, and horse camping is available.

Tuskegee National Forest
125 National Forest Road 949, Tuskegee, AL 36083
334-727-2652
http://www.fs.fed.us/r8/alabama/tuskegee
Located in east central Alabama, Tuskegee is the smallest national forest in the country. In its 11,000 acres, it offers camping and miles of trails for riders.

Arkansas

Ozark National Forest
605 West Main, Russellville, AR 72801
479-968-2354
http://www.fs.fed.us/oonf/ozark/index.html
Covering 1.2 million acres and home to the tallest mountain in the state, Mount Magazine, this forest in the Ozarks features miles of riding trails and several horse camps. Check out the popular Huckleberry Mountain and Moccasin Gap horse trails.

Florida

Ocala National Forest
2715 State Highway 80, Sherburne, NY 13460
607-674-4036
http://www.dec.state.ny.us/website/dlf/publands/stateforests/reg7/brookfield.html
This trail system in central New York consists of 130 miles of trails over 13,000 acres of state forests. There is an assembly and camping area that accommodates 150 horses and campers.

Picayune Strand State Forest
2121 52nd Avenue South, Naples, FL 34117
239-348-7557
http://www.fl-dof.com/state_forests/picayune_strand.html
Located in southwest Florida, this state forest offers 22 miles of trails, primitive camping, and horse rentals. It is part of the Florida Division of Forestry Trailtrotter program (visit http://www.fl-dof.com/forest_recreation/trailtrotter_index.html for more).

Georgia

Chattahoochee/Ocoonee National Forest
1755 Cleveland Highway, Gainesville, GA 30501
770-297-3000
http://www.fs.fed.us/conf
Ride on 200 miles of trails and roads, including the Willis Knob Trail in Georgia and the Rocky Gap Trail in South Carolina. Horse camps are located near both trails.

Louisiana

Hodges Garden Park and Wilderness Area

Hodges Gardens, PO Box 340, Florien, LA 71429
318-586-3523
http://www.hodgesgardens.com/home.htm
Located halfway between Shreveport and Lake Charles, this private horticultural and recreational facility is run by the nonprofit A. J. and Nona Triggs Hodges Foundation. It features 4,700 acres for riding, biking, and hiking; and camping with horses can be arranged.

High line at a trailhead

SOUTH TRAVEL SECTION

IF YOU ARE TRAVELING WITHOUT YOUR HORSE, OR IF YOUR HORSE IS BOARDED SAFELY AT A STABLE, ENJOY THE SITES IN THE NEIGHBORING TOWNS. BELOW, YOU'LL FIND A MILEAGE CHART LISTING THE DISTANCES BETWEEN THE TRAILS AND ALL THE AREAS DISCUSSED IN THE FOLLOWING TRAVEL SECTION. THE AREAS CLOSEST TO THE TRAILS ARE INDICATED BY AN **X**. FOR AREAS WHERE NEITHER STABLING NOR HORSE RENTALS ARE AVAILABLE, NO SIGHTSEEING OPTIONS ARE LISTED.

COAST TO COAST	Columbus, Ga.	Garfield, Ark.	Natchez Trace National Scenic Trail, Bienville, Miss.	Natchitoches, La.	Orlando, Fla.	Ozark-St. Francis National Forest, Russelville, Ark.	Pine Mountain, Ga.	Robeline, La.	Titusville, Fla.	Warm Springs, Ga.
Bienville National Forest (Miss.)	290 miles	610 miles	**X** * miles	275 miles	685 miles	455 miles	495 miles	350 miles	725 miles	325 miles
Canaveral National Seashore (Fla.)	425 miles	1225 miles	725 miles	935 miles	**X** 40 miles	1070 miles	595 miles	950 miles	**X** * miles	450 miles
Devil's Den State Park (Ark.)	725 miles	**X** 50 miles	560 miles	460 miles	1135 miles	105 miles	805 miles	460 miles	1175 miles	760 miles
F. D. Roosevelt State Park (Ga.)	**X** 35 miles	790 miles	305 miles	665 miles	430 miles	635 miles	220 miles	815 miles	470 miles	**X** 15 miles
Kisatchie National Forest (La.)	595 miles	555 miles	230 miles	**X** 60 miles	750 miles	405 miles	705 miles	**X** 70 miles	880 miles	630 miles

*The area to visit is the same as or is within 10 miles of the trails.

MUST SEE / MUST DO

ARKANSAS

DEVIL'S DEN STATE PARK AREA

You'll find other great places to ride in the general vicinity of Devil's Den. There are horse trails in the massive **Ozark-St. Francis National Forest** (605 West Main, Russellville, AR 72801; 479-964-7200; http://www.fs.fed.us/oonf/ozark/), and the **Pea Ridge National Military Park** (15930 Highway 62, Garfield, AR 72732; 479-451-8122; http://www.nps.gov/peri). The forest is open year-round, and there are no fees for riding the trails. Pea Ridge National Military Park is open year-round from 8:00 a.m. to 5:00 p.m., and entry fee is $5 maximum per vehicle.

FLORIDA

CANAVERAL NATIONAL SEASHORE AREA

The space coast is not lacking in things to do. In addition to riding at the seashore, you can hike, bird-watch, kayak, swim, fish, relax in the sun, and more. Around Titusville, immerse yourself in the area's space history by visiting the **U. S. Space Walk of Fame Museum** (3550 South Washington Avenue #27, Titusville, FL 32782; 321-264-0434; http://www.nbbd.com/godo/spacemuseum). It is open Monday through Friday from 10:00 a.m. to 5:00 p.m. and on Sunday from noon to 5:00

Rocket Garden

p.m. Admission is free. And visit the **Air Force Space and Missile Museum** at Cape Canaveral Air Force Station (321-452-2121 or 321-853-9171 for the curator; http://www.patrick.af.mil).

The huge **Kennedy Space Center** (321-867-5000; http://www.ksc.nasa.gov), near the intersection of State Road 405 and State Road 3, is a must-see. The more than 140,000-acre facility, six times the size of Manhattan, is NASA's launch headquarters. Learn about America's amazing leading role in the exploration of space, and find out more about the space shuttle and the International Space Station in behind-the-scenes tours. Steep yourself in the history of space and man's flight to the moon at the Apollo/Saturn V Center.

Astronaut Hall of Fame

Visit the Rocket Garden, where Redstone, Atlas, and Titan rockets "blast off" into space, and the *Space Mirror*—a memorial to the heroic astronauts who have given their lives for space exploration. You can even meet or have lunch with an astronaut and get a taste of what his or her job is like at the interactive **Astronaut Hall of Fame**. You can easily spend a day here, so be sure to schedule enough time for your visit. The center is open daily from 9:00 a.m. to 7:00 p.m., except Christmas and some launch days. Standard admission is $31 for adults and $21 for children three to eleven, but other admission options are offered with additional activities and tours. Admission for visiting the Astronaut

Hall of Fame only is $17 for adults and $13 for children three to eleven. The Astronaut Hall of Fame is open from 10:00 a.m. to 8:00 p.m. Contact the Visitor's complex at 321-449-4444 or

Shuttle lifting off

at http://www.kennedyspacecenter.com.

Within an hour of Canaveral National Seashore is Orlando, home to world-famous **Disney World** and its various resorts and parks. For the full range of activities available at Disney World, visit http://www.disneyworld.disney.go.com.

GEORGIA

F. D. ROOSEVELT STATE PARK AREA

Visit the Little White House in Pine Mountain that Franklin Delano Roosevelt built after coming to Georgia seeking treatment for polio. Preserved much as FDR left it, the house, guesthouse, servant's quarters, sentry houses, and garage are open to the public. **The Little White House State Historic Site** (401 Little White House Road, Georgia Highway 85 Alternate, Warm Springs, GA 31830; 706-655-5870; http://www.fdr-littlewhitehouse.org), a 12,000-square-foot museum that opened in 2004, features exhibits about the president and items from his life. The site is open from 9:00 a.m. to 4:45 p.m. seven days a week; closed Thanksgiving Day, Christmas Day, and New Year's Day. Admission is $7 for adults, $6 for seniors, and $4 for children six to eighteen (free for children under five). Drinks and snacks are available in the gift store, and there is a picnic area.

Another historical attraction in Pine Mountain is **Butts Mill Farm** (2280 Butt Mill Road, Pine Moun-

tain, GA 31822; 706-663-7400; http://www.buttsmillfarm.com). Built in the 1830s as the site of a grist mill, the farm today provides a host of family fun. Just a few of the things you can do here include rent horses, fish, take a hayride, swim, see farm and wild animals, picnic, and play a round of miniature golf. Open Monday through Friday and on Sunday from 10:00 a.m. to 5:00 p.m.; open Saturday from 10:00 a.m. to 6:00 p.m. General admission prices are $11.95 for adults and $9.95 for children three to nine (free for children two and under). Horseback riding for a 45-minute to a 1-hour ride is an additional $20.00.

Callaway Gardens (Georgia Highway 18/354, Pine Mountain, GA 31822; 800-225-5292; http://www.callawaygardens.com) is a popular visitors' spot in Pine Mountain. This 13,000-acre resort, garden, and nature preserve features a variety of activities as well as events throughout the year. It offers biking, golf, and other recreational activities and a butterfly center, horticultural center, bird of prey show, and more. Callaway Gardens opens daily at 9:00 a.m. and closes at 5:00 p.m. in fall and winter; it's open until 6:00 p.m. in spring and summer. General admission is $13.00 for adults and $6.50 for children six to twelve. Children under six are admitted free.

Of special interest to horse enthusiasts is the **Steeplechase at Callaway**. Held each year on the first Saturday in November, the Steeplechase at Callaway, sanctioned by the National Steeplechase Association, is one of the top five steeplechase events in the country. For more information, contact The Steeplechase at Callaway (1017 Second Avenue, Columbus, GA 31902; 706-324-6252; http://www.steeplechaseatcallaway.org).

LOUISIANA

KISATCHIE NATIONAL FOREST AREA

Not far from the forest is the city of **Natchitoches**, which is the oldest permanent settlement in the Louisiana Purchase Territory. The city features a great assortment of Creole architecture, lots of scenic beauty, and many historic sites. One such site is the **St. Jean Baptiste State Historic Site** (155 Rue Jefferson, Natchitoches, LA 71457; 318-357-3101 or 888-677-7853; http://www.lastateparks.com/fortstj/ftstjean.htm.). The site portrays the history and culture of French Colonial Louisiana. Located on the Cane River, which passes through the center of the city, the fort replicates the original fort built in 1732 to prevent the Spanish from advancing from Texas into French Louisiana. Another site that portrays the history of the Spanish and French in Louisiana is **Los Adaes State Historic Site** (Highway 485, Robeline, LA 71449; 318-472-9449 or 888-677-5378; http://www.lastateparks.com/losades/losadaes.htm). Dating back to the early 1700s, Los Adaes was once the capital of Texas. Today, visitors to the site can take a guided tour of the archaeology lab and see its changing displays. Historic demonstrations and special programs are offered throughout the year. A walking trail is available to visitors to study the natural and cultural features, which are an integral part of the site. For more on the city of Natchitoches, contact the Natchitoches Area Convention & Visitors Bureau at 781 Front Street, Natchitoches, Louisiana 71457; 800-259-1714; http://www.historicnatchitoches.com.

MISSISSIPPI

BIENVILLE NATIONAL FOREST AREA

In addition to riding in the national forest, equestrian visitors to Mississippi will also enjoy riding the **Natchez Trace National Scenic Trail**. If you stay with your horse at Oakdale Farms while in the Bienville area, you can experience a guided ride at Natchez Trace. Currently, 63 miles of the national scenic trails are open for use along the 444-mile-long Natchez Trace Parkway, which winds through Alabama, Mississippi, and Tennessee, commemorating an ancient

Natchez Trace Trail commemorative sign

trail that connected southern portions of the Mississippi River to salt licks in central Tennessee. It experienced its heaviest use as a foot trail for boatmen returning from markets in Natchez and New Orleans. Through the centuries, Native Americans, including the Choctaw and the Chickasaw, traveled the trail. Visitors can ride, drive, bike, and hike the trail and scenic byway. Several locations along the trail accommodate horse trailers. Contact the National Park Service (2680 Natchez Trace Parkway, Tupelo, MS 38804; 800-305-7417; http://www.nps.gov/natt/index.htm) for information on how to access trailheads for the four sections of the National Scenic Trail. The trail is open all year, and there are no fees for using it.

Scenery along the Natchez Trace Trail

WHERE TO STAY & STABLE

ARKANSAS

DEVIL'S DEN STATE PARK AREA

Horses and Riders:
Devil's Den Horse Camp
Located in the park
479-761-3325
http://www.arkansasstateparks.com/devilsden
$13 per night; $6 during winter
The horse camp, located off of Highway 220, near the Old Road Horse trailhead, has forty-three campsites, picnic tables, charcoal grills, a bathhouse, water, and electricity. It accommodates both tent and RV camping. Horses must be picketed.

Perry's Passin' Thru
21365 Perry Road
Springdale, AR 72764
479-756-6969
http://www.perryspassinthru.com
$90–$135 per night; $65–$100 per night for the Monday through Thursday special; $20 per night for RV hookup/one-horse stall, $5 for each additional stall per night
About thirty minutes from Devil's Den, this cattle ranch offers a two-bedroom minilodge for travelers and their pets. Rooms have private baths, sport cedar decks, and overlook a lake. Continental breakfast is included in the room rate. Four-legged critters are very welcome here. Horses will enjoy their own stalls and plenty of green pasture for riding—the ranch has more than 100 acres of land.

FLORIDA

CANAVERAL NATIONAL SEASHORE AREA

Horses and Riders:
Flying D Ranch
2720 South Street
Titusville, FL 32780
321-268-5955
http://www.flyingdranchonline.com
$15 per night for stabling
Flying D Ranch offers overnight horse boarding as well as camping for horse owners with self-contained living quarters in their RVs or trailers (there is no water available to campers). Or horse owners can opt to stay at the nearby Best Western Space Shuttle Inn at a reduced rate by mentioning that they are boarding at Flying D Ranch. Stabling facilities include 12 x 12–foot stalls, a large arena, a round pen, and extensive riding trails. Flying D Ranch also offers horse rentals on their trails. Reservations required.

T Shot Ranch
3350 Retdor Road
Cocoa, FL 32926
321-632-3020
$50 per night for cottage rental; $20 per horse for stalls
This private ranch approximately thirty minutes from Canaveral National Seashore offers a small cottage and stable on the same property. The cottage has a bathroom

and kitchen. Bring your own feed for your horse. No drop-ins; at least 24-hour notice required.

Best Western Space Shuttle Inn
3455 Cheney Highway (Route 50)
Titusville, FL 32780
321-269-9100/Reservations only: 800-523-7654
http://www.spaceshuttleinn.com
$59–$135 per night

The Best Western Space Shuttle Inn offers all the amenities you would expect to find at this hotel chain as well as a barbeque area, tennis and volleyball courts, and a pets-allowed policy. It is located near Kennedy Space Center and offers special attraction packages that include admission to the Kennedy Space Center. There is a restaurant on site. Equestrians who board their horses at the Flying D Ranch receive a discount on accommodations here.

Dickens Inn Bed & Breakfast
2398 North Singleton Avenue
Mims, FL 32754
321-269-4595/877-847-2067
http://www.dickens-inn.com
$95–$115 per night, includes full breakfast and evening glass of wine

The Dickens Inn, built in 1860, was the original manor house to a 15,000-acre citrus plantation. Today, the inn still sits amid grapefruit and orange trees, and fruit from the trees is served with breakfast when they are in season. Four charmingly decorated rooms with bathrooms are available for travelers. Watch space shuttle launches from the front porch (reservations are required far ahead for launches), or even say hello to a former owner and resident ghost some have claimed to have seen walking its halls.

Riverview Hotel
101 Flagler Avenue
New Smyrna Beach, FL 32169
800-945-7416/386-428-5858
http://www.riverviewhotel.com
$100 per night for a room to $225 for a three-bedroom guest house

This 1885 Victorian inn is a former drawbridge tender's home along the Intracoastal Waterway. It offers eighteen guest rooms as well as a cottage and a guesthouse. Continental breakfast is served in your room. The hotel also includes a four-star waterfront restaurant, Kelsey's Riverview, and a spa for relaxing in after hours of riding on the beach.

GEORGIA

F. D. ROOSEVELT STATE PARK AREA

F. D. Roosevelt State Park Campgrounds
Located in the park
Reservations 800-864-7275
http://www.gastateparks.org
$18–20 for campsites per night; $65–$135 for cottages; $400–$500 for group camps (sleeps 75 and 120); $3 per person for backcountry campsites

There are 140 tent, trailer, and RV campsites available in the park and 22 cottages. Campsites feature picnic tables, grills, and fire rings. Cabins include bed linens.

Amenities may vary by cabin and may include fireplaces, screened porches, coffee makers, fully equipped kitchens, and more.

Pine Mountain Tourism Association
101 East Broad Street, PO Box 177
Pine Mountain, GA 31822
706-663-4000/800-441-3502
http://www.pinemountain.org
Prices vary
The Pine Mountain Tourism Association can provide you with information on a variety of accommodations in the area, including hotels, motels, inns, and bed-and-breakfasts.

Horses Only:
Roosevelt Stables
Located in the park
1063 Group Camp Road
Pine Mountain, GA 31822
877-696-4613 for reservations
http://www.rooseveltstables.com
$17 per night for overnight stabling; $5 for using the riding trails
The stables are for housing only; owners must provide feed and feed buckets and are responsible for all horse care. The stable also offers rentals and a variety of different rides, including one geared to moms and a ranger-led ride.

LOUISIANA

KISATCHIE NATIONAL FOREST AREA

Horse and Riders:
Ahtus Melder Hunter Camp
Calcasieu Ranger District Office, 9912 Highway 28 West
Boyce, LA 71409
318-793-9427
http://www.fs.fed.us/r8/kisatchie/kisatchie_national_forest/calcasieu_rd/calcasieu_rd_home
.html
Free camping
This tent campsite offers primitive camping with no water or sanitary facilities in an open pine-stand setting. It accesses the Clairborne multiuse trails.

Cane Camp and **Oak Camp**
Kistachie Ranger District Office, 106 Old Highway 6 West
Natchitoches, LA 71457
318-352-2568
http://www.fs.fed.us/r8/kisatchie/kisatchie_national_forest/kisatchie_rd/kisatchie_rd_home
.html
$3 per night to stay at Cane Camp; free to stay at Oak Camp
Cane Camp offers tent and RV camping with flush toilets and drinking water. Oak Camp provides RV and tent camping in more primitive conditions with vault toilets and no drinking water. Horse trails in this district include the Sandstone Trail, the Caroline Dorman Recreation Trail, and the Kisatchie Hills Wilderness Area.

Gum Springs Horse Camp
Winn Ranger District Office, 9671 US Highway 84 West
Winnfield, LA 71483
318-628-4664

http://www.fs.fed.us/r8/kisatchie/kisatchie_national_forest/winn_rd/winn_rd_home.html
$3 per day
This campground, with access to the Gum Springs Horse Trail, offers tent and RV camping. It has vault toilets.

Kisatchie National Forest Backcountry Camping
Catahoula Ranger District, 5325 LA Highway 8
Pollock, LA 71407
318-765-3554
http://www.fs.fed.us/r8/kisatchie/kisatchie_national_forest/catahoula_rd/catahoula_rd_home.html
$2–$3 parking fee
There are no designated horse camps in this district, but backcountry camping with horses is allowed. Contact the ranger district for more information.

Riders Only:
Andre's Riverview Guesthouse
612 Williams Avenue
Natchitoches, LA 71457
318-357-0423
http://www.andresriverview.com
$98.75 per night and up, breakfast included
Andre's Guesthouse is a three-story cottage on the east bank of the Cane River. It was built in the 1950s. Amenities include whirlpool tubs and ceiling fans in its three suites. Each of the suites—the Tree House Suite, Library Suite, and River Room—is uniquely decorated.

MISSISSIPPI

BIENVILLE NATIONAL FOREST AREA

Horses and Riders:
Oakdale Farms
245 Loydale Drive
Brandon, MS 39047
601-825-2612/Cell: 601-260-8671
http://www.oakdalefarmsbedandboard.com
$79–$89 per night for rooms for one or two people (extra charge for more people or pets); $25–35 per night for stalls (shed row barn or main barn)
This horse boarding and training facility offers guest accommodations in the main house and stalls for overnight stabling. The facility also has a round pen, a lighted arena, and a 10-acre pasture. English and western riding lessons and training are available, as are bed-and-breakfast riding packages and guided trips to the Bienville Forest and Natchez Trace Trail or on the farm property. Guided trips can be arranged on the facility's horses or on your own. Oakdale Farms is approximately forty-five minutes from Bienville Forest.

Shockaloe Trail Camps
Located in the forest
601-469-3811
http://www.fs.fed.us/r8/mississippi/bienville
$7 per night, includes camping and use of the trail
Base Camp 1 is located a quarter mile north of US 80 on Forest Service Road 513 and is open April through October. Base Camp 2 is approximately 5 miles farther north of FSR 513 and is open year-round. The camps have restrooms, picnic tables, grills, hitch rails, drinking water, and an area for parking and camping.

WHERE TO WINE & DINE

ARKANSAS

DEVIL'S DEN STATE PARK AREA

AQ Chicken House
Highway 71 Business
Springdale, AR 72762
479-751-4633
http://www.aqchicken.com
$5.99–$15.99
AQ Chicken House is popular with the locals. It first opened its doors in Springdale in 1947. The restaurant serves four different kinds of chicken—pan fried, over-the-coals, barbecued, and fire roasted—as well as sandwiches, ribs, steaks, and more.

Jose's
324 West Dickson Street
Fayetteville, AR 72701
479-521-0194
http://www.oleforjoses.com
$5.49–$15.99
The original Jose's in Fayetteville celebrated its twenty-five-year anniversary in 2005. Known locally for great margaritas and food, the restaurant expanded to Springdale, opening Jose's Southwest Grille (5240 W. Sunset, Springdale, AR 72762; 479-750-9055). Both restaurants feature live music.

FLORIDA

CANAVERAL NATIONAL SEASHORE AREA

GinSeng Chinese Restaurant
8501 Astronaut Boulevard
Cape Canaveral, FL 32920
321-868-3440
Approximately $10 for dinners
GinSeng Chinese Restaurant serves delicious Chinese food in a casual setting. There is a pick-up window for those wishing to grab a quick meal to go. Delivery is available also. The owner's flagship restaurant, Yen Yen (2 N. Atlantic Avenue, Cocoa Beach, FL 32931; 321-783-9512), serves the same delicious fare, and more, in a more formal setting. It is open for lunch and dinner.

J. B.'s Fish Camp and Restaurant
859 Pompano Avenue
New Smyrna Beach, FL 32169
386-427-5747
http://www.jbsfishcamp.com
$4.75–$20.95
Watch a launch or the sunset as you dine at this restaurant overlooking the Indian River, north of Canaveral National Seashore's north entrance. J. B.'s is a local favorite, specializing in blackened, Cajun, and other seafood. The seafood gumbo is ranked tops by the locals.

Mangroves
6615 N. Atlantic Avenue
Cape Canaveral, FL 32920
321-783-4548
$8.95–$26.50 for dinner
Mangroves serves large entrée portions of pasta, meat, and seafood that satisfy a hunger built up by a day riding on the beach. Features live entertainment on weekends. Call ahead to be sure you get a table. Mangroves serves lunch Monday through Friday, and dinner Monday through Saturday.

GEORGIA

F. D. ROOSEVELT STATE PARK AREA

Carriage & Horses
607 Butts Mill Road
Pine Mountain, GA 31822
706-663-4777
http://www.cometodagher.com
$4.95–$20.95
Carriage & Horses features pastas, seafood, prime rib, grilled dishes, and more with live entertainment. Enjoy your meal while watching horses grazing in the pasture. The restaurant is open for lunch and dinner, Tuesday through Sunday. Reservations are suggested.

The Rose Cottage
111 East Broad Street
Pine Mountain, GA 31822
706-663-7877
$6.25–$7 for lunch; $15 per person plus 20 percent tip for English tea
Stop in for a sandwich or make an appointment for a full English tea. In addition to being a great place for a meal, The Rose Cottage also sells wine by the bottle, antiques, and gifts in its store. Open seven days a week. Full English tea is served by reservation made forty-eight hours in advance. The Rose Cottage also offers breakfast items and specialty coffees.

LOUISIANA

KISATCHIE NATIONAL FOREST AREA

The Landing Restaurant and Bar
530 Front Street
Natchitoches, LA 71457
318-352-1579
http://www.thelandingrestaurantandbar.com
$9.95–$21.95
This highly rated restaurant, which has been praised in *Southern Living Magazine*, the *Los Angeles Times*, and other publications, serves everything from fried green tomatoes and crawfish to steaks and pastas. Sunday brunch is also offered. Don't miss it while in the area.

Mariner's Restaurant
5948 Highway 1 Bypass
Natchitoches, LA 71457
318-357-1220
http://www.marinersrestaurant.com

$11.95 and up

Mariner's serves something for everyone. This family-owned restaurant features pastas, seafood, beef, poultry dishes, and Cajun and Creole cooking. There is a full cocktail bar with a wine list containing more than fifty different wines.

MISSISSIPPI

BIENVILLE NATIONAL FOREST AREA

Waffle House

105 Octavia Drive
Brandon, MS 39042
601-824-5001
http://www.wafflehouse.com
$3–$10

This chain restaurant (with locations at 905 W. Government Street, 601-824-3769; and 5452 Highway 25, 601-919-2746) originated in Georgia in 1955. It features waffles, as the name suggests, as well as other Southern-accented breakfast, lunch, and dinner items, with service twenty-four hours a day. Since the chain opened, it has served more than 495 million waffles.

Riding with friends

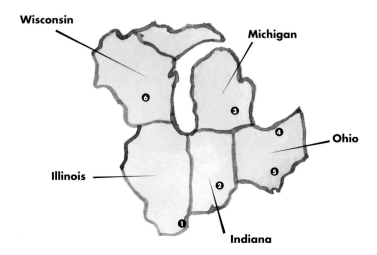

Wisconsin

Michigan

Illinois

Ohio

Indiana

MIDWEST MAP LEGEND

Illinois
❶ Shawnee National Forest

Indiana
❷ Brown County State Park

Michigan
❸ Brighton Recreation Area

Ohio
❹ Cuyahoga Valley National Park

❺ Hocking State Forest

Wisconsin
❻ Wildcat Mountain State Park

THE MIDWEST

ou'll find many enjoyable places to ride in the Midwest, from pastoral hills to rugged terrain marked by steep gorges. You can ride near the city of Cleveland, Ohio, along miles of bridle trails, or you can get away from it all and head to rural Indiana, where you'll find a recognized gourmet restaurant featuring a hitching post outside that beckons passing riders to stop in for a meal. You can also enjoy an Amish meal in Ohio, which contains the largest Amish population in the country. Or try cantering down an old wagon road that brought the pioneers out West or doing the Sore Seat Saunter, a ride offered by a local rental stable. If your interest in riding in the country's heartland isn't piqued enough yet, consider that you can also check out a cave in which a Civil War veteran lived and died and is believed to be buried.

Sometimes the Midwest is considered to be a larger region that also includes many of the states that are found in the following chapter about the Great Plains states. The Midwest as discussed here includes the states of Illinois, Indiana, Michigan, Ohio, and Wisconsin.

ILLINOIS

SHAWNEE NATIONAL FOREST

When avid trail riders talk about their favorite places to ride in the country, Shawnee National Forest is often mentioned. Located in southern Illinois, this 277,506-acre national forest has some of the most spectacular scenery in the Midwest. Much of Illinois consists of gently rolling farmland, but there is nothing gently rolling about Shawnee. The forest lies in the rough, unglaciated area of the state known as the Illinois Ozark and Shawnee Hills. Located between the Mississippi and Ohio rivers, its topography ranges from the floodplains at about 325 feet above sea level to 1,064 feet at Williams Hill, in Pope County. Meadows and woodlands; stone bluffs and canyons; unique rock formations; and streams, waterfalls, and wetlands all converge here, giving riders and other visitors a chance to commune with the diversity of nature's work. In addition to horseback riding, Shawnee National Forest draws people for fishing, boating, hiking, backpacking, swimming, camping, mountain biking, and other recreational activities. All-terrain vehicle use is prohibited here.

Dramatic landscape is not all that Shawnee offers. Visitors may also catch a glimpse of one of the many wild creatures who live here in the forest. More than 500 species of wildlife are found in Shawnee. These include 237 birds, 109 fish, 57 amphibians, 52 reptiles, and 48

Baby striped skunk

mammals. Five nationally threatened and endangered animal species live here, as well as many animals considered regionally sensitive. The five threatened and endangered species include the bald eagle, peregrine falcon, least tern, and gray and Indiana bats. More common for visitors to see are white-tailed deer, finches, squirrels, and other small mammals.

Shawnee's Garden of the Gods

Riding is allowed in many areas of the forest. There are many miles of trails and roads that offer equestrians a view of several interesting and scenic areas. Two popular trails to check out include the One Horse Gap Trail and the River-to-River Trail. The One Horse Gap Trail is an easy to moderate 10-mile trail system located in the Vienna/Elizabethtown Ranger District. It gets its name from its short loop trail known as the gap trail. This trail has a narrow gap in the bluffs that allows only one horse to pass through at a time. Along the One Horse Gap Trail, you'll sometimes ride on old wagon roads, and some of the interesting things you'll see include old cemeteries and stone foundations from old homesites. This trail system provides access to the River-to-River Trail, a 160-mile trail that

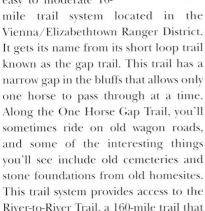

One Horse Gap Trail

spans southern Illinois. There are many other access points for this long, linear trail, and the level varies from easy to difficult. The River-to-River Trail is part of the longer American Discovery Trail that runs from California to Delaware. If you want to see some of the most beautiful scenery in the country, ride the River-to-River Trail. One point to remember is that, if you don't like sharing the trail with lots of other horses and riders, you should avoid the One Horse Gap and River-to-River trails in late July and early August, when the annual Nine Mile Trail Ride takes place. It draws approximately two thousand horses and riders for nine days of riding and camping. If you don't mind crowds, join the ride and join in the fun!

SNAPSHOT - SHAWNEE NATIONAL FOREST

Description: The Shawnee National Forest is a must ride for avid trail riders. There are a number of horse-related accommodations in the area. Visit these southern Illinois tourism Web sites for more horse camping and lodging facilities as well as information on "people only" hotels in the area: http://www.adventureillinois.com and http://www.southernmostillinois.com. There are several horse camps as well as overnight boarding facilities for horses in the forest. Several stables on the Shawnee provide rental horses for horseless riders.

Open: Year-round

Address: 50 Highway 145 South, Harrisburg, IL 62946

Phone: 618-253-7114

Web site: http://www.fs.fed.us/r9/forests/shawnee

Getting there: Located on the southern tip of Illinois: Take Interstate Highway 57 South from Chicago. (Visit the U.S. Forest Service Web site for Shawnee for directions to specific areas in the forest.)

Fees/permits: No fees to ride trails

Horse rentals: Available in the forest and locally

Horse camping: Available in the forest and locally

Trail conditions/level of difficulty: Moderate to difficult; very hilly

NEED A HORSE?

Want to ride the trails of the Shawnee but don't have a horse? Several rental stables in the area offer guided and unguided rides for all levels of equestrians.

✪ **Giant City Stables**, 235 Giant City Road, Makanda, IL 62958; 618-529-4110; http://www.dnr.state.il.us/lands/education/INTERPRT/giant_city/equestrian.htm. The stable is located in the Giant City State Park, which is inside Shawnee National Forest. It's open March to November and offers one- to three-hour guided trail rides for beginning to advanced riders. The Giant City State Park also offers a horse camp.

✪ **Honey Bee Stables**, Route 2, Box 130, Golconda, IL 62938; 618-949-3791; http://www.honeybeestables.com. It offers one-hour, half-day, or all-day rides to small groups (two to four people) through the Shawnee National Forest. It specializes in honeymooners and couples. A picnic lunch is provided. Reservations are required. Open year-round.

✪ **Kosmic Acres Stables**, off Highway 127 on Prospect Street, Alto Pass, IL 62905; 618-893-2347; http://www.centaur.org/kosmic. This stable offers trail rides for groups of one to four people through the forest. Guided tours also are available for people traveling with their own horses. Open year-round.

✪ **Lake Glendale Stables**, 201 Lake Glendale Road, Golconda, IL 62938; 618-949-3737; http://www.lakeglendalestables.com. This stable rents horses for guided or unguided trail rides on stable property and in the national forest. It offers everything from hourly rentals to overnight pack trips. Accommodations are also available in the lodge or camp. Overnight guests get discount rates on rental horses. Open year-round.

INDIANA

BROWN COUNTY STATE PARK

The Little Smokies is an affectionate name for Brown County State Park, located in Indiana's rolling hills approximately 50 miles south of Indianapolis. The largest state park in Indiana, at 15,696 acres, it got its nickname because of the mists that rise from its steep and wooded ravines and

Fall in Brown County

hover at the tops of its trees. Its real name comes from Major General Jacob Brown, a hero in the war of 1812, for whom the county is named.

The acreage that now makes up Brown County State Park was originally a game reserve early in the twentieth century, before administration as a state park began in the 1940s. Game birds were raised here, and white-tailed deer were released; they are still very common today. Although this region was once isolated by its densely forested hills and poor roads, it is now a major tourist attraction. Artists and craftspeople are concentrated in the nearby town of Nashville, which is worth an afternoon's visit to stroll through its galleries. That being said, don't get the idea that you are visiting a citified area. The county, especially the park, still retains a distinctly rural feel. There is even a small town in the area with the delightfully unsophisticated name of Gnaw Bone, and the area where the park is headquartered is called Weed Patch Hill. The park's north entrance, through which many of the park's amenities are located, has a covered bridge that dates to 1838.

With its 70 miles of hilly bridle trails and the state's largest horse camp,

Enjoying quiet woods

the park is a dream come true for horseback riders. Much of its southwestern and eastern sectors can be reached only on horseback or by foot. Trails that vary in length from .5 mile to 10.9 miles wind through strands of walnut, black locust, and sassafras trees and cross many streams. Even more of a bonus to riders, the 200,000-acre Hoosier National Forest with 211 miles of horse trails is directly next door, so you can

Riding in fall

ride out of the state park and enjoy those trails as well. (Riders over the age of sixteen on Hoosier National Forest trails are required to have a trail permit, available for $3 at the forest.)

If you don't have your own horse and still want to experience the beauty of this park via equine locomotion, the Brown County State Park Saddle Barn offers guided trail rides, pony rides for young children, and hayrides from March through November. The barn is located inside the north entrance to

SNAPSHOT - BROWN COUNTY STATE PARK

Description: Brown County State Park features the largest horse campground in the state and also has a rental stable, the Brown County State Park Saddle Barn (812-988-8166), that offers guided trail rides. And you can ride to a nearby gourmet restaurant; tie up your horse at the hitch rail; and enjoy a delicious breakfast, lunch, or dinner.

Open: Year-round

Address: 1405 State Road 46 West, Nashville, IN 47448

Phone: 812-988-6406

Web site: http://www.in.gov/dnr/parklake/parks/brownco.html

Getting there: From Indianapolis: Take State Highway 135 South. From Columbus: Take Highway 46 West. From Bloomington: Take Highway 46 East.

Fees/permits: Annual horse tag is $20 (required for any horse using Indiana Department of Natural Resources properties, including one-time visitors), $5 daily; gate fee is $4 Monday–Thursday for vehicles with Indiana license plates, $5 on Friday–Sunday and on holidays, $7 for nonresident vehicles, $2 for visitors entering on horseback, on bicycle, or on foot

Horse rentals: Available in the park

Horse camping: Available in the park

Trail conditions/level of difficulty: Easy to difficult; very hilly, rugged terrain, so horses need to be in good condition

the park, and its hours are 9:00 a.m. to 5:00 p.m. daily, weather permitting. Trail rides are 2.2 or 3.3 miles long. Other things to do in the park include hiking, tennis, swimming in the Olympic-size pool, fishing, boating, picnicking, walking through the nature center, and watching the kids enjoy the park's playground equipment. The park also features a lodge and cabins.

Great times to visit the park are in early fall—you'll see one of the most beautiful displays of changing leaves in the country—and spring, when the wildflowers are blooming. In spring, though, there is more water in the streams on the horse trails than in the summer months.

MICHIGAN

BRIGHTON RECREATION AREA

The Brighton Recreation Area is centrally located between Detroit and Lansing. It is approximately 50 miles west of Detroit and 45 miles east of

Detroit skyline

Lansing. Although it is in proximity to Michigan's largest city and the state's capitol, Brighton Recreation Area is a world away from the hubbub of urban life. In its 4,947 acres are high, irregular ranges of hills, with oak forests, thick hedgerows, and open spaces blending on the uplands. Its lowlands consist of grassy marshes, shrub masses, and dense swamp timber. As is characteristic of the state of Michigan, there are several lakes in the park. (The state's name comes from Lake Michigan, which is believed to have come from the Chippewa Indian word *meicigama* for "great water.")

SnapShot - Brighton Recreation Area

Description: Ride the nearly 5,000-acre Brighton Recreation Area. There is a horse campground in the park as well as rental horses. The Brighton Recreation Area Riding Stable, located inside the park at 6660 Chilson Road, offers guided, themed trail rides to all levels of riders. Beginners will be comfortable with the slower-paced Turtle Trot ride, whereas more advanced riders will enjoy the longer, hillier, faster Dude's Delight ride. Or try the stable's standard ride, the Sore Seat Saunter. You can contact the stable by phone at 810-225-2225 or visit its Web site at http://www.brightonridingstable.com.

Open: Year-round, 8:00 a.m. to 10:00 p.m.

Address: 6360 Chilson Road, Howell, MI 48843

Phone: 810-229-6566

Web site: http://www.michigandnr.com/parksandtrails/ParksandTrailsInfo.aspx?id=438

Getting there: Located between Lansing and Detroit: Take I-96 to exit 147 at Brighton, go west approximately 6 miles to Chilson Road, drive south 1.5 miles to Bishop Lake Road to park.

Fees/permits: Daily admission is $6 for Michigan residents, $8 for nonresidents

Horse rentals: Available in the park

Horse camping: Available in the park

Trail conditions/level of difficulty: Easy to moderate

Horseback riders will especially enjoy Brighton Recreation Area because of its 18 miles of horse trails, an equestrian camp, a staging area, and a rental stable for horseless riders. This area is known among local horse people as one of the best places to ride in the state. The Brighton Trail Riders Association, a local equestrian organization, works in cooperation with the state to ensure that the horse trails and horse camp are maintained and even improved upon and that more area is potentially opened up to horses. The association also organizes group rides and competitive trail rides here.

White-tailed deer

Wildlife watchers may see ruffed grouse, pheasant, quail, white-tailed deer, geese, rabbits, ducks, and more. Several campgrounds and rustic cabins are available for visitors seeking all sorts of recreational opportunities.

OHIO

CUYAHOGA VALLEY NATIONAL PARK Centrally located between the major metropolitan areas of Akron and Cleveland, the Cuyahoga Valley National Park protects 33,000 acres

Waterfall at Cuyahoga

along the Cuyahoga River. The valley sits in the transition zone between the central lowlands to the west and the Appalachian plateau to the east, serving as a natural dividing line between the zones of the western prairie and eastern mountains. The park is located in Summit and Cuyahoga counties.

The word *Cuyahoga* (pronounced cai-a-HO-ga) is Native American for "crooked," although other accepted translations are "place of the jawbone" and "place of the wing." Native Americans gave the name Cuyahoga to the river and have a long history in this valley. Human presence goes back as early as 12,000 to 10,000 BC, not too long after the glaciers that carved the valley receded in 13,000 BC. These early prehistoric natives, known as Paleo-Indians, were nomadic: they followed and lived off the herds of mastodons and mammoths that roamed the valley. Over the years, the once-nomadic Native Americans became semipermanent residents. Before the first Europeans arrived in the area in the seventeenth century, the natives had become permanent residents, farming the land and living in protected villages. The original inhabitants of the valley disappeared forty years before the European arrival, which is confirmed by radiocarbon dating of native sites, most recently from 1620, and by accounts of early fur traders beginning in 1640. There have been different theories about their disappearance, but the currently held view is that a series of Iroquoian raids displaced the native inhabitants.

The settlement of the valley by European Americans would not fully take hold until the completion of the Ohio and Erie Canal in 1832. The canal was originally proposed by George Washington, who recognized the need for a transportation system into the country's interior, tied Ohio to the rest of the young nation and also opened the interior of the country to southern and eastern markets. Towns began cropping up along the canal, and it was the primary mode of north-south transportation until the arrival of the railroad in the late 1800s, which competed with the canal for commerce. In 1913, the canal stopped operating after a devastating flood.

Cuyahoga National Park

Remains of the Ohio and Erie Canal can still be seen at the park today. Visitors to the park can either hike or bike the Towpath Trail, although horses are allowed on only some sections of the trail. Equines were not always excluded from the trail, however, as it was mules who powered the canal boats. Customarily, three mules were hitched to the boats by towlines, and they worked eight hours a day pulling 80 tons of cargo.

You will find plenty of designated horse trails in the park to keep you busy for a day or two, including the Wetmore Valley, Riding Run, and Langes Run trails. Riding is easy to moderate on these well-marked and well-maintained trails that traverse rolling hills. Expect

SnapShot - Cuyahoga Valley National Park

Description: Ride day-use horse trails in Cuyahoga Valley National Park. For even more riding fun, visit the adjoining Cleveland MetroParks district and ride its trails. There are no horse rentals in the park or in the Cleveland MetroParks district, and there are no campgrounds and no backcountry camping in the park. But you'll find plenty of wildlife. Horse stabling can be arranged at Cleveland MetroParks stables, dependent on availability.

Open: Daily; some areas of the park close at dusk; visitor centers are closed Thanksgiving Day, Christmas Day, and New Year's Day

Address: 15610 Vaughn Road, Brecksville, OH 44141

Phone: 216-524-1497/800-445-9667

Web site: http://www.nps.gov/cuva

Getting there: Located between Cleveland and Akron: The park can be accessed by many different highways, including I-77, I-271, I-80 (Ohio Turnpike), and State Route 8.

Fees/permits: Admission is free

Horse rentals: None

Horse camping: None

Trail conditions/level of difficulty: Easy to moderate

Riders at Cuyahoga

to see plenty of deer along your ride, as there is no hunting allowed here. There are also several bridle trails within the national park that are managed by the Cleveland MetroParks district, a separate political subdivision of the state of Ohio. The Cleveland Metro-Parks district has nearly 82 miles of designated equestrian trails.

HOCKING STATE FOREST

If you enjoy rugged trail riding, check out the 40 miles of trails in the 9,266-acre Hocking State Forest. Located southeast of Columbus, Hocking offers some of the best horseback riding in the state along with some very special

scenery. You'll marvel at the soaring Black Hand sandstone cliffs that represent a time hundreds of millions of years past when a shallow sea covered the area. As the land uplifted over time, streams eroded the sandstone to carve the overhanging cliffs of today. There are so many cliffs in the forest that it closes at dark to prevent anyone from falling. The name Black Hand comes from a giant drawing of a human hand found sketched in soot on a river gorge

Hocking State Forest

cliff face near Newark, Ohio. The hand, destroyed by canal builders in the 1820s, was believed to have been drawn by prehistoric peoples to point the way to flint deposits in the area.

In addition to the magnificent cliffs, another natural attraction in Hocking State Forest, one of twenty state forests in Ohio, is its natural vege-

Grooming at the trailer

tation. Plants typical of both northern and southern Ohio are found here. Species of plants that are usually found farther north mix it up with species more typical of southern Ohio, providing an unusual variety of native plant life. In the dry ridge areas, you'll see Virginia and pitch pines; sassafras; and black, scarlet, white, and chestnut oaks.

The moist, deep gorges include communities of yellow and black birches, eastern hemlocks, and Canada yews, remnants of an ice age when glaciers threatened the area but were stopped by hills to the north. The glaciers came close enough, though, to inspire passing Wyandot hunters in the 1700s to name the river for which the park gets its name, *Hockhocking*. The name means "bottle river" for the river's bottle-shaped valley, which gained its shape after being blocked by glacial ice.

How did this special area come to be protected by the state? In 1924, the Ohio Agricultural Experiment Station (OAES), predecessor to today's Ohio Department of Natural Resources (ODNR), began buying land in the area

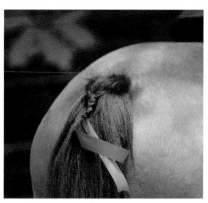

Careful: the horse kicks!

to demonstrate the practical value of forestry. Much of the land had been cut over, and the stands of trees that were left were not in good shape. After acquiring the land, the OAES replanted trees in fields that had once been used for farming corn, wheat, and hay. The organization regulated timber harvest and controlled erosion as well as re-introduced native wildlife such as turkey and beaver to the forest. The Civilian Conservation Corp also helped make improvements to the area. The ODNR was formed in 1949, and the

SnapShot - Hocking State Forest

Description: The trails in Hocking State Forest are considered among the best in Ohio. There is a horseman's camp in the state forest as well as a staging area adjacent to the camp for day-use riders. Additional camping and other accommodations for horses and riders are available at the nearby Palmerosa Horseman's Camp, which offers rental horses for guided trail rides as well. Horse rentals are also available at Stone Valley Ranch (31606 Fairview Road, Logan, OH 43138; 800-866-5196; http://www.hockinghillshorses.com) and Happy Trails Horseback Rides (25851 Big Pine Road, Rockbridge, OH 43149; 740-380-6372; http://www.hthorsebackrides.com).

Open: Year-round; the forest closes at dark; riding is not permitted after dark

Address: 19275 State Route 374, Rockbridge, OH 43149

Phone: 740-385-4402

Web site: http://www.dnr.state.oh.us/forestry/Forests/stateforests/hocking.htm

Getting there: From Columbus: Take US Highway 33 southeast to State Highway 664. Forest headquarters are located off of State Highways 374 and 664, northeast of Laurelville.

Fees/permits: No fees to ride trails

Horse rentals: Available locally

Horse camping: Available in the forest and locally

Trail conditions/level of difficulty: Moderate to difficult (unless taking guided rides from a rental facility)

Ohio is Amish country.

Hocking Hills State Park was created, becoming a separate entity from the Hocking State Forest. There are no horse trails in Hocking Hills State Park, and horses are not allowed there. Additionally, there are three designated nature preserves in the forest.

The horse trails in Hocking State Forest are not for beginners, unless they are accompanied by an experi-enced guide from one of the rental facilities. The trails are marked by rugged terrain, open meadows, and the steep gorges that characterize the forestland. To help riders and others find their way, different colors of paint on the trails designate their use. Red-, orange-, and purple-blazed trails des-ignate the main bridle trails, and green indicates side trails open to horses. Blue designates the Buckeye Trail, which allows horses. Although horses are not allowed in Hocking Hills State Park, there is an exception for riders traveling the Buckeye Trail in Hocking State Forest. There is a horseman's bypass on the Buckeye Trail that goes around the east end of Old Man's Cave and Cedar Falls through the state park.

WISCONSIN

WILDCAT MOUNTAIN STATE PARK
Wildcat Mountain State Park is located in southwestern Wisconsin, which is known as the driftless area of the state.

Wildcat Mountain State Park

Wild bergamot at Wildcat

This part of the state gained its name because the glaciers that covered most of the state did not come through this area. It provides a picture of what Wisconsin looked like before the Ice Age changed much of its topography 10,000 years ago. The driftless area is the only part of the state that has no natural lakes. Sandstone hills and exposed bluffs add to the area's rugged

SNAPSHOT - WILDCAT MOUNTAIN STATE PARK

Description: Equestrians enjoy riding on the wooded trails at Wildcat Mountain State Park. The spring and fall seasons are especially beautiful here, with colorful wild-flowers in spring and colorful leaves in the fall. In addition to marked horse trails that take riders on looped routes, there are 25.8 miles of hiking trails and 17.5 miles of trails for snowshoeing during winter. There are no rental stables inside the park, but there are rental horses available locally, although they do not ride into the park: Kickapoo Valley Ranch (E11761 County Road P, La Farge, WI 54639; 608-625-6222; http://www.kvranch.com), Circle S Trail Rides (23936 Logan Road, Wilton, WI 54670; 608-435-6975), and Red Rock Trail Rides (13597 Katydid Ave., Sparta, WI 54656; 608-823-7865).

Open: Horse trails open May 1 through Nov. 15

Address: E 13660 State Highway 33, PO Box 99, Ontario, WI 54651

Phone: 608-337-4775

Web site: http://www.dnr.state.wi.us/org/land/parks/specific/wildcat

Getting there: From the north: Take State Highway 131 South from I-94 near Tomah about 20 miles to Ontario. From the south: Take State Highway 131 North from US Highway 14 at Readstown about 23 miles to County Highway F, go right (east) on Highway F about 1.5 miles to State Highway 33, turn left (west) on Highway 33, and drive less than a mile to the park entrance.

Fees/permits: Daily vehicle admission is $7 for Wisconsin residents, $10 for nonresidents; daily trail pass for riders sixteen and older is $4 for residents and nonresidents. Children younger than 16 are free and do not require a trail pass.

Horse rentals: Available locally

Horse camping: Available in the park and in adjacent Kickapoo Valley Reserve

Trail conditions/level of difficulty: Hilly trails, some difficult and steep; horses need to be in condition

and horseback riding. The Kickapoo River (*kickapoo* is an Algonquin Indian word for "that which goes here, then there"), which meanders through the park, is the longest tributary of the Wisconsin River. It is a popular spot for canoeing, and there are several canoe rentals in the town of Ontario for people wishing to explore the river.

Horse campground at Wildcat

Equestrians will enjoy the 15 miles of looping trails in the park. Most of the horse trails are color coded. The Red Loop starts at the park's horse camp and travels through its hills and valleys. The Yellow and Blue loops connect to the Red Loop and take riders farther from the park's more populated areas. Another trail, the Rock Johnson Loop, starts north of the camp and heads up a high ridge connecting to the Red Loop. Horses should be well conditioned for riding on these tree-lined, hilly trails. The trails can be challenging, especially in the summertime when it is hot and there are steep hills to climb.

scenic wonder. The park is located on approximately 3,600 wooded acres that offer a variety of recreational pursuits. Especially popular here are canoeing

Safely penned at Wildcat

OTHER GREAT PLACES TO RIDE

Illinois

Shenandoah Riding Center
200 N. Brodrecht Road, Galena, IL 61036
815-777-2373
http://www.shenandoahridingcenter.com
This private riding facility may be a little pricier than riding on public lands, but it features 40 miles of groomed trails, a cross-country course, and indoor and outdoor lighted arenas. Overnight boarding and rental horses are also available.

Wolf Creek State Park
RR 1, Box 99, Windsor IL, 61957
217-459-2831
http://www.dnr.state.il.us/lands/landmgt/PARKS/R3/WOLFCREK.HTM
Located not far from Springfield and Champaigne on the shore of Lake Shelbyville, Wolf Creek State Park offers 15 miles of scenic trails, including access to a beach. Horse camping and horse rentals are also available here.

Indiana

Tippecanoe River State Park
4200 N. US 35, Winamac, IN 46996
574-946-3213
http://www.in.gov/dnr/parklake/parks/tippecanoeriver.html
Ride 12 miles of winding trails through the trees. The horse camp has hitching posts, water, and lots of shade. There is also a day-use area for riders and horses.

Whitewater Memorial State Park
1418 South State Road 101, Libertyville, IN 47353
765-458-5565
http://www.in.gov/dnr/parklake/parks/whitewater.html
This state park in Indiana features horse camping and easy to moderate bridle trails. There is also a horse rental barn in the park.

Michigan

Michigan Shore-to-Shore Riding and Hiking Trail
Michigan Trail Riders Association, 3010 North M-52, Stockbridge, MI 49285
517-851-7554
http://www.mtra.org
This popular trail stretches east and west from Lake Huron to Lake Michigan and north and south from Grayling to Mackinac. It is open to riders and foot traffic only. There are campgrounds about every 18 to 25 miles of trail.

Yankee Springs Recreation Area
2104 S. Briggs Road, Middleville, MI 49333
269-795-9081
http://www.michigandnr.com/parksandtrails/ParksandTrailsInfo.aspx?id=511
This 5,200-acre park has approximately 19 miles of riding trails and a rustic equestrian camp with twenty-five sites.

Ohio

Wayne National Forest
13700 US Highway 33, Nelsonville, OH 45764
740-753-0101
http://www.fs.fed.us/r9/wayne
This is the only national forest in Ohio, and it is right next door to Hocking State Forest. It has more than 300 miles of trails for horseback riding, hiking, and other recreational pursuits. Trails are closed to all but hikers from December through April.

Wisconsin

Chequamegon-Nicolet National Forest
1170 Fourth Avenue South, Park Falls, WI 54552
715-762-2461
http://www.fs.fed.us/r9/cnnf
Riding trails abound in these two national forests, located in northern Wisconsin. Camping along the trails is permitted.

In Cuyahoga Valley National Park

MIDWEST TRAVEL SECTION

IF YOU ARE TRAVELING WITHOUT YOUR HORSE, OR IF YOUR HORSE IS BOARDED SAFELY AT A STABLE, ENJOY THE SITES IN THE NEIGHBORING TOWNS. BELOW, YOU'LL FIND A MILEAGE CHART LISTING THE DISTANCES BETWEEN THE TRAILS AND ALL THE AREAS DISCUSSED IN THE FOLLOWING TRAVEL SECTION. THE AREAS CLOSEST TO THE TRAILS ARE INDICATED BY AN **X**. FOR AREAS WHERE NEITHER STABLING NOR HORSE RENTALS ARE AVAILABLE, NO SIGHTSEEING OPTIONS ARE LISTED.

COAST TO COAST	Alto Pass, Ill.	Brighton Recreation Area, Mich.	Hocking Hills State Park, Ohio	Kickapoo Valley Reserve, La Farge, Wisc.	Nashville, Ind.	Northfield, Ohio	North Randall, Ohio	Peninsula, Ohio	Pittsfield, Ill.
Brighton Recreation Area (Mich.)	570 miles	**X** * miles	270 miles	505 miles	355 miles	205 miles	195 miles	205 miles	505 miles
Brown County State Park (Ind.)	295 miles	360 miles	265 miles	505 miles	**X** 15 miles	350 miles	355 miles	365 miles	350 miles
Cuyahoga Valley National Park (Ohio)	590 miles	200 miles	185 miles	600 miles	355 miles	**X** * miles	**X** 20 miles	**X** * miles	585 miles
Hocking State Forest (Ohio)	495 miles	270 miles	**X** * miles	650 miles	260 miles	190 miles	200 miles	165 miles	515 miles
Shawnee National Forest (Ill.)	**X** 60 miles	580 miles	450 miles	575 miles	270 miles	530 miles	540 miles	525 miles	285 miles
Wildcat Mountain State Park (Wis.)	565 miles	510 miles	660 miles	**X** * miles	490 miles	605 miles	600 miles	600 miles	435 miles

*The area to visit is the same as or is within 10 miles of the trails.

Must See / Must Do

ILLINOIS

SHAWNEE NATIONAL FOREST AREA

So Illinois doesn't come to mind when you think of fine wine? Well guess what? The state has nearly sixty wineries, and several of them are located in southern Illinois in the heart of Shawnee National Forest. And the **Illinois Wine** Web site (http://www.illinoiswine.com) even claims that some wines from the Prairie State have bested California wines in competition. If your seat is sore and you need a break from the saddle, sample a bit of the grape along the Shawnee Hills Wine Trail, the Rend Lake Wine Trail, or at other wineries in the

Shawnee Wine Trail

area. Visit both the Illinois Wine Web site and the Shawnee Hills Wine Trail Web site (http://www.shawneehillswine.com) for maps and information.

INDIANA

BROWN COUNTY STATE PARK AREA

While in the area, spend some time in nearby **Nashville** (Brown County Convention and Visitors Bureau, 10 North Van Buren Street, Nashville, IN 47448; 800-313-0842; http://www.brown county.com), enjoyable for its quaint specialty shops, art galleries, entertainment, and historic homes. In Nashville is the last home and studio of Indiana artist T. C. Steele, a member of the noted Hoosier group of American impressionist painters. You can visit the **T. C. Steele State Historic Site**

at 4220 T. C. Steele Road (Nashville, IN 47448; 812-988-2785; http://www.tcsteele.org). Hours are 9:00 a.m. to 5:00 p.m. Tuesday through Saturday, and 1:00 p.m. to 5:00 p.m. on Sunday. The site is closed on Mondays and holidays (except July 4th and Labor Day). Standard admission is $3.50 for adults, and group tours of the buildings are an additional $3.00.

Riders can also enjoy trotting the trails at **Yellowwood State Forest**, located in Nashville (772 So. Yellowwood Road, Nashville, IN 47448; 812-988-7945; http://www.in.gov/dnr/forestry/stateforests/ylwwd.htm). There is a $15 fee for an annual horse tag to use the trails. Horseless riders can rent mounts for riding the forest trails from **Schooner Valley Stables** (2282 West State Road 46, Nashville, IN 47448; 812-988-2859; http://www.schoonervalleystables.homestead.com). The stables are open seven days a week from March through mid-November and on weekends and holidays December through February. The fees are $20–$40 for rides from one to two hours.

Entrance to T. C. Steele house

MICHIGAN

BRIGHTON RECREATION AREA

Making use of the great waters in this park are people who come here for the boating and fishing. **Boat launches** are located on Appleton, Bishop, Chilson, and Shenango lakes. **Fishing sites** are available at Murray, Reed, and Shenango lakes. Other fun pastimes here are **mountain biking** and hiking.

Michigan birch trees

There are two mountain biking trails, the Murray Lake Trail and the Torn Shirt Mountain Bike Trail, which accommodate beginning through advanced riders. The Murray Lake Trail is also open to **hiking**. Two additional hiking trails, the 2-mile Kahchin (meaning short) and the 5-mile Penosha (meaning long), offer hikers (no horses) even more space to get away from the frenzy of the city. So if your horse is securely stabled and you want to hoof the trail yourself, this is a great place to do it.

OHIO

CUYAHOGA VALLEY NATIONAL PARK AREA

If you want to see the Cuyahoga Valley National Park and the general area via some very serious horsepower, try taking a ride on the **Cuyahoga Valley Scenic Railroad** (PO Box 158, Peninsula, OH 44264; 800-468-4070; http://www.cvsr.com.) Fares for adults vary from $6 to $25 depending on the destination. In addition to offering the regular rides, the railroad holds seasonal events, including a wine-tasting train, various historical storytelling events, and themed holiday rides.

You can also watch Thoroughbred racing and harness racing while in the area. To see Thoroughbreds, visit **Thistledown** (21501 Emery Road, North Randall, OH 44128; 216-662-8600; http://www.thistledown.com.) There is live racing April through December as well as simulcasting during the year. General admission and

Apple blossom, Michigan state flower

Rock House

parking are free. To see trotters and pacers, go to **Northfield Park** (10705 Northfield Dr., Northfield, OH 44067; 330-467-4101; http://www.northfield park.com). The track has live racing throughout the year as well as simulcast races 364 days a year. Grandstand admission is $1.75 except Monday, Wednesday, Friday, and Saturday, when admission (until 6:00 p.m.) and parking (until 5:30 p.m.) are free. Free parking, admission, and television carrels are offered all day and night on Sunday, Tuesday, and Thursday except during Tuesday live racing.

Hocking State Forest Area

If you feel like taking a riding break, visit the beautiful **Hocking Hills State Park**, which is surrounded by the Hocking State Forest (19852 Street, Route 664, South Logan, OH 43138; 740-385-6842; http://www.dnr.state.oh .us/parks/parks/hocking.htm). Visit Old Man's Cave, where a Civil War–era hermit named Richard Rowe lived and was buried. You can also hike to the Rock House, a cave halfway up a 150-

foot cliff with a 200-foot-long tunnel-like corridor. Legend has it that horse thieves, robbers, and other miscreants hid here after committing their crimes. The park has a restaurant, a swimming pool, and other amenities. There is no entry fee, and the park is open year-round, from half an hour before sunrise to half an hour after sunset.

WISCONSIN

Wildcat Mountain State Park Area

When visiting Wildcat Mountain, don't miss the bordering 8,569-acre **Kickapoo Valley Reserve**, which offers approximately 40 miles of horse trails. There are also horse camping opportunities in the reserve, including the Willow and Mule campgrounds, which are popular with riders. For more information on the Kickapoo Valley Reserve, contact the Kickapoo Valley Reserve Visitor Center (S3661 State Highway 131, La Farge, WI 54639; 608-625-2960; http://www.kvr.state.wi.us/home).

WHERE TO STAY & STABLE

ILLINOIS

SHAWNEE NATIONAL FOREST AREA

Horses and Riders:

Bay Creek Ranch Horse Camp
Route 1, Box 189
Simpson, IL 62985
618-695-2670
http://www.baycreekranch.com
$20 per night for camping with hookups; $30 per adult, $10 per child up to age thirteen for the lodge; $10 per night for stalls; $10 per night for pens, limit four horses per pen; $2 per horse for day-use parking
This family-run operation, near the River-to-River Trail, has direct access to the national forest. It provides a tack and gift store, shower house, and laundry facilities.

Bear Branch Horse Camp
PO Box 40, Highway145
Eddyville, IL 62928
618-672-4249
http://www.BearBranch.com
$12–$24 per night for camping; $39–$69 per night for cabins and bunkhouses; $8 per night for stalls; $2 per person for day use
Located near Eddyville, Illinois, this horse camp offers camping and other lodging for riders. Campsites feature water and electricity; most cabins have private bathrooms and refrigerators. The camp has a general store, tack store, and restaurant on site.

Camp Cadiz (National Forest Service campground)
Vienna/Elizabethtown Ranger District, 602 N. 1st Street
Vienna, IL 62995
618-658-2111
http://www.fs.fed.us/r9/forests/shawnee/recreation/camping/cadiz/
$5 per night
This national forest campsite has water and vault toilets, and it allows horses. It is a trailhead on the River-to-River Trail. Open year-round.

Johnson Creek Group Camping (National Forest Service campground)
Jonesboro/Murphysboro Ranger District, 521 North Main Street
Jonesboro, IL 62952
618-833-8576
http://www.fs.fed.us/r9/forests/shawnee/recreation/camping/johnson
$5–$12 per night
This camp has water and flush toilets from May through September and vault toilets year-round.

34 Ranch
PO Box 38
Herod, IL 62947
618-264-2141
http://www.34ranch.com
$15–$20 per night for camping; $10 per night for stalls; $5 per night for pens; $3 per person for day use

This 500-acre private horseman's camp located in the Shawnee National forest has nearly two hundred graveled sites with electrical and water hookups, modern restroom and shower house, show arena, dance barn, and other amenities. It also has tether posts and box stalls available at some campsites.

Trail of Tears Lodge and Sports Resort
Old Cape Road, 1575 Fair City Road
Jonesboro, IL 62952
618-833-8697
http://www.trailoftears.com
$65–$85 per night with breakfast for the lodge; $125 per night for cabins; $20 per night for camping with hookups; $10 per night for primitive camping; $10 per night for horse stalls plus $3 unloading fee per horse; $25 per hour for horse rentals for registered guests only
Adjacent to the Shawnee National Forest, this rustic lodge is located on 445 acres of land. It features a restaurant, a gift shop, a swimming pool, a game room, and laundry facilities.

Riders Only

Main Street Bed and Breakfast
300 N. Main Street
Anna, IL 62906
618-833-7422
http://www.mainstreetbandb.com
$85 per night, breakfast included
This small Victorian bed-and-breakfast includes two rooms with private baths, decorated in period furnishings. There is a common area with a full kitchen, a living room with a gas fireplace, and an enclosed porch with a hot tub.

Shawnee Hills Bed & Breakfast
290 Water Valley Road
Cobden, IL 62920
618-893-2211
http://www.shawneehillbb.com
$60–$150 per night, continental and full breakfasts optional
The Shawnee Hills Bed & Breakfast is located in the heart of Shawnee National Forest. All guest rooms have private baths and decks and are decorated with antique furnishings. There is an 1860 barn, now an antique store, on site and a blacksmith shop below the barn.

INDIANA

BROWN COUNTY STATE PARK AREA

Horses and Riders

Brown County State Park Horsemen's Campground
Located in the park off State Route 135, 7 miles south of State Route 46
866-622-6746
http://www.indiana.reserveworld.com/Campgrounds/search.cfm
$26 per night January 1 through May 4, $31 per night May 5 through October 29, $28 per night October 30 through December 31 for modern electric campground; $8 per night January 1 through May 4, $13 per night May 5 through October 29, $11 October 30 through December 31 for primitive campsites
The park has 118 horse camping sites with electric hookups and a modern bathroom with hot showers. It also has 86 primitive sites. The campsites fill up fast, especially on weekends, so be sure to call ahead for reservations. From January 1 through April 28, no reservations are accepted. There is a day-use parking area near the campsite.

Rawhide Ranch
1292 State Road 135 South
Nashville, IN 47448
812-988-0085
http://www.rawhideranchusa.com
$89 and up per night for rooms; beginning at $10 for stalls for horses of ranch guests
Rawhide Ranch accommodates guests with and without horses. Horseless visitors can enjoy trail rides on trails bordering Brown County State Park. Guided one-hour trail rides are $15 per person for overnight guests and $25 per person for those who are not guests of the ranch. Riders with horses can take their horses into the park, on ranch trails, or to other riding venues in the area. Guests will find comfortable accommodations in Western-themed rooms, and horses of guests will enjoy their stay in the thirty-two-stall "horse-tel."

Riders Only:
Abe Martin Lodge and Cabins
PO Box 547
Nashville, IN 47448
812-988-4418/Toll free: 877-265-6343
http://www.in.gov/dnr/parklake/inns/abe/index.html
$52–$119 per night
The lodge is named for cartoon character Abe Martin, who was the main character in humorist Kin Hubbard's cartoons, which appeared in *The Indianapolis News* from 1905 to 1930 and were also syndicated nationwide. Although Abe Martin belonged to no particular locality, in the February 3, 1905, column he announced, "I'm goin' ter move ter Brown County Tewmorrow," and the next day he was depicted in a wagon piled high with household goods along with the words, "By cracky, it's sum travelin' ter git ter Brown County." He has been the favorite son of the county ever since. The lodge's cottages feature names of characters from the cartoon. There is a restaurant on the premises.

MICHIGAN

BRIGHTON RECREATION AREA

Horses and Riders:
Brighton Recreation Area Equestrian Campground
Located in the park
810-229-6566
http://www.michigandnr.com/parksandtrails/ParksandTrailsInfo.aspx?id=438
$17 per night
This rustic campground has twenty-five campsites and is open April through October. It features hitching posts, vault toilets, and hand pumps.

Happy Hollow Ranch
4773 Mack Road
Howell, MI 48843
517-546-3351
http://www.zfarms.com
$125 per night, including meals, three-night minimum stay
This working ranch near the Brighton Recreation Area specializes in breeding Egyptian Arabians. Visitors who stay here can lease these horses for riding at the 100-plus-acre ranch or bring their own equine companions to ride. The ranch has 5 miles of trails, box stalls, 40 acres of pasture, twenty-five paddocks, and an indoor riding arena. English and western riding lessons are also offered. Guests sleep in the fourteen-bed bunkhouse. Open April through October.

Amerihost Inn and Suites
4121 Lambert Drive
Howell, MI 48843
517-546-0712
http://www.amerihostinn.com
$71–$120 per night
The inn features suites with whirlpool tubs and daily continental breakfast. The inn also has an indoor pool, a spa, and a fitness center.

Best Western of Howell
1500 Pinckney Road
Howell, MI 48843
517-548-2900
http://www.bestwestern.com
$80–$135 per night
This Best Western has a breakfast restaurant on the premises. There is also a game room as well as an outdoor heated pool.

Kensington Inn
124 Holiday Lane
Howell, MI 48843
517-548-3510
http://www.kensingtoninn.com
$69–$99 per night
The Kensington Inn features continental breakfast and an outdoor swimming pool. Pets are allowed.

OHIO

CUYAHOGA VALLEY NATIONAL PARK AREA

The Inn at Brandywine Falls
8230 Brandywine Road
Sagamore Hills, OH 44067
330-467-1812
http://www.innatbrandywinefalls.com
$119–$298 per night for two people, $20 less per night for one person, includes breakfast
This charming 1848 inn, which is located inside the boundaries of the national park, is listed on the National Register of Historic Places. It overlooks the 67-foot Brandywine Waterfall. The inn's guest rooms and public rooms are decorated in antiques.

Brecksville Stables
11921 Parkview Road
Brecksville, OH 44134
440-526-6767
http://www.valleyriding.org
$15 per night for stalls, including bedding and feed three times a day
This stable, along with Rocky River Stables, is run by Valley Riding, Inc., and is located in the Cleveland MetroParks district. Both stables offer overnight boarding based on availability of stalls, so be sure to make reservations before you take your trip.

Rocky River Stables
19901 Puritas Avenue
Cleveland, OH 44135
216-267-2525
http://www.valleyriding.org
$15 per night for stalls, including bedding and feed three times a day
Like Brecksville Stables, Rocky River Stables is located in the Cleveland MetroParks district. Boarding is based on availability of stalls, so make reservations before you take your trip.

HOCKING STATE FOREST AREA

Horses and Riders:

Hocking State Forest Horsemen's Camp
Located in the park, off of Laurel Township Road 231
877-247-8733
http://www.dnr.state.oh.us/forestry/Forests/stateforests/hockingbridle.htm
No fee for camping
This primitive campground has twenty-three campsites, water for horses, hitching posts, and room for rig parking. Campsites are available on a first-come, first-served basis, and users must register at the self-registration booth.

Palmerosa Horseman's Camp
19217 Keifel Road
Laurelville, OH 43135
740-385-3799
http://www.palmerosa.com
$12 per night for tent camping for one to four guests; $20 per night hookups for one to four guests; $35 per night double occupancy, $5 each additional guest per night, and $40 per night on holidays for bunkhouses; $100–$150 per night for cabins; $2 per night for horse picketing at the campsite; $12 per night for stalls; $2 per horse for day-ride parking; $25 per hour to $350 per week for horse lease for registered campers; $25 per hour for guided horse rentals
Located next to Hocking State Forest, this horseman's camp offers everything from tent camping to romantic cabin getaways. Hot showers and outhouses are available for campers and those folks staying in the bunkhouses. Horses can stay in the barn—recommended for those guests who are planning to spend time doing "nonhorsey" things in the area—or be picketed at your campsite. The camp has permanent picket lines, so there is no need to bring your own. There is a farrier on call, and other pets are welcome for a one-time $5 fee.

WISCONSIN

WILDCAT MOUNTAIN STATE PARK AREA

Horses and Riders:

End of the Trail Equine Campground
E13722 Cass Valley Road
Ontario, WI 54651
608-337-4738
http://www.endofthetrailcampground.com
$20 per night camping with electricity, $15 without; $7 per night for box stalls, including bedding
This private horse camp with 50 miles of trails is located between Wildcat Mountain and the Kickapoo Valley Reserve trails. It has box stalls and permanent high lines, a round pen, showers, picnic tables, and fire rings. Open May 1 through November 15.

Highland Quarter Horses
E7630 Rognstad Ridge Road
Cashton, WI 54619
608-634-3035
$10 per night for camping; $5 per night for box stalls; $5 per person for day use
Ride on more than 12 miles of trails at the farm, or stay here and trailer your horse a short distance from Wildcat Mountain State Park. The camp has water, showers, fire pits, and horse pens. No electricity. Reservations are required.

Horsetrail Campground
Located in Wildcat Mountain State Park
608-337-4775
http://www.dnr.state.wi.us/org/land/parks/specific/wildcat
$8 per night, $2 additional on weekends and holidays
The horse campground is located inside the park in a valley northeast of the park office. It has twenty-four campsites, twenty of which can be reserved; the others are on a first-come, first-served basis. The campground has a corral, hitching posts, parking pads and a large parking lot, loading ramps, drinking water, vault toilets, picnic tables, and fire rings. There are restrooms with showers at the nonhorse camp that horse campers are allowed to use.

WHERE TO WINE & DINE

ILLINOIS

SHAWNEE NATIONAL FOREST AREA

The Creek Bar and Grill
Highway 146
Golconda, IL 62938
618-683-2227
http://www.thecreekbar.com
$2.25–$19.95
The Creek Bar and Grill serves a varied menu, from hamburgers to dinner entrées such as catfish and crab legs, with all the sides. It also features pool tables, dart boards, video games, and live music.

Peach Barn Café
560 Chestnut Street
Alto Pass, IL 62905
618-893-4923
http://www.peachbarn.com/cafe.htm
$4.25–$12.85 for the Café; $110–$115 for the bed-and-breakfast
Authentic Swedish cuisine is served at the Peach Barn Café, located within the Shawnee National Forest. The café is part of the Hedman Orchard and Vineyards. The orchard sells a variety of peaches and table grapes, and wine grapes are also grown on the property. The winery sells both red and white wines. There is also a bed-and-breakfast, called the Peach Barn Suite, that features a two-room suite that can sleep up to four guests. Reservations are required.

INDIANA

BROWN COUNTY STATE PARK AREA
Abe Martin Lodge and Cabins

PO Box 547
Nashville, IN 47448
812-988-4418/toll free: 877-265-6343
http://www.in.gov/dnr/parklake/inns/abe/index.html
$3–$17
The restaurant on the premises serves American fare. It is open for breakfast, lunch, and dinner; no alcoholic beverages are served.

Artists Colony Inn
PO Box 1099, Corner of Van Buren and Franklin streets
Nashville, IN 47448
812-988-0600
http://www.artistscolonyinn.com
$7–$15
The Artists Colony Inn is open for breakfast, lunch, and dinner. In good weather, you can enjoy your meal outside on the porch. The inn is also a bed-and-breakfast with rooms starting at $75 per night.

The Story Inn
6404 South State Road 135
Nashville, IN 47448
800-881-1183/812-988-2273
http://www.storyinn.com
$21–market price for dinner; $9–$14
for lunch; $6–$13 for breakfast

From the outside, the Story Inn doesn't look much like with its scruffy, tin-roofed façade, but step inside the restaurant and it's as if you've entered another world. Formerly a turn-of-the century country store, the inn is now a well-known gourmet restaurant that has been given rave reviews in such publications as *The New York Times*, the *Chicago Sun-Times*, and *Midwest Living*. Dinner entrées include breast of duck with pumpkin ravioli, salmon with artichoke hearts, and filet au poivre—a 10-ounce Angus filet mignon hand cut and finished with a rich peppercorn sauce. Casual dress is fine; ride your horse right up to the hitch rail at the back door. The inn is open Tuesday through Sunday for breakfast, lunch, and dinner; dinner reservations are required.

MICHIGAN

Brighton Recreation Area

Blue Willow Tea Room
113 N. Michigan Avenue
Howell, MI 48843
517-540-1589
http://www.bluewillowtearoom.com.nationprotect.net/index.htm
$4.95–$14.95
The name for this charming tearoom came from a set of antique Blue Willow China belonging to the owner's grandmother. The tearoom offers lunch, afternoon tea, scones, and desserts. The lunch menu changes weekly and includes such delectable fare as quiche, sandwiches, soups, and salads. Open Tuesday through Saturday; afternoon tea is served Tuesday, Thursday, and Saturday at 2:30; closed Sunday and Monday. Reservations are required for afternoon tea; reservations are necessary for lunch for groups of four or more.

Cleary's Pub
117 East Grand River Avenue
Howell, MI 48843
517-546-4136
http://www.clearyspubhowell.com
$12–$20 for entrées
Enjoy seafood, steaks, and casual American fare in a relaxed atmosphere while sipping Irish beer. Open for lunch and dinner; takeout is available. Friday evenings feature live music.

OHIO

Cuyahoga Valley National Park Area

Eddie's Creekside Restaurant & Market
8803 Brecksville Road
Brecksville, OH 44141
440-546-0555
http://www.eddiescreekside.com
$7.95 and up
Variety is the spice of life, and you'll find it at Eddie's Creekside Restaurant & Market. The menu features several styles of waffles for breakfast as well as egg dishes; lunch includes pot roast to portobello sandwiches; and for dinner you'll find pizzas, steaks, chicken, Italian specialties, and more.

Ken Stewart's Grill
1911 N. Cleveland
Akron, OH 44333
330-666-8881
$20 and up
Ken Stewart's Grill and Ken Stewart's Lodge (1970 W. Market Street, Akron, OH 44333; 330-867-2555) feature fine dining in a comfortable atmosphere. They serve seafood, steaks, and more.

Hocking State Forest Area

The Olde Dutch Restaurant
12791 Street Route 664
S. Logan, OH 43138
740-385-1000
http://www.oldedutch.com
$4.99–$13.99

Although many people think of Pennsylvania when they think of the Amish, Ohio actually has the largest Amish population in the country. (See Amish buggies at right.) Enjoy an Amish meal with your choice of meat and sides served family style (the entire party eats the same family meal), or order individually from the menu. A sampling of the menu items includes a family-style sampler, the house specialty of roasted chicken, country-cured ham, spaghetti and meat balls, and even a vegetarian platter. The restaurant also offers picnic baskets in summer. Open seven days a week.

Trail's End Grill
25851 Big Pine Road
Rockbridge, OH 43149
740-380-6372
http://www.hthorsebackrides.com/Index3.htm
$1.50–$2.50
Trail's End Grill serves hamburgers, chicken fingers, chicken sandwiches, apple dumplings, ice cream, and other snack foods. Horseback riders at Happy Trails Horseback Rides, which is on the same property, receive 10 percent off their meals. Open seasonally, beginning in April.

WISCONSIN

WILDCAT MOUNTAIN STATE PARK AREA

Dorset Valley School Restaurant & Bakery
26147 Highway 71
Wilton, WI 54670
608-435-6525
http://www.dorsetvalleyrestaurant.com
$2.95–$6.95 for breakfast; $5.95 for average lunch; $9.95 for average dinner
This restaurant, located approximately 12 miles north of Wildcat Mountain State Park, is located in an old country schoolhouse, which was built in the 1800s. It serves Italian food, Mexican meals, country dishes, and more. During the summer, fifteen varieties of pies are available. Open seven days a week in summer and fall. Open Friday through Sunday from January 1 through April 30.

Rockton Bar and Restaurant
Highway 131 between Ontario and La Farge
608-625-4395
http://www.rocktonbar.com
$2–$10 for lunch; $6–$15 for dinner
This casual restaurant and bar is popular with riders of horses and of motorcycles. Try the barbecue chicken, a specialty of the house. You'll also find burgers, sandwiches, and more on the menu. It is open seven days a week, except from the end of November through April when it is closed on Mondays.

Grazing by a pond

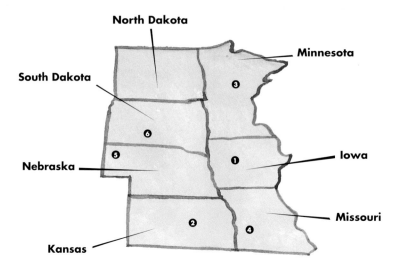

North Dakota

Minnesota

South Dakota

Iowa

Nebraska

Missouri

Kansas

GREAT PLAINS MAP LEGEND

Iowa
❶ Brushy Creek State
Recreation Area

Kansas
❷ Kanopolis State Park

Minnesota
❸ Chippewa National Forest

Missouri
❹ Harry S. Truman Dam
and Reservoir

Nebraska
❺ Fort Robinson State Park

South Dakota
❻ Badlands National Park

THE GREAT PLAINS

hen you ride in the Great Plains states, even if you've never visited, the landscape may look strangely familiar. If you've ever watched a Western movie and seen the bad guys in their black hats galloping away from the good guys in their white hats, you've been here before—though you may not have ever set foot in any of these states.

These are the lands that Wyatt Earp, Wild Bill Hickock, and other great gunslingers roamed. These are the lands of the wild and wicked cow towns, where disagreements were settled at the end of a gun barrel and questions asked later, after some poor cowboy's body was lying prone in the dirt. This is the land of Chief Crazy Horse and of military outposts that sought to quell Indian "uprisings" as the country's natives were relocated to reservations.

It is also a place where wild horses galloped, buffalo roamed, and, in the far northern lakes lands, mythical Paul Bunyan felled trees with his mighty ax. Today, it is a place to enjoy the country's frontier history while making a little trail riding history of your own.

IOWA

BRUSHY CREEK STATE RECREATION AREA

With more than 6,000 acres, Brushy Creek, located in central Iowa, is one of the state's largest tracts of public recreation land. Approximately 50 miles of multiuse trails pass through woodlands, fields, and valleys. Riders, hikers, and mountain bikers enjoy this recreation area in milder weather, but when winter's white wonderland arrives, cross-country skiing and snowmobiling are the area's focus. A human-made 690-acre lake welcomes boaters, swimmers, and fishing enthusiasts, who catch walleyes, both largemouth and smallmouth bass, muskies, crappies, red-ear sunfish, channel catfish, and bluegill sunfish. A fishing tournament takes place on the lake almost every weekend here. If you'd rather swim with the fish than hook them, you'll find a designated swimming beach to

Brushy Creek

A nice day on the trail

enjoy. There are also two shooting ranges in the park, and seasonal hunting is allowed.

Planning for this recreation area was launched in the 1960s, when the Iowa Conservation Commission began a study of areas of the state conducive to constructing large recreational lakes. With its location along a tributary of the Des Moines River and abundant natural resources that made it a good candidate for protection, the site along Brushy Creek was a natural choice. The area also boasted significant archaeological sites and geological formations as well as being a habitat for a threatened vole species. By 1968, land was being acquired and environmental studies were being performed. By 1998, the lake was com-

Lake at the recreation area

plete, and the rest is history. Today, Iowa residents and visitors to the Hawkeye State have a ruggedly beautiful area to enjoy getting away from it all.

KANSAS

KANOPOLIS STATE PARK

Want to get a flavor of what riding in the Old West was like? Visit Kanopolis State Park, Kansas's oldest park. It is located in central Kansas and covers more than 1,600 acres of rolling hills, bluffs, and woods. The park is divided

Inside Kanopolis

into two areas of the 35-acre Kanopolis Reservoir, Langley Point and Horsethief on the southern and north-

Kanopolis mule riders

eastern shores, respectively. In addition to these areas, managed by the Kansas Department of Wildlife and Parks, there is a wildlife area and thousands of acres of U.S. Army Corps of Engineers property that, combined with the state park, encompass approximately 16,000 acres of recreational area. The park is located in Ellsworth County and near the town of Ellsworth, which was a major cow town in the early 1870s.

The intriguingly named Horse-thief Canyon is full of caves and crevices, where you can still imagine horse thieves and others hiding out in the area's wilder days. Today, equestrians, hikers, and mountain bikers share 25 miles of trails in Horsethief Canyon, and there is a campground reserved exclusively for horses and their riders, the Rockin' K campground, where campers can access the trails. (Day

SNAPSHOT - BRUSHY CREEK STATE RECREATION AREA

Description: More than 6,000 acres of open land beckon riders to enjoy the trails of Brushy Creek State Recreation Area. In addition to the trails, equestrian users enjoy two well-equipped, modern campgrounds that have 125 horse campsites. There are also day-use staging areas with restrooms located near each of the campgrounds. The south staging area also features a picnic shelter. No horse rentals are available at Brushy Creek.

Open: Year-round

Address: 3175 290th Street, Lehigh, IA 50557

Phone: 515-543-8298

Web site: http://www.iowadnr.com/parks/state_park_list/brushy_creek.html

Getting there: Located south of US Highway 20, 15 miles southeast of Fort Dodge, IA

Fees/permits: No fees to ride trails or use staging areas

Horse rentals: None

Horse camping: Available in the recreation area

Trail conditions/level of difficulty: Easy to moderate; gentle to moderate slopes

riders use trailhead B, Horsethief Canyon). The trails loop through canyons, trees, high prairie, and the sandstone Red Rock Canyon. Northern loops that extend onto the

Sign to Rockin' K

wildlife area have many water crossings and give riders views of extensive open prairie. Riding here varies from easy to challenging. Trails outside the state park are closed from November 1 through January 31 because of hunting in the area; park trails are open year-round. Riding in Kansas in the summer is hot, so consider coming in fall or spring for best conditions.

Also in Horsethief Canyon is the 1.5-mile-long Buffalo Track Canyon Nature Trail. The trail follows Bison Creek, once a watering hole for wild horses and buffalo, and offers an educational tour of the plants, animals, and geology of the canyon. It is open only to hikers but is worth a visit if you feel like stretching your legs after a long day in the saddle. You'll see yucca, or "soap-

weed" plant, its leaves used by Native Americans to weave baskets and its roots used as shampoo; Dakota sandstone that has been shaped by the elements into animal-like sculptures; and marks in the sandstone that local lore says are tracks from buffalo who came into the canyon looking for water. Box Canyon, toward the end of the trail, was used by Native Americans to trap wild horses and buffalo and was named when Pawnee

Trail marker at Kanopolis

SNAPSHOT - KANOPOLIS STATE PARK

Description: Visit Kansas's centrally located Kanopolis State Park, the oldest of twenty-five state parks in the Sunflower State, with 25 miles of horse, hiking, and mountain biking trails that take you through trees, canyon, and prairie and past caves and sandstone walls. There is one horse campground in the park. If you don't have a horse but want to travel through the area the way the cowboys, Native Americans, and pioneers did, horse rentals and covered wagon and stagecoach rides are available in the park at the Goverland Stage Stop (785-826-0743 or 785-826-0789), located in the Horsethief area.

Open: Year-round

Address: 200 Horsethief Road, Marquette, KS 67464

Phone: 785-546-2565

Web site: http://www.kdwp.state.ks.us/news/state_parks/locations/kanopolis

Getting there: From Salina, Kansas: Travel 33 miles southwest via State Highway 140 to State Highway 141.

Fees/permits: Admission is $5.50 October 1 through March 31, $6.50 April 1 through September 30

Horse rentals: Available in the park

Horse camping: Available in the park

Trail conditions/level of difficulty: 90% easy to moderate, 10% difficult (horses must cross water in places)

hid horses stolen from a Cheyenne village there.

Be sure to see the prairie dog town located in the Horsethief Canyon area. For food, camping supplies, and fuel, visit the full-service marina that is located in the park.

Riding at Kanopolis

MINNESOTA

CHIPPEWA NATIONAL FOREST

Up here in north central Minnesota in the Chippewa National Forest, it's not hard to imagine lumberjack Paul Bunyan and his blue ox, Babe, striding with giant footsteps through the dense trees. The forest's history begins in prehistoric times, after the glaciers retreated and the first native peoples moved in, living off the rich land and its mammals, fish, and plant food staples such as wild rice. It continues with the early logging era in the mid to late 1800s—when the north country was stripped of its trees—through its establishment as a national forest in 1908 and the subsequent reforestation effort, which was aided by the Civilian Conservation Corp. Originally called Minnesota National Forest, the 660,000-acre forest was renamed the Chippewa National Forest in 1928 to honor its original inhabitants, the Chippewa Indians, who were also known as the Ojibwa. The forest's gross boundary is 1.6 million acres, and the acreage that is not managed by the U.S. Forest Service is state, county, Native American, or private.

THE WICKEDEST COW TOWN IN KANSAS

Kanopolis State Park is deep in the heart of an area that was once a thriving cattle market. It is located in Ellsworth County, which gained its name from the town of Ellsworth, established in 1867 and now the county seat. The town of Ellsworth became a thriving railhead in the 1870s after the town fathers devised a plan to lure the Texas cattle trade away from the more well-known cow town of Abilene, Kansas, of which the famous Wild Bill Hickock was marshal.

With more cows came more people to Ellsworth, all seeking to benefit from the profitable longhorn trade. Respectable businessmen, along with gamblers, thieves, prostitutes, and gunmen, moved into town. Ellsworth quickly became known as the "wickedest" of the cow towns, with drunken cowboys running rampant, frequent shootings, and even the killing of the town's sheriff Chauncey B. Whitney in 1873. The point-blank shooting occurred when Whitney sought to break up a dispute between several drunken gamblers. A notable personality who is said to have witnessed the shooting and caught one of the men involved, even as the sheriff's own deputies cowered, was Wyatt Earp, who was allegedly then offered the job of town marshal but refused it.

The year Whitney was shot was also the year that Ellsworth reached its apex in the cattle trade. That year, 220,000 head of longhorn were shipped from the town. By 1875, the cattle market was moving south as more railroad track was completed, and the cow trade died out in Ellsworth.

Ellsworth's original commercial district still remains. Visitors can see a small log cabin, an 1878 Victorian home, an early livery stable, an 1880s church, and more.

Taking in the fall colors

Water is abundant in this lake country. The forest has 1,300 lakes, 923 miles of streams, and 400,000 acres of wetlands. Naturally, water sports take center stage here, and canoeing, waterskiing, swimming, lakeside camping, and fishing for walleyes, northern pikes, bass, muskies, and sunfish are popular activities. Ice fishing takes place in the frozen winter months. Other activities in the winter are cross-country skiing, dog sledding, and snowmobiling.

Chippewa is also involved in helping restore our national bird's popula-

A bald eagle calls out.

tion. It is home to one of the largest breeding populations of bald eagles in the continental United States and has banded and surveyed the birds since 1962. There are about 178 nesting pairs of eagles found each year. Spend some time on the lakes here and you may spot an eagle. The best viewing is on Leech Lake, Cass Lake, and Lake Winnie. If you spot an eagle feather, though, leave it alone. It's illegal to possess the feathers, but tribal members are allowed, with appropriate permission, to use bald eagle feathers for ceremonial purposes. Also living here are other raptors, such as hawks, ospreys, and great gray owls, and other birds, such as swallows, sparrows, ruffled grouse, and loons. Another animal that is here, but that you are unlikely to see, is the wolf. There are approximately thirteen wolf territories estimated in the forest.

Logging still takes place in Chippewa, although on a much smaller scale than in the past. Timber is harvested from about 1 percent of the

SNAPSHOT - CHIPPEWA NATIONAL FOREST

Description: Ride on 120 miles of trails near Cut Foot Sioux Horse Camp in the southeast portion of the Chippewa. As you ride, keep your eyes open for bald eagles, as the forest is home to one of the largest breeding populations of bald eagles. Day riders can park off of Highway 46 in a large day-use and group area. Or stay in a private horse camp near the town of Bemidji, and enjoy horse trails there (see Where to Stay & Stable).

Open: Year-round

Address: 200 Ash Avenue, Cass Lake, MN 56633

Phone: 218-335-8600

Web site: http://www.fs.fed.us/r9/chippewa

Getting there: From the north: Take US Highway 71. From the east and west: Take US Highway 2. From the Minneapolis area: Take US Highway 10 to Highway 371.

Fees/permits: None

Horse rentals: Available locally

Horse camping: Available in the forest

Trail conditions/level of difficulty: Easy to moderate

MISSOURI

A wolf surveys his territory.

Chippewa National Forest each year. Common in the old days was using horses to pull logs out of the forest. In nonmotorized areas of the forest today, this use of horses still takes place.

A great place to stay if you want to ride horses in the forest is at the Cut Foot Sioux Horse Camp, which is surrounded by more than 120 miles of mostly flat, grassy recreation trails and numbered forest roads. The trails, ranging in length from 1 to 20 miles, take riders through the Cut Foot Experimental Forest, an outdoor laboratory for studying pine forest management, and through some of the forest's most scenic countryside. Moondance Ranch and Adventure Park (Highway 371 South, Walker, MN 56484; 218-547-1055; http://www.moondanceranch .com), Rising Star Ranch (Highway 71, Park Rapids, MN 56470; 218-732-1749/888-900-1749), and Stein's Winding River Guest Farm (14185 Teddy Road NW, Pinewood, MN 56676; 218-243-2629; http://www.steinsguest farm.com) all offer horses to rent for guided rides through the Chippewa forest.

HARRY S. TRUMAN DAM AND RESERVOIR

The U.S. Army Corp of Engineers planned, designed, built, and manages the Harry S. Truman Dam and Reservoir, commonly referred to as Truman Lake. The reservoir is located within the Osage River Basin of west central Missouri, approximately 100 miles southeast of Kansas City. Its main purpose is flood control, but it is also important as a source of hydroelectric power production, wildlife and fish management, and recreation. First authorized in 1954 as the Kaysinger Bluff Dam and Reservoir, construction began in 1964. Completing the massive project included the relocation of roads, towns, and cemeteries. The reservoir was renamed by the U.S. Congress in 1970 in honor of President Harry S. Truman, who was born in Lamar, Missouri, in 1884.

This reservoir is the largest flood control reservoir in Missouri, with a stor-

Truman Dam and Reservoir

age capacity of 5 million acre-feet (1 acre-foot equals 325,000 gallons). During flooding periods, Truman Reservoir operates in conjunction with other reservoirs to help protect the floodplains of the lower Osage, Missouri, and Mississippi rivers. The power plant at Truman contains six turbine generators and churns out 160,000 kilowatts of electrical energy, which is used to help meet energy

Unloading the horses

demand during peak periods when conventional power plants cannot. The lake and its surrounding land are managed for fish and wildlife with involvement from the Missouri Department of Conservation. Wetlands' development, native grass reintroduction, and improvement of fishery habitats are a few of the management projects. Truman Lake is a popular recreation destination for boating, fishing, swimming, camping, hiking, using off-road vehicles, hunting, and horseback riding.

Riders can enjoy nearly 50 miles of trails here, with the most extensive being those leading from the Berry Bend Equestrian Campground, a camping area that is exclusively for horses and riders. There are two trail loops: the West Trail and the East Trail. Both trails have mile markers to help you determine your distance from the campground. The West Trail is the more challenging of the two trails, as it traverses many steep ridges and valleys. The East Trail is a

SNAPSHOT - HARRY S. TRUMAN DAM AND RESERVOIR

Description: Ride 50 miles of horse trails in two separate trail systems at Harry S. Truman Dam and Reservoir. Day-use riders and overnight horse campers are welcome. You'll find food and supplies at the lake's marinas and groceries in the gateway town of Warsaw. The Berry Bend horse trails and campground are closed for one weekend in November when the annual Truman Managed Deer Hunt for hunters with physical disabilities takes place.

Open: Year-round

Address: Harry S. Truman Project Office, U.S. Army Corps of Engineers, 15968 Truman Road, Warsaw, MO 65355

Phone: 660-438-7317/Fax: 660-438-7815

Web site: http://www.nwk.usace.army.mil/harryst/hst_home.htm

Getting there: Access to the area is provided by US Highways 65 and 54, and Missouri Highways 7 and 13: From Kansas City: Take Highway 7 southeast through Clinton to Route UU. From Springfield: Take US Highway 65 north to Warsaw, then take Highway 7 West 9 miles to Route UU.

Fees/permits: $8–$17 camping fee in season, $7–$13 off-season; $8.50 reservation fee

Horse rentals: None

Horse camping: Available at the reservoir

Trail conditions/level of difficulty: Moderate to difficult; rocky terrain, so horses must be shod and in good condition

bit more level and over-looks the lake in several spots. Day-use riders to the Berry Bend area trails can access the trails from the Berry Bend #1 Picnic Shelter area.

Another trail system is located across the lake, around 12 miles southwest of the Berry Bend trails. It is called the Smith Bend Equestrian Trail and has 13 miles of trails and trailhead parking. Horses should be well conditioned and must wear shoes for these trails, as the terrain is rocky. You'll be happy to note that only hikers share the trail with equestrians; wheeled vehicles, including mountain bikes, are not permitted.

A welcome drink

Truman Dam

NEBRASKA

FORT ROBINSON STATE PARK

Nebraska's largest state park, at 22,000 acres, is steeped in U.S. military and Native American history. Fort Robinson, located in the northwestern part of the state in the Pine Ridge region, served as a military outpost from 1874 to 1948, a time period that ranges from the nineteenth-century Indian Wars until after World War II. The U.S. government authorized the establishment of the fort in March 1874 at the Red Cloud Agency, which had been established as a reservation for the

HISTORY OF ARMY ENGINEERS

You may know that the U.S. Army Corps of Engineers provides civil and military design, engineering, and construction services for the country. But have you every wondered how the corps—made up of 34,600 civilian and 650 military engineers, scientists, biologists, hydrologists, and other professionals—got started?

Truman Dam and Reservoir turbines

The U.S. Army Corps of Engineers traces it origins to the Revolutionary War, specifically June 16, 1775, when the Continental Congress organized an army with a chief engineer and two assistants. Colonel Richard Gridley became General George Washington's first chief engineer, but it was not until 1779 that Congress created a separate Corps of Engineers. Army engineers, including several French officers, were instrumental in some of the hard-fought battles of the Revolutionary War, including Bunker Hill, Saratoga, and the final victory at Yorktown.

Despite several proposals that a peacetime military establishment that includes engineers be retained after the Revolutionary War, Congress allowed all but a token force of infantry and artillery to muster out of service by the end of 1783. In 1794, Congress organized a Corps of Artillerists and Engineers, but it was not until 1802 that it reestablished a separate Corps of Engineers. The Corps of Engineers has been in continuous existence ever since.

Exploring Fort Robinson

Sioux and others under Chief Red Cloud. The outpost is where the famous Sioux Chief Crazy Horse was imprisoned in 1877, the year following his defeat of Custer at Little Bighorn, and was later stabbed and killed by a soldier. A plaque marks the spot of his death. The 1879 Cheyenne breakout took place here. In 1878, three hundred Cheyenne had left their reservation in Oklahoma to return to their native land near the area's White River. About half of them were captured and imprisoned here. After months of their refusing to return to the Oklahoma reservation, the fort's commanding

SnapShot - Fort Robinson State Park

Description: Ride 20 miles of horse trails in the historic Fort Robinson State Park. There are two barns for horse stabling, and riders can stay in one of the campgrounds, in the lodge, or in cabins. (Horses are not allowed in the campgrounds.) Horse trailers are parked by the horse barns, except for trailers that include living quarters, which can be parked in the camps. Guided rides are offered on the park's horses from Memorial Day through Labor Day. Sign up at the park's information booth located at the park entrance.

Open: Park trails are open year-round; the restaurant is open Memorial Day through Labor Day; camping with hookups and water is open April through November, electricity is available at camps year-round; cabins and lodge rooms are available April through November

Address: PO Box 392, Crawford, NE 69339

Phone: 402-944-2703 or 308-665-2900

Web site: http://www.ngpc.state.ne.us/parks/guides/parksearch/showpark.asp? Area_No=77

Getting there: Located in northwestern Nebraska, 3 miles west of the town of Crawford on US Highway 20

Fees/permits: Admission is $3

Horse rentals: Available in the park

Horse camping: None; stabling is available in the park

Trail conditions/level of difficulty: Easy to difficult, from flat to hilly

officer tried to starve them into submission. Some of the younger warrior's escaped, but cavalry soldiers tracked them down after a couple of weeks, and a fight ensued that left sixty-four Cheyenne and eleven soldiers dead. With its high number of casualties, this turned out to be one of the major conflicts in the Indian Wars.

Fort Robinson House

The fort served as a cavalry remount station and a garrison for the Buffalo Soldiers, black soldiers of the 9th and 10th Cavalry Regiment. During World War II, K-9 war dogs were trained here, and German prisoners of war were kept here as well. In addition to having a military history, the fort was a training site for the U.S. Olympic Equestrian team in the 1930s.

Equestrians coming here today may not be training for the Olympics, but they'll enjoy riding here just as well. Keep an eye out for the park's bison and longhorn herds as you meander down the park's 20 miles of horse trails and fire service roads. Wranglers take horseless visitors on walking rides as they discuss the fort and its history. Rides include the ninety-minute Butte Country Ride ($16) and the fifty-minute Soldier Creek Ride ($12).

In addition to horseback riding, hiking and mountain biking are popular activities in the park. There are 60 miles of hik-

Riding in Fort Robinson

ing trails and 20 miles of biking trails. There is also a swimming pool and a sundeck for cooling off and relaxing in after a long day's riding, hiking, or biking adventure.

Along the trail

SOUTH DAKOTA

BADLANDS NATIONAL PARK

Many terms have been used over the years to describe the area of South Dakota that is now the 244,000-acre Badlands National Park. The Lakota Sioux called the area *mako sica*, or "land bad." French-Canadian trappers, who were the first nonnatives to see the area, labeled them *les mauvaises terres traverser*, or "bad land to travel across." General George A. Custer described the Badlands as "hell with the fires burned out." In our modern age, the words *moonscape* or *lunar* are often used to describe the Badlands. Although the phrase *bad land* stuck and became its moniker, and although this waterless land certainly does look inhospitable and otherworldly with its strangely shaped pinnacles and spires, eroded buttes and ridges, and deep canyons and valleys, it somehow still seems to resist being labeled.

Badlands National Park

Could that be because there is so much more here than its landscape seems to indicate?

Badlands National Park contains one of the world's richest Oligocene fossil beds, dating back twenty-three to thirty-five million years. It is considered to be a birthplace of vertebrate paleontology. The skeletons of early horses, pigs, sheep, saber-toothed cats, camels, rhinoceroses, and other animals have been found in its geologic layers, indicating that sometime long ago the Badlands had ample water. Their discoveries help scientists reconstruct the environmental and climatic changes the area has gone through over the millennia. A paleontologist on staff at the park works with university and museum researchers to prepare fossils and to survey and document the rich fossil history contained here.

The park has the largest protected mixed-grass prairie in the United States. There are fifty-six different types of grasses here, most of them

A pronghorn buck

native, that have developed over millions of years. These grasslands were seen to be inhospitable and desolate to early pioneers making their way west. In

A bison rolls in the dirt.

reality, the grasses support wildflowers, desert plants, and occasionally trees, all of which provide habitat for a diverse assembly of creatures, including birds, reptiles, amphibians, insects, and mammals such as the prairie dog. Benefiting from the prairie dog's presence is the black-footed ferret, considered to be the most endangered land mammal in North America. Badlands National Park is a reintroduction site for this endangered species, which is dependent on its prey base of prairie dog colonies for survival. Approximately twenty-five to thirty black-footed ferrets now live in the park.

Riders in the Badlands may see other wildlife such as bison, coyotes, and bighorn sheep. The bison, or buffalo, were reintroduced to the area in the early 1960s, after an absence of one hundred years. There are now about six hundred bison in the Sage Creek wilderness area of the park. (If you see any, enjoy them from a distance as they can be dangerous if approached.) This wilderness area consists of 64,000 acres of spires and prairie perfect for riding. The nearby Sage Creek campground is designated for horse use. Although most riders prefer the wilderness area, riding is allowed anywhere in the park except on marked trails, roads, highways, and developed areas. Day-use riders can park vehicles and trailers at parking areas and overlooks.

SNAPSHOT - BADLANDS NATIONAL PARK

Description: The scenery in the 244,000-acre Badlands National Park is like nothing you've seen before. Horseback riders most enjoy riding in the Sage Creek wilderness area, and the horse camp is there. Backcountry camping with horses is also available. Camps must be at least .5 mile from all roads, developed areas, or marked trails. Horses of backcountry campers are allowed to graze. Water is scarce here, so be sure to pack enough for both you and your horse: 1 gallon of water per person per day, and 5 gallons of water per horse per day are recommended. Although the park does not have horse rental facilities, area outfitters may offer overnight backcountry horse packing trips. Ask at the visitor centers about currently licensed outfitters.

Open: Year-round, twenty-four hours a day, seven days a week

Address: 25216 Ben Reifel Road, PO Box 6, Interior, SD 57750

Phone: 605-433-5361

Web site: http://www.nps.gov/badl/index.htm

Getting there: I-90 to exit 110 or 131 to access Highway 240 (Badlands Loop Road); Highway 44 West from Rapid City provides an alternate scenic route to the park.

Fees/permits: Admission is $10 for a seven-day pass

Horse rentals: None

Horse camping: Available in the park

Trail conditions/level of difficulty: Easy (flat, top area trails) to difficult

OTHER GREAT PLACES TO RIDE

Kansas

Eisenhower State Park
29810 S. Fairlawn Road, Osage City, KS 66523
785-528-4102
http://www.kdwp.state.ks.us/news/state_parks/locations/eisenhower
Approximately 35 miles south of Topeka, Eisenhower State Park, named for the thirty-fourth president, Dwight D. Eisenhower, features miles of horse trails, including the 20-mile Crooked Knee Horse Trail named for the knee injury Eisenhower received at West Point. There is also horse camping at the Cowboy Campground and at part of the Westpoint Campground.

Minnesota

St. Croix State Park
30065 St. Croix Park Road, Hinckley, MN 55037
320-384-6591
http://www.dnr.state.mn.us/state_parks/st_croix/index.html
Ride near the St. Croix River, with 75 miles of horse trails, open April 15 through the first snowfall. It offers horse camping with room for up to one hundred horses, with drinking water, showers, and corrals.

Missouri

Blue and Gray Park Reserve
300 S. Bynum Road, Lone Jack, MO 64070
816-503-4800
http://www.co.jackson.mo.us/rec_tr_bg.shtml
This 1,733-acre county park located near Kansas City is popular with equestrians. Facilities added to this otherwise undeveloped park because of horseback riding interest include a parking lot with pull-through capability for trailers as well as restrooms, picnic tables, and shelters.

Nebraska

Indian Cave State Park
65296 720 Road, Shubert, NE 68437
402-883-2575
http://www.ngpc.state.ne.us/parks/guides/parksearch/
showpark.asp?Area_No=91
Indian Cave features 3,052 acres bordering the Missouri River. Just 10 miles south of Brownville, Indian Cave is home to a variety of hardwood trees. There are 16 miles of horse trails, and horse camping and seasonal horse rentals are available.

Rock Creek Station State Historical Park
57426 710th Road, Fairbury, NE 68352
402-729-5777
http://www.ngpc.state.ne.us
This former pony express station, where it is said Wild Bill Hickock got his start as a gunfighter, is now a state historical park. Horse trails here and at the adjoining state recreation area offer a flavor of riding in the Wild West. There is a horse campground in the recreation area.

North Dakota

Maah Daah Hey Trail
U.S. Forest Service, 240 W. Century Avenue, Bismarck, ND 58503
701-250-4443
http://www.fs.fed.us/r1/dakotaprairie/mdhtl.htm
This multiuse trail begins in McKenzie County and runs 97 miles to Billings County in the south. There are four campgrounds along the trail that riders may use.

Theodore Roosevelt National Park
Box 7, Medora, ND 58654
701-623-4466
http://www.theodore.roosevelt.national-park.com
Miles of horse trails and cross-country riding make for an enjoyable riding adventure. Horse camps, backcountry camping, and horse stabling at the park's horse livery are available in the park. Guided rides are available from the livery (701-623-4568). There is also a herd of wild horses in the park.

South Dakota

Custer State Park
HC83, Box 70, Custer, SD 57730
605-255-4515
http://www.sdgfp.info/parks/Regions/Custer/Index.htm
Stay at French Creek Horse Camp and ride through 71,000 acres of pine-covered mountains and rolling prairie foothills. Call 605-255-4531 for information on horse rentals and trail rides.

GREAT PLAINS TRAVEL SECTION

IF YOU ARE TRAVELING WITHOUT YOUR HORSE, OR IF YOUR HORSE IS BOARDED SAFELY AT A STABLE, ENJOY THE SITES IN THE NEIGHBORING TOWNS. BELOW, YOU'LL FIND A MILEAGE CHART LISTING THE DISTANCES BETWEEN THE TRAILS AND ALL THE AREAS DISCUSSED IN THE FOLLOWING TRAVEL SECTION. THE AREAS CLOSEST TO THE TRAILS ARE INDICATED BY AN **X**. FOR AREAS WHERE NEITHER STABLING NOR HORSE RENTALS ARE AVAILABLE, NO SIGHTSEEING OPTIONS ARE LISTED.

COAST TO COAST	Bemidji, Minn.	Fort Dodge, Iowa	Fort Robinson State Park, Neb.	Hot Springs, S.D.	Mushroom Rock State Park, Kans.	Park Rapids, Minn.	Walker, Minn.
Badlands National Park (S.D.)	755 miles	595 miles	130 miles	**X** 65 miles	645 miles	700 miles	730 miles
Brushy Creek State Recreation Area (Iowa)	435 miles	**X** 15 miles	685 miles	620 miles	485 miles	405 miles	400 miles
Chippewa National Forest (Minn.)	**X** 65 miles	445 miles	955 miles	890 miles	870 miles	100 miles	**X** 70 miles
Fort Robinson State Park (Neb.)	830 miles	670 miles	**X** ∗ miles	75 miles	540 miles	780 miles	810 miles
Harry S. Truman Dam and Reservoir (Mo.)	770 miles	400 miles	790 miles	880 miles	**X** 315 miles	745 miles	735 miles
Kanopolis State Park (Kans.)	835 miles	505 miles	565 miles	615 miles	**X** ∗ miles	785 miles	840 miles

∗*The area to visit is the same as or is within 10 miles of the trails.*

MUST SEE / MUST DO

IOWA

BRUSHY CREEK STATE RECREATION AREA

If you have some extra time, visit the **Fort Museum** in Fort Dodge to learn more about the history of Northwest Iowa (http://www.fortmuseum.com). The frontier outpost was built in 1851. Each year in June, the three-day Frontier Days festival is held at the

Japanese archer Misa Tsuyoshi

museum and in other parts of the town. Open mid-April to mid-October from 9:00 a.m. to 5:00 p.m. Monday through Saturday and Sunday from 11:00 a.m. to 5:00 p.m. Admission is $6 for adults and $3 for students (six to eighteen). Children five and under are free.

Of special interest to horse enthusiasts will be the **International Horse Archery Festival** held each year in Fort Dodge. The festival features three days of demonstrations by horseback archery experts from throughout the world. There are also workshops, lectures about archery traditions in various countries, archery games, youth programs, and more. The dates of the festival vary each year, so be sure to

Horse archery in action

check the organization's Web site for information on dates, location, and current admission prices (http://www.intlhorsearchery.org).

Visit the Fort Dodge Chamber of Commerce at 1406 Central Avenue, Box T, Fort Dodge, Iowa 50501 (515-955-5500; http://www.dodgenet.com/~chamber), which is 15 miles northwest of the recreation area, off Highway 20, for more information on things to do in the area.

KANSAS

KANOPOLIS STATE PARK AREA

Just a stone's throw from Kanopolis State Park is **Mushroom Rock State Park** (200 Horsethief Road, Marquette, KS 67464; 785-546-2565; http://www.kdwp.state.ks.us/pmforum/kanopolis.html). Although this is the smallest state park in Kansas at approximately 5 acres, it is also the most unique. Its rock formations resemble giant mushrooms rising above the horizon. Native

Mushroom Rock State Park

Americans and early pioneers such as Kit Carson and John C. Fremont used these unusual formations as meeting places. They're definitely worth a visit while you're in the area. The park has picnic tables and vault toilets.

MINNESOTA

CHIPPEWA NATIONAL FOREST AREA

The whole family can have fun at **Moondance Ranch and Adventure Park** (Highway 371 South, Walker, MN 56484; 218-547-1055; http://www .moondanceranch .com) even if you aren't renting a horse there. Other activities that put the adventure in the park include viewing wildlife, playing miniature golf, riding go-carts, and going down the water-

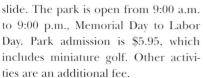

Fort Robinson stable

slide. The park is open from 9:00 a.m. to 9:00 p.m., Memorial Day to Labor Day. Park admission is $5.95, which includes miniature golf. Other activities are an additional fee.

If you are visiting the area during July, don't miss the **Headwaters of the Mississippi Rodeo** in Park Rapids, held over the July 4th holiday each year at the Flying J Ranch, Route 1 Box 378 A, Park Rapids, Minnesota 56470; 800-JOKELA1.

For a feel of Northern Minnesota history, visit the town of **Bemidji**. It is home to the famous statues of **Paul Bunyan** and his blue ox, Babe, which was placed on the National Register of Historic Places in 1988. You can also see the statue of **Chief Bemidji**, the namesake for the town, and its first permanent settler. You can visit the **Great Northern Depot Museum**; the historic district, noted for its architecture; and nearby Camp Rabideau, one of three remaining Civilian Conservation Corp camps. Contact Visit Bemidji for more information (PO Box 66, Bemidji, MN 56619; 800-458-2223 Ext. 105; http://www.visitbemidji.com).

NEBRASKA

FORT ROBINSON STATE PARK AREA

When your horse is happily munching hay in his stall or if you're visiting without a horse, take advantage of some of

Paul Bunyan and Babe

Black Hills wild horses

the many things to see and do at Fort Robinson. You can learn more about the fort's history and the area by visiting the **Fort Robinson Museum** and exhibit buildings. **The Trailside Museum**, run by the University of Nebraska, is worth a look to learn about the paleontology and geology of the region. Feel like learning about the park in Old West style? Short **stagecoach tours** leaving on the hour give visitors a quick overview of the park. There are also jeep tours, hayrides, pony rides for kids, bike rentals, a nature center, a souvenir store, cookouts, and rodeos two evenings a week in summer. Inquire at the information booth at the park's entrance for information on activities or to sign up.

Home on the range

SOUTH DAKOTA

BADLANDS NATIONAL PARK AREA

The **Black Hills Wild Horse Sanctuary** (PO Box 998, Hot Springs, SD 57747; 800-252-6552; http://www.wildmustangs.com) supports more than five hundred wild mustangs on its 11,000 privately owned acres. The sanctuary is managed by Dayton O. Hyde's Institute of the Range and American Mustang (IRAM), a nonprofit organization whose mission is to give freedom and a better quality of life to America's wild horses. It is supported through tourism, donations, bequests, and the sale of paint horses. Although it is a couple of hours from Badlands National Park, horse lovers may find it worth their while to make the trip here. For $20 (less for seniors and children), visitors can take a two-hour guided bus tour to

Greeting the horses

see the wild horses on the sanctuary's lower prairie. Very committed wild horse supporters can take a tax deductible private working tour ($750 for no more than three people) to set out salt licks and monitor water in the rugged terrain of the upper plateau, where the wildest of the mustangs choose to stay, rather than coming down to summer on the lower prairie. The sanctuary is open seven days a week, April 1 through October 31; tours are by reservation (800-252-6652) November 1 through March 31.

WHERE TO STAY & STABLE

IOWA

BRUSHY CREEK STATE RECREATION AREA

Horses and Riders:
Brushy Creek Recreation Area Horse Campground
Located in the northern area
515-543-8298
http://www.iowadnr.com/parks/state_park_list/brushy_creek.html
No fee for campers
In the northern area of the park, just inside the west entrance, is a campground with showers and restrooms, a playground, and 125 campsites, 50 with electricity. Sites have picnic tables, grills, hitch rails, and fire pits. There is also a riding arena, drinking water, and horse wash area in the campground.

Brushy Creek Recreation Area Horse Campground
Located in the southern area
515-543-8298
http://www.iowadnr.com/parks/state_park_list/brushy_creek.html
$14 per night for campsites without electricity, $19 per night for those with electricity; rates may be lower in the off-season
The southern campground has a shower and restroom with 105 sites, 70 with electrical hookups, and amenities similar to those of the northern campground.

KANSAS

KANOPOLIS STATE PARK AREA

Horses and Riders:
Rockin' K Campground
Located in the park
785-546-2565
http://www.kdwp.state.ks.us/pmforum/kanopolis.html
$17 per night with electricity, $13 without
This horse camp has thirty-five sites with drinking water and electrical hookups. The campground has lake access, a shower building, and vault toilets. There are tie-ups, corrals, horse-washing stations, and a group camping area and group shelter. The campsite also has a camp host to answer any questions. Open year-round, but water to the shower building is shut off in October.

Riders Only:
Ira E. Lloyd House Bed and Breakfast
1575 Avenue JJ
Ellsworth, KS 67493
785-472-5100
http://www.iraelloydhouse.com
$65–$80 per night
This three-story colonial revival home was built in the late 1800s by Ira E. Lloyd, a

prominent attorney in the area. There are three guest rooms. The owner is president of the National Chisholm Trail Association.

MINNESOTA

CHIPPEWA NATIONAL FOREST AREA

Horses and Riders:

Cut Foot Sioux Horse Camp
Deer River Ranger District, 1037 Division Street, Box 308
Deer River, MN 56636
218-246-2123
http://www.fs.fed.us/r9/chippewa/flyer/cfhorse.htm
$12 per night
From the camp, you'll have access to 120 miles of trails. Most of them are grassy trails and old logging roads. The camp has vault toilets, hand water pumps, and a manure dump. The sites have fire pits, picket lines, and picnic tables. There are no portable corrals permitted. Open April 14 through October 1.

Maple Beach Resort
6876 Maple Beach Court, NE
Bemidji, MN 56601
218-586-2955/888-620-8790
http://www.maplebeachresort.com
$24 per night and $135 per week for camping
This lodge on Big Lake in the Chippewa National Forest features cabins and camping for horseless visitors as well as a horse camp in the woods. The horse camp has a corral, hitching posts, water and electricity, and access to trails in the forest's northwestern region. Horse campers make use of the shower house at the main resort.

Stein's Winding River Guest Farm
14185 Teddy Road Northwest
Shevlin, MN 56676
218-243-2629
http://www.steinsguestfarm.com
$60 and up per night for rooms; $15 per hour for trail riding for guests, $20 per hour for nonguests; $5 per night for horses, portable corral is provided
Both horseless riders and riders with their horses are welcome at the 240-acre Stein's Winding River Guest Farm. You can stay in one of four guest rooms or rent the entire guest house. Continental breakfast is available upon request. Riders bringing their own horses must supply hay.

MISSOURI

HARRY S. TRUMAN DAM AND RESERVOIR AREA

Horses and Riders:

Berry Bend Equestrian Campground
Located in the reservoir
660-438-3812/Reservations: 877-444-6777 or online
http://www.ReserveUSA.com
$12–$25 per night for camping, depending on amenities
All users of the Berry Bend Equestrian Campground must have horses with them; it is not open to nonequestrians. The campground has eighty-nine campsites with fire rings. Electrical hookups are available at twenty-four campsites, and water hydrants

are placed throughout the campground. There are restrooms, a shower building with laundry facilities, a children's playground, picnic tables, lantern hangers, a sanitary dump station, corrals, and overhead tie posts. Open year-round, except one weekend in November when it is closed for a managed deer hunt.

NEBRASKA

FORT ROBINSON STATE PARK AREA

Horses and Riders:

Ponderosa Ranch
PO Box 472, 680 Saw Log Road
Crawford, NE 69339
308-665-1585
http://www.ponderosaranch.net
$75 for one night for cabins, $50 per night for two nights or more; $10 per night for horse boarding; $20–$50 per person for one- to five-hour rides for horse rentals, riders must have some experience; $125 per person per night for the vacation package, which includes lodging, meals, and riding
Stay and ride on this working cattle ranch. It offers one-bedroom cabins with a living room—both rooms have twin beds. Cabins have refrigerators, and meals are also available in the main house for an extra fee (no extra cost in the vacation package). Horses are accommodated in the pasture, corrals, pens, or barn.

Riders Only:

Fort Robinson Lodge
Located in the park
402-944-2703/Reservations: 308-665-2912
http://www.outdoornebraska.org
$35–$40 per night for rooms; $80–$200 per night for cabins
The lodge offer rooms in the 1909 "enlisted men's quarters" as well as cabins dating from 1874 to 1909 in the former officer's quarters; they range from two to nine bedrooms. Cabins have kitchens, baths, living rooms, and bedrooms and include cooking utensils, blankets, towels, stoves, and refrigerators. Campgrounds and cabins feature grills and picnic tables.

Red Cloud Campground
Located in the park
308-665-2900
http://www.outdoornebraska.org
$10 per night for tent camping; $18 per night for full hookups for RVs
Campsites can be reserved up to a year in advance.

Soldier Creek Campground
Located in the park
308-665-2900
http://www.outdoornebraska.org
$14 per night
This campground is the nearest to the horse stables at about three city blocks distance. It has electricity and a shower house.

Horses Only:

Fort Robinson State Park Horse Barns
Located in the park
402-944-2703/308-665-2912
http://www.outdoornebraska.org

$10 per night for stalls
Horses visiting the park are accommodated in two barns, each with forty-six stalls. Owners are responsible for bedding, feeding, and cleaning prior to leaving. Horse stalls can be reserved up to one year in advance.

SOUTH DAKOTA

BADLANDS NATIONAL PARK AREA

Horses and Riders
Circle View Guest Ranch
20055 E. Highway 44
Scenic, SD 57780
605-433-5582
http://www.circleviewranch.com
$70–$125 per night, depending on the season and the number of guests, home-cooked breakfast included; $8 per night for stabling
The owner of this 3,000-acre ranch, situated near both the Badlands and the Pine Ridge Indian Reservation, was born here and now runs approximately 150 head of cattle. Charming guest rooms with private baths keep visitors cozy. Guests also have use of the kitchen.

Jobgen Ranch Homestead Bed & Breakfast
24800 Sage Creek Road
Scenic, SD 57780
605-993-6201
$85 per night (20 percent off November through April) for the guesthouse with ranch-style or continental breakfast; $10 for dinner (half price for small children), extra fee for sack lunches; $5 per day without feed, $7 per day with feed for horse corrals
This 5,500-acre working ranch, established in 1906 as a 160-acre homestead, is nestled on the edge of the Badlands. From here, you can visit Badlands National Park or ride and relax on the ranch. The guesthouse has two bedrooms and one bath. Children are welcome. Reservations are preferred, but walk-ins are welcome per availability.

Sage Creek Campground
Located in the park; accessible from Sage Creek Rim Road
605-433-5361
http://www.nps.gov/badl/exp/facilities.htm#campgrounds
No fee
This primitive campground is open to horse use and is available on a first-come, first-served basis. There are hitching posts and pit toilets, but the campground has no water, so be sure to bring your own. To get to the campground on the unpaved Sage Creek Rim Road, your vehicle must have high clearance.

WHERE TO WINE & DINE

IOWA

BRUSHY CREEK STATE RECREATION AREA

Amigo's
280 1st Avenue North
Fort Dodge, IA 50501
515-576-0142

$4–$6
Amigo's serves lunch and dinner in a relaxed atmosphere. Mexican food, hamburgers, sandwiches, and other casual fare will fill you up after a long trail ride. The restaurant is open year-round, Monday through Friday, from 11 a.m. to 1:30 p.m. for lunch and from 5:00 p.m. to 10:00 p.m. for dinner. It is open for dinner only on Saturday and closed on Sunday.

The Cellar
Junction of 169 and D20
Fort Dodge, IA 50501
515-576-2290
$9.95–$16.95
The Cellar is known for its fine dining in Fort Dodge. It features a full bar with a long wine list and serves dinner entrées such as seafood, steaks, pork chops, pastas, and poultry. The restaurant serves dinner only, opening at 4:00 p.m., and is closed on Sundays. Seating is on a first-come, first-served basis.

Kristine's
26 North 27th Street
Fort Dodge, IA 50501
515-955-7663
$5–$12
Kristine's serves Italian-American dishes for lunch and dinner. It is open seven days a week, except from June to August when it is closed on Sundays. This local favorite features a full bar, can accommodate large groups for family-style meals, and will deliver to large groups visiting Brushy Creek.

KANSAS

KANOPOLIS STATE PARK AREA

Dairy Queen
Highway 40 and 156
Ellsworth, KS 67439
785-472-4104
$2.50–$6.50
This chain restaurant offers burgers, sandwiches, beverages, ice cream concoctions, and other fast-food items.

Pizza Hut
Highway 156
Ellsworth, KS 67439
785-472-3134
$3.25–$20.00
Another chain restaurant, this pizza place offers the usual pizzas and sides.

MINNESOTA

CHIPPEWA NATIONAL FOREST AREA

Peppercorn Restaurant and Lounge
1813 Paul Bunyan Drive
Bemidji, MN 56601
218-759-2794
http://www.peppercornrestaurant.com
$6.99–$25.99

You'll find just about anything you could want—American, Mexican, Italian—on this menu, which features chops, steaks, ribs, poultry, seafood, pastas, fajitas, and more. The restaurant also features a full wine list and a lounge with a full bar and bar food. Open seven days a week, lunch and dinner.

Rafael's Bakery Café
319 Minnesota Avenue
Bemidji, MN 56601
218-759-2015
http://www.gr8buns.com
$3–$5
Stop by for a quick sandwich, salad, or bowl of soup, and be sure to take a loaf of fresh-baked bread with you. This bakery specializes in several different varieties of bread, using natural ingredients. Rafael's is open for lunch Monday through Friday from 11:00 a.m. to 2:00 p.m.; the coffee shop is open on Saturday from 7:00 a.m. to 2:00 p.m.

MISSOURI

HARRY S. TRUMAN DAM AND RESERVOIR AREA

The Benton House
29205 Benton House Avenue
Warsaw, MO 65355
660-438-6676
$8.95–$34.00
Prime rib is the specialty of the house at The Benton House, although this well-known restaurant serves a wide variety of entrées, including seafood, various steaks, chops, poultry, and sandwiches, all in large portions. Located near the access road to the Truman Dam, the restaurant, which opened in 1981, serves dinner seven days a week. Seating is on a first-come, first-served basis. The restaurant opens on Sundays at 11:30 for early dining. There is a lounge and a wine list. The dress is casual.

Gasoline Alley
324 W. Main
Warsaw, MO 65355
660-438-4170
http://www.gasoline-alley.net
$2.50–$6.00
Enjoy a sandwich and a beer in this unique restaurant and museum, and then take a look at the gasoline memorabilia and the renovated old-time Texaco gas station. There are at least two hundred oil cans representing different companies on display.

NEBRASKA

FORT ROBINSON STATE PARK AREA

Fort Robinson Lodge
Located in the park
402-944-2703/308-665-2912
http://www.outdoornebraska.org
$5.25–$14.50
The varied menu features such items as lasagna, chicken strips, buffalo tacos and burgers, and more. Portions are large and prices are reasonable.

Staab's Drive Inn
W. Highway 20 (112 McPherson Street)
Crawford, NE 69339
308-665-1210
$1.50–$14

This casual eatery features roasted chicken by the bucket, shrimp, sandwiches, shakes, malts, sundaes, and more. Seating is outside at picnic tables, or you can get your food to go. Staab's is open seven days a week from mid-February to mid-November and closed for the winter. Hours are 10:00 a.m. to 10:00 p.m.

SOUTH DAKOTA

BADLANDS NATIONAL PARK AREA

Cedar Pass Lodge & Restaurant
Inside the park's north unit near Ben Reifel Visitor Center
605-433-5460
$5–$10

This is the park's only restaurant. It serves buffalo burgers, fish, steaks, and other fare. It is open daily for breakfast, lunch, and dinner, but it closes from late October to mid-April.

Wall Drug Store
510 Main Street
Wall, SD 57790
605-279-2175
http://www.walldrug.com
$4–$13, coffee is 5¢

Visit the famous Wall Drug Store, which started as a small country pharmacy in 1931. After the founders, Ted and Dorothy Hustead, began advertising free ice water on roadside signs to people heading to Mount Rushmore and Yellowstone, the store's business took off. Over the years, signs throughout the state, the country, and the

world have advertised how far it is to Wall Drug Store. Today, "the store" is a 76,000-square-foot tourist spot with dozens of shops, Old West–inspired attractions, a museum and art gallery, and three cafeterias seating 530 people. Enjoy a country breakfast, sandwiches, burgers and steaks, sodas and shakes, and more. And don't forget the ice water; it's still free. Wall's is open year-round, seven days a week, except New Year's Day, Easter, Thanksgiving Day, and Christmas Day.

Cowboy country

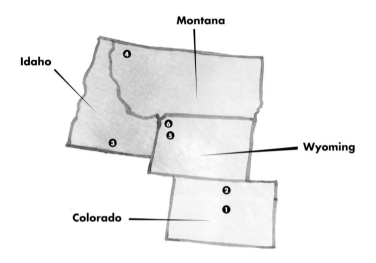

Montana

Idaho

4

Wyoming

6
5

3

2

1

Colorado

WEST MAP LEGEND

Colorado
1 Pike National Forest

2 Rocky Mountain
National Park

Idaho
3 City of Rocks National
Reserve

Montana
4 Glacier National Park

Wyoming
5 Grand Teton
National Park

**Wyoming, Montana,
and Idaho**
6 Yellowstone National Park

THE WEST

*I*n 1872, President Ulysses S. Grant signed a law stating that Yellowstone would forever be "dedicated and set apart as a public park or pleasuring ground for the benefit and enjoyment of the people." Thus the world's first national park was born, and with it came a growing recognition of the need to preserve the country's magnificent lands. During the early twentieth century, President Theodore Roosevelt, a dedicated horseman and conservationist, added 150 million acres of land to the public domain, establishing the U.S. Forest Service in 1905. Over the years, federal and state governments have set aside additional lands to be saved for the enjoyment of future generations. Glacier became a national park in 1910, Rocky Mountain in 1915, and Grand Teton in 1929. Pike became a national forest in 1908. City of Rocks was designated a national reserve in 1988.

Every open space preserved in this country has characteristics that make it special and unique. There is something about the wide-open spaces of the West, though, that especially calls to that place of freedom and independence in the human spirit and harkens back to a time when wild horses and buffalo thundered across the land.

Majestic, grand, and *breathtaking* are words you might exclaim as you ride your own horse through any of these wild places. Whether galloping through a verdant meadow or winding up a mountain trail, the dramatic beauty of these locales will continue to inspire you, even long after your trip is over. Visit for a day's ride or pack into the backcountry for nights of camping under the stars: endless open space, abundant wildlife, blue skies, shimmering mountain lakes, beautiful vistas—just you, your horse, and nature's majesty. What could be better?

COLORADO

PIKE NATIONAL FOREST

Pike National Forest encompasses more than one million acres of land in the Front Range and Mosquito Mountains of south central Colorado. It is one of eleven national forests in the state. Stretching into six counties, Pike is marked on its north end by the 14,264-foot Mount Evans, which is surrounded by the 74,401-acre Mount Evans Wilderness. The wilderness is located in both the Pike and Arapaho national forests. Pikes Peak, Colorado's most famous mountain, is a popular destination and, at 14,110 feet, it can't be missed looming among six other "fourteener" peaks (more than 14,000 feet high), including the previously mentioned Mount Evans and Mounts Bierstadt, Democrat, Lincoln, Cameron, and Bross.

Forest wildflowers

Pikes Peak and Pike National Forest is named for Zebulon Montgomery Pike, an explorer and U.S. Army officer who led an expedition exploring the southwestern border of the Louisiana Purchase in 1806 and 1807. He attempted to climb Pikes Peak but was unable to and became convinced that the mountain could not be scaled. Pike died in action during the Battle of York, in the War of 1812. The mountain stayed officially unclimbed until 1820, when two members of the exploring party of U.S. Army Major Stephen H. Long successfully scaled its towering heights in the first recorded ascent. Although Long named the mountain for Dr. Edwin James, a New York botanist and doctor who was traveling with the party, James Peak never stuck, and Pikes Peak was used in military maps. In 1858, Mrs. Julia Archibald Holmes became the first woman to climb Pikes Peak. She became known as the bloomer girl because of the bloomers she wore while ascending the mountain.

Today's equestrian explorers who come to admire Pikes Peak and all that Pike National Forest has to offer will find a vast variety of landscapes here. You'll be taken by the beauty and drama of the area's great domelike forms, spires, and turrets in the Garden

Pikes Peak

Road to Garden of the Gods

of the Gods; by the windblown, bleak bristlecone pine forests; by the cascading snow-fed creeks; by the golden grass and prairies dotted with aspens. There is plenty of true wilderness left in Pike National Forest, and much of its acreage is accessible only by horseback, foot, or four-wheel drive. In some areas in the forest, you can still see the remains of early stagecoach routes and mining railroads.

Hundreds of miles of riding trails of varying difficulty await, some that will challenge you as the mountain chal-

lenged its early climbers, and some that you will find easy to moderate, such as the 4-mile Platte River Trail, the 2.3-mile Lizard Rock Trail, and the 1.3-mile

Lunch along the trail

SNAPSHOT - PIKE NATIONAL FOREST

Description: In Pike National Forest, gold-medal fishing streams, wilderness areas, campgrounds, scenic byways, ski resorts, and hundreds of miles of trails are available to nature lovers intent on appreciating this beautiful wilderness. There are several options for vacationing with your horse, including trailside camping, working ranches, and bed-and-barns. If you don't have your own horse, rentals and pack trips are available locally.

Open: Year-round

Address: 1920 Valley Road, Pueblo, CO 81008

Phone: 719-545-8737

Web site: http://www.fs.fed.us/r2/psicc

Getting there: Pike National Forest is northwest of Colorado Springs. To get there, take Interstate Highway 25.

Fees/permits: Admission is free

Horse rentals: Available locally

Horse camping: Available in the forest

Trail conditions/level of difficulty: Easy to difficult

Hardrock Trail. There are many, many more trails of all levels to choose from. Park rangers can provide brochures and additional trail information.

ROCKY MOUNTAIN NATIONAL PARK
Mountain man Rufus Sage spent four years exploring the Colorado Rockies, and in 1843 he wrote this account of the area that is now Rocky Mountain National Park: "beautiful lateral valleys, intersected by meandering watercourses, ridged by lofty ledges of precipitous rock, and hemmed in upon the west by vast piles of mountains climbing beyond

The park's stately trees

the clouds." As the tenth oldest national park, Rocky Mountain holds everything that the Colorado high country has to offer in its 416 square miles, most notably the "vast piles of mountains climbing beyond the clouds" that Sage waxed poetic about. With at least 60 mountains exceeding 12,000 feet, the highest being 14,259-foot-high Longs Peak, one-third of the entire park is above the tree line. The names given to some of the tallest mountain peaks, such as Cirrus, Chiefs Head, Isolation, Mummy, and Storm, are eminently worthy of this dramatic landscape that nature has produced

Rocky Mountain National Park

PIKE NATIONAL FOREST RANGER DISTRICTS

Check with the ranger districts for details on horse camping and permit information:

Pikes Peak Ranger District U.S. Forest Service
601 South Weber Street
Colorado Springs, CO 80903
719-636-1602/Fax: 719-477-8273

South Park Ranger District U.S. Forest Service
320 Highway 285, PO Box 219
Fairplay, CO 80440
719-836-2031

South Platte Ranger District U.S. Forest Service
19316 Goddard Ranch Road
Morrison, CO 80465
303-275-5610

USDA Forest Service
2840 Kachina Drive
Pueblo, CO 81008
719-553-1400

over the millennia. More than 110 of the mountain peaks in the park that rise above 10,000 feet in elevation have already been named, with only a few peaks that are still wait-

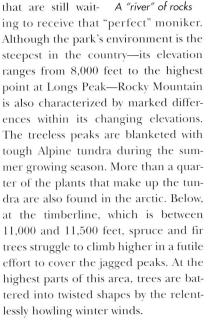

A "river" of rocks

ing to receive that "perfect" moniker. Although the park's environment is the steepest in the country—its elevation ranges from 8,000 feet to the highest point at Longs Peak—Rocky Mountain is also characterized by marked differences within its changing elevations. The treeless peaks are blanketed with tough Alpine tundra during the summer growing season. More than a quarter of the plants that make up the tundra are also found in the arctic. Below, at the timberline, which is between 11,000 and 11,500 feet, spruce and fir trees struggle to climb higher in a futile effort to cover the jagged peaks. At the highest parts of this area, trees are battered into twisted shapes by the relentlessly howling winter winds.

Dense forests cover the mountain slopes as does snow blown from the mountaintops, which accumulates into banks among the trees, eventually melting and then feeding streams that rush down to rivers and lowland lakes. The wetland ecosystem in the park is made up of 150 lakes and 450 miles of streams. Wildlife is attracted to these lakes, and in winter, when higher elevations are unreachable, many animals make their homes in the lowlands among the trees and snow-blanketed meadows. Elk, mule deer,

A black bear cub

FINDING INSPIRATION ON PIKES PEAK

In 1893, Katharine Lee Bates, a professor of English Literature at Wellesley College, was in Colorado Springs to teach a summer session at Colorado College. There she saw the Rockies for the first time and at the end of the school session took a carriage to the summit of Pikes Peak with several other visiting faculty members. Horses got them to the halfway point, and a team of mules finished the climb to the steep 14,110-foot summit. The group stayed on the summit only a short time because one of its members suffered from altitude sickness, but the brief look at the stunning view was enough to inspire Katharine to write the lyrics to "America the Beautiful."

"It was then and there, as I was looking out over the sealike expanse of fertile country spreading away so far under those ample skies, that the opening lines of the hymn floated into my mind," she later said.

The words of "America the Beautiful" first appeared in print in 1895 and gained instant attention when it was set to music by Silas G. Pratt (the popular version of today, however, was set to music by Samuel A. Ward). Other countries such as Australia, Canada, and Mexico found inspiration in the song, borrowed the lyrics—which Katharine freely gave permission to do—and substituted their country's names in place of America. Katharine rewrote the four-stanza hymn several times over the years, with the final version written in 1913.

bighorn sheep, black bears, coyotes, cougars, beavers, eagles, and hawks, to name only some of the creatures that live here, all call the park home.

The diverse ecosystems found in Rocky Mountain National Park com-

A deer pauses

bine to create a horseback rider's heaven. More than 350 miles of trails traverse the park and provide endless opportunities for exploration. More than 260 miles of these trails are open to horses. Park rangers can advise you as to which trails are open or closed to stock use. And hundreds of campsites are available to campers.

The comforts of civilization are found in Estes Park and Grand Lake, the towns that flank the park on the

east and west sides, respectively. For more information, contact the Chamber of Commerce of the towns: Estes Park Chamber Resort Association, Estes Park, Colorado 80517, 800-44-ESTES, http://www.estesparkresort .com; Grand Lake Chamber of Commerce, PO Box 429, Grand Lake, Colorado 80447-0057, 970-627-3402, http://www.grandlakechamber.com.

Ready for rain

SnapShot - Rocky Mountain National Park

Description: The park maintains more than 260 miles of trails open to private and commercial horse users. Horses and guides can be hired at two locations inside the park on the east side or from a number of liveries outside the east and west park boundaries during the summer seasons. To ensure that the natural beauty of Rocky Mountain National Park is not disrupted by its visitors, there are no lodgings or dining facilities within the park. However, campgrounds, food, and supplies are available, and there is a snack bar at Fall River Pass. Lodging is available in the gateway towns of Estes Park and Grand Lake.

Open: Year-round, twenty-four hours a day

Address: Backcountry Office, Rocky Mountain National Park, Estes Park, CO 80517

Phone: 970-586-1242/970-586-1206

Web site: http://www.nps.gov/romo

Getting there: Approach from the east via US Routes 34 or 36 through Estes Park, the gateway to the park, or from the south from I-70 and US Route 40 to US Route 34.

Fees/permits: Admission is $15 for a seven-day automobile pass (individuals and families); $15 for backcountry camping permits

Horse rentals: Available both in the park and locally

Horse camping: Available in the park

Trail conditions/level of difficulty: Most easy to moderate, some difficult

One note of interest to visitors is that the weather is changeable at the park. Warm and sunny summer mornings often turn into stormy afternoons. In summer, temperatures drop from the seventies and eighties in the daytime to the forties at night, so be prepared, especially if you are camping. In spring and fall, snowfall is not uncommon.

A view in the park

SYMBOL OF THE ROCKIES

Bighorn sheep once lived in the wild from southwest Canada to California and northern Mexico. Today, due to habitat destruction, disease, and excessive hunting, the sheep, aptly named for the male's large curved horns, are found only in remote mountainous areas and in national parks. One of these national parks is Rocky Mountain, where as many as six hundred of the bighorns now live.

View of bighorn country

The animals are perfectly suited for life in the difficult conditions of the Rockies. Their cloven hooves, soft and spongy on the inside, ensure a strong grip on rocky surfaces as they climb and jump on ledges and cliffs seeking shelter and safety from predators. Coarse, double-layered coats, which are shed in spring, help the sheep survive the bitterly cold winters in the mountains. With teeth that grow throughout life and a complex four-chambered stomach, the sheep are perfectly designed to grind down and digest the often tough forage they feed on. With such a tough constitution, their survival in Rocky Mountain National Park would seem assured, but that has not always the case.

In the mid-nineteenth century, bighorns numbered in the thousands in the area. When settlers and hunters arrived, as was happening throughout the bighorn's total range, the population of bighorn in the park area dropped rapidly. The sheep were shot by the hundreds, and their meat and horns were sold. Ranchers moving into the mountain valleys altered the habitat and brought in domestic sheep, which carried diseases such as pneumonia and scabies. This double whammy further reduced bighorn numbers, and over the years the combination of all these factors continued the sheep's decline. In the 1950s, research showed that only about 150 bighorn remained in the park's area, and they were limited to isolated locations in the high country. As hunting and disease declined in the ensuing two decades, however, the populations increased. To further increase the sheep's numbers, wildlife managers reintroduced bighorns to areas where they had once ranged. The reintroduced herds and the original herds continue to grow.

Visitors to the park in late spring and early summer have a good chance of seeing the sheep. During these times, the bighorns come down from the Alpine areas of the Mummy Range to graze in the meadows of Horseshoe Park near Sheep Lakes. They also eat the soil here because it contains necessary minerals not found in their high-country home. To reach this feeding ground, the sheep must cross Highway 34 on the north side of Horseshoe Park. Protecting the sheep through their highway crossings are park rangers who control traffic at the Bighorn Crossing Zone, in Horseshoe Park. Between 9:00 a.m. and 3:00 p.m., groups of from one to sixty sheep move from the ridge on the valley's north side, cross the road, graze for two to three hours, and then cross back over to return to the high country.

IDAHO

CITY OF ROCKS NATIONAL RESERVE

City of Rocks National Reserve is located in Almo on the northern edge of the Great Basin Desert, in southern Idaho. Clustered in a romantic valley within the Albion Mountain Range are 100- to 600-foot-high granite rock spires that resemble a Stone Age city against the clear Idaho sky. At 2.5 billion years old,

City of Rocks

the granite rock formations are among the oldest in the continental United States. The formation developed through an erosion process called exfoliation in which thin rock plates and scales sloughed off along joints in the rock.

In the early 1800s, beaver trappers were the first non–Native Americans to note the City of Rocks. The country's westward migration along the California Trail also passed the City of Rocks. Emigrants heading west to Oregon, Washington, and California began passing through in the 1840s. They marked the City of Rocks and the passage over nearby Granite Pass as milestones in their progress toward a new life. Some of their names, written in axle grease, are still visible on the rock faces. An emigrant named James Wilkins was among the first wagon travelers to fix the name City of Rocks to the area. He wrote in 1849 that it looked like "a dismantled, rock-built

city of the Stone Age" and referred to camping "at the city of the rocks." Other people saw animals and even faces in the shapes. In the year 1852, more than fifty thousand people passed through the City of Rocks on their way to seeking fortunes in California's gold fields. By the late 1800s, settlers were homesteading the area.

Shoshone and Bannock tribes had been in the area long before the first fur trappers passed through. Like that of Native Americans throughout the West, however, their way of life was forever changed by the onset of westward migration. Although most emigrants on the California Trail never saw the native peoples, some did write in their journals about seeing smoke signals coming from the surrounding hills and mountains.

In addition to its significance to the history of the country's westward migration, City of Rocks today has a reputation as a world-class climbing destination, rivaling Yosemite National Park as a favorite in the West. With seven hundred different climbing routes described to date, one of them appropriately named Bloody Fingers,

One of the park's namesakes

City of Rocks is one of the finest granite-cragged rock climbing sites anywhere. The spires are also a sanctuary, as part of Idaho's Minidoka Bird Refuge, for eagles, falcons, hawks, vultures, and many other birds. Many mammals such as mountain lions, mule deer, bobcats, and coyotes also live in the City of Rocks.

Equestrians will find the reserve to be an inspi rational sanctuary. Trails meander throughout its 14,300 acres among the weathered granite rock formations, the piñon and juniper tree stands, and the Alpine-like meadows. There are about seventy-five designated campsites in the reserve, and three group sites are available. There is one potable water source in the reserve. Most of the campsites among the rock formations are accessed from the road. Sites are equipped with picnic tables and fire rings. There are no hookups, showers, or dump stations. Vault toilets are located throughout the reserve. Bring your own wood, or purchase wood at the visitor cen-

Sharing an apple trailside

Heading out

ter, as gathering firewood is not allowed.

Indian Grove Outfitters (800-844-3246) features trail rides through the dramatic City of Rocks, where you can marvel at time's effect on the landscape, and along the California Trail. Enjoy a delicious dinner waiting for you at the end of your ride. Overnight pack trips and fishing trips are also offered. In spring and fall, organized ranger-led trail rides take place in the reserve. Participants can bring their own horses or rent horses from Indian Grove to view the reserve's scenic vistas. The spring ride takes place in May and the fall ride in September; the specific dates are dependent on the weather. The rides are several hours long and include a stop for an Old West

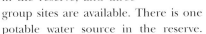

SNAPSHOT - CITY OF ROCKS NATIONAL RESERVE

Description: City of Rocks National Reserve is notable for its towering granite rock spires. It is a primitive area with relatively little civilization to fall back on. Ranger-led rides are offered twice yearly. Campsites are available in the park, but the horse site—which includes a corral and water trough—is limited, so call ahead to ensure availability and make reservations. Be prepared for limited lodging and dining options in the vicinity of the reserve.

Open: Year-round, but most pleasant for outdoor recreation April through October

Address: PO Box 169, 3035 Elba Almo Road (off Idaho 77), Almo, ID 83312

Phone: 208-824-5519/Fax: 208-824-5563

Web site: http:// www.nps.gov/ciro

Getting there: From Boise and points west: Take I-84 to the Declo exit south to Idaho Route 77, proceed through Albion and Elba to Almo. From Pocatello, Idaho Falls, and points east: Take I-86 to I-84 to the Declo exit south to Route 77, proceed through Albion and Elba to Almo. From Salt Lake City and points south: Take I-84 to north of Snowville, proceed west on Utah Routes 30 and 42.

Fees/permits: Admission is free; free backcountry passes are available at the visitor center

Horse rentals: Available in the reserve

Horse camping: One site in the reserve

Trail conditions/level of difficulty: Easy to moderate (children as young as 8 can ride)

Dutch-oven lunch. Reservations are required, and space is limited to no more than twenty to twenty-five horses and riders. Contact City of Rocks for more information.

MONTANA

GLACIER NATIONAL PARK

Uncrowded and blessed with some of the world's most beautiful scenery, Glacier National Park contains 1.4 million acres of spectacular landscape created eons ago by slow-moving glaciers. Located in northeastern Montana, the park is perhaps the last vestige of pristine wilderness left in the continental United States. The park shares its border with the smaller Waterton Lakes National Park, in Alberta, Canada. In 1932, as a gesture of friendship, the countries designated the two parks the world's first International Peace Park. Although the parks are administered separately, scientific research, some visitor services, and wildlife management is shared.

More than 70 species of mammals and 260 species of birds inhabit Glacier National Park. Mountain goats climb its dizzying cliffs, mule deer munch on its wildflowers, marmots hibernate during its long winters, and

Bald Eagle at Glacier

white-tailed ptarmigans change their coloring from brown in summer to white in winter to blend in with its snowy landscape. Grizzlies, wolves, and mountain lions all live in Glacier, the only area in the continental United States where the three roam the same turf.

For people wishing to roam the park, one of the world's most scenic highways, the Going-to-the-Sun Road, which opened in 1932 and was designated a National Historic Landmark in 1997, leads you through the park's grand vistas. Hundreds of miles of hiking and horse trails take you through Alpine meadows and forests, up majestic glacier peaks, and past sky-reflecting lakes. Horse travel is inherent to the history of the park. Long before the Going-to-the-Sun Road opened, the only way for tourists to see the interior

Resting in Glacier National Park

of the park was via horses or hiking. A typical visit to the park involved a train ride to its boundaries, followed by several days on horseback and nights spent in the park's lodges, built for tourist use by the Great Northern Railway. During that period, the horse livery at Glacier was the largest of its kind in the world. Today's horse rental concession, Mule Shoe Outfitters, carries on the tradition of allowing visitors to see the park by horseback.

Other visitors came via train and then traveled by stagecoach to Lake McDonald, Glacier's largest lake, where they boarded a boat for an 8-mile trip to the Snyder Hotel. Boats are still an integral part of the Glacier National Park experience, as they provide the ultimate opportunity to enjoy its pristine lakes and scenery.

Taking in the view

Approximately 700 miles of trails in Glacier are open to horses and other stock animals as well as to foot travel (see the Web site for a list of trails that are open and closed to horses). Overnight use of the backcountry is controlled through Backcountry Use Permits, which are issued for periods of

SNAPSHOT - GLACIER NATIONAL PARK

Description: "Little Switzerland of America" is what Glacier is often called. With 1 million-plus acres of forests, Alpine meadows, and lakes surrounded by majestic glacier peaks straddling the border of northwestern Montana and Canada, it is a fitting description. Reservations for backcountry campsites may be made in advance beginning in April for the upcoming summer. Call 403-653-3009 for more details. If you aren't bringing your own horse, contact Mule Shoe Outfitters (Lake McDonald, 406-888-5121; Many Glacier, 406-732-4203; or Winter, 928-684-2328) for one-hour, two-hour, half-day, and full-day guided rides. Alpine Stables in Waterton Lakes National Park also offers horse rentals and overnight horse boarding (see Where to Stay & Stable). Note that special restrictions apply if you are crossing the international boundary with horses. From the United States into Canada, you must obtain a horse use permit from Carway Customs; each animal must have had a Coggins test endorsed by a veterinarian and must enter and exit at Carway. Length of stay is seventy-two hours.

Open: Year-round; visitor facilities are open from late May to mid-September; roads may be inaccessible in fall and winter

Address: PO Box 128, West Glacier, MT 59936

Phone: 406-888-7800

Web site: http://www.nps.gov/glac

Getting there: Located in northwestern Montana on the U.S./Canadian border: Access to the park is from the east and west along US Highway 2; park headquarters is located in West Glacier.

Fees/permits: Admission is $5 for a seven-day individual pass; $20 for a seven-day single vehicle pass; Backcountry Use Permits are required if camping in the backcountry: permits are $4 or $24 if making a reservation in advance ($20 reservation fee plus $4 for camping)

Horse rentals: Available in the park and locally

Horse camping: Available in the park

Trail conditions/level of difficulty: Trails for all levels, from easy to difficult

McDonald Creek in Glacier

up to six nights and may be obtained at visitor centers and major ranger stations. Backcountry campgrounds have designated capacities for numbers of people and animals. From July to mid-August, competition for space is very keen at some areas, so riders are encouraged to plan overnight trips at later dates, when trails and campgrounds are less crowded and in better condition for horse travel, and when

GIVING GLACIER NATIONAL PARK ITS NAME

How do glaciers develop? They form in areas that are cold enough for snow to remain on the ground year-round. When more snow falls each winter than melts each summer, the fresh snow compacts the bottom layers of snow that haven't melted into ice. As the layers pile up over time, the pressure of the ice in the upper layers causes the compacted ice in the lower layers to move. As the snow and ice mass flows downhill, encouraged by gravity, a glacier is born. Rocks are pulled into the mix as the glacier heads downhill. Over the eons, glaciers carve and reshape the landscape. The churning rock and ice slowly scour the landscape into wide valleys, lake-filled basins, and pointing peaks.

A glacial lake

The approximately fifty or so small glaciers in Glacier National Park today are relatively young, having formed in only about the last five thousand years. However, much older glaciers have long been at work here. Several times over the last two million years, huge glaciers formed and then melted away as climatic conditions changed from cooler to warmer and then back again. About twenty thousand years ago, during the last ice age, scientists theorize that the climate became cooler or wetter, or both. This climate change allowed for giant glaciers to form, filling the valleys with massive sheets of ice thousands of feet thick. These rivers of ice, which melted around ten thousand years ago with the end of the last ice age, sculpted the mountains and valleys into the forms you see today. The glaciers' legacies are traced not only to the sculptured land but also to the brilliant blue lakes that occupy the lower ends of the glacial valleys.

For an education on the ways that glaciers form the land, take a look at some of the park's mountains, lakes, and other features. Reynolds Mountain provides an excellent example of a glacial horn. Horns are steep mountain peaks caused by glaciers carving three or more sides of the same mountain. Mount Clements offers another view of a horn. When two glaciers carve opposite sides of the same mountain wall, leaving only a narrow ridge, the formation is called an arête, which is French for "fish bone." Cirque lakes, such as Avalanche, Gunsight, and Iceberg lakes, occur when the ice from a glacier melts and the water accumulates in the depression left by the glacier. The material transported by glaciers and left in piles after the glaciers have melted are called moraines; the rock and gravel visible along the fronts and sides of the park's current glaciers are moraines. Hanging valleys are also found throughout Glacier. They appear as steppes on the sides of the mountains and were created by tributary glaciers that scoured smaller side canyons as large glaciers worked on the main valleys.

High country snow

there are fewer insects. Campgrounds are open June through September. An information sheet with details about parking and loading ramps for west-side trailheads is available upon request. There are a number of campsites outside of the park for horses and riders and a boarding facility in Waterton Lakes National Park, in Alberta, Canada. There are also a number of inns and lodges in Glacier National Park for riders only.

In addition to backcountry horse camping and other campgrounds, the stately historic lodgings built by the Great Northern Railroad are still available to tourists. Their authentic rustic feel, combined with the unique transportation system made up of 1930s red "jammer" buses (so named by locals in the old days for the sound of the manual transmissions jamming as drivers shifted), give visitors the flavor of the romantic era gone by.

Commercial services within Glacier National Park are operated by private companies under contract with the National Park Service. These ser-

vices provide opportunities for visitors to stay overnight in the park, to travel from place to place within the park, or to see the park from the differing perspectives afforded by horses and boats, just as earlier visitors did. Dining facilities are available in most areas, as are markets and gift shops.

WYOMING

GRAND TETON NATIONAL PARK

Grand Teton National Park is located in the northwestern corner of Wyoming near Idaho and Montana, bordering Yellowstone National Park. The two parks are connected by the John D.

Grand Teton peaks

Rockefeller, Jr. Memorial Parkway, which contains 23,700 acres and is managed by Grand Teton National Park as a recreation area.

The main feature of the park is the Teton Range, a 40-mile-long mountain front that includes eight peaks more than 12,000 feet high. The grandest of

A trail at Grand Teton

these peaks is Grand Teton, which towers at 13,770 feet. These magnificent mountains were born through periodic earthquake activity over the centuries, beginning any time from two to thirteen million years ago. As the range rose, the land to the east sank, forming a valley now known as Jackson Hole. The valley was

The Teton range

named for fur trapper David E. Jackson, who reportedly spent the winter of 1829 there, and the term *hole* was coined by trappers to describe a high-altitude plateau surrounded by mountains. From Jackson Hole, the Tetons appear as an abrupt wall of mountains thrusting upward with no gentle foothills to mute their dramatic skyscraping effect. Seven morainal lakes mark the range's base and reflect the mountain peaks, adding even further drama to their towering presence.

If you and your horse want to escape civilization and experience the unspoiled wilderness of the Old West,

Grand Teton is for you, as it contains no towns or villages within its 485 square miles. And desolation seems to come naturally to this area. Because of its geographic location and its soils and climate, farming and ranching was risky, so Jackson Hole remained unsettled until late into the nineteenth century. By 1890, however, the valley claimed a population of sixty-four. The first permanent homesteaders, John Holland and John Carnes, settled north of the present town of Jackson. Since then, of course, the area's population has increased significantly. Tourism supports the local economy, and Grand Teton National Park offers a variety of outdoor activities—from skiing and snowshoeing to hiking and biking—that keep visitors coming.

With hundreds of miles of horseback trails meandering through the park, riders can still find plenty of unpopulated land to explore. Because many of the high-country trails are blocked by snow

SNAPSHOT - GRAND TETON NATIONAL PARK

Description: In Grand Teton National Park, horseback riders can ride and camp in the unspoiled wilderness of the Old West amid some of the world's most incredible scenery. Five backcountry campsites within the park allow horses. For horseless riders, multiple stables with horse rentals are located at Jackson Lake Junction, Coulter Bay Village, and Flagg Ranch. Long winters and heavy snow mean that sometimes trails are impassable; check with the park before visiting for information on possible trail closures.

Open: Year-round

Address: PO Drawer 170, Moose, WY 83012

Phone: 800-443-2311

Web site: http://www.nps.gov/grte

Getting there: Off state highway 191

Fees/permits: Admission is $20 for a seven-day vehicle pass

Horse rentals: Available locally

Horse camping: Available in the park

Trail conditions/level of difficulty: Easy; flat, guided trails

into July and are impassable to horses, people traveling with their horses often stay at adjoining national forests and the John D. Rockefeller, Jr. Memorial Parkway, and then take day rides into the park. The parkway connects Grand Teton with Yellowstone and includes a roadway as well as land for riding and other recreation.

WYOMING, MONTANA, AND IDAHO

YELLOWSTONE NATIONAL PARK

Yellowstone National Park offers many things to many different people. It holds clues to the lives of early nomadic peoples and the honorable position as the world's first national park, and it is therefore the model for hundreds of other national parks around the world. Its more than 2.2 million acres are located mostly in Wyoming but also sprawl into Montana and Idaho, straddling the Continental Divide. People have lived in the area that is now Yellowstone since the end of the last ice age, which was about eleven thousand years ago, as artifacts found at early campsites attest. And they didn't live alone. Animals that are still found in

Entrance to Yellowstone

Old Faithful

Yellowstone such as elk, bison, bighorn sheep, and black bears were prevalent, and some long gone creatures also lived here, including sloths, early camels, and woolly mammoths.

The park is also a geologic mecca to professional and amateur scientists alike, with its gushing geysers and hot springs powered by volcanic activity deep beneath Earth's surface. The park has more geysers and other thermal features within its boundaries than anywhere else on the planet. In fact, it contains almost 60 percent of the entire world's geysers. Perhaps the best known of these is Old Faithful, located in the Upper Geyser Basin and named for its consistent eruptions. This large geyser has an average interval of ninety-one minutes between eruptions. Although there are other, smaller geysers in the park that erupt more frequently, none have the towering majesty of Old Faithful.

Wildlife lovers will find an abundance of animals. Yellowstone has more

Riding at Yellowstone

free-roaming wildlife than any other national park in the country, and it is the only park in the lower forty-eight states where a herd of bison has existed since prehistoric times. In 1902, 50 native bison remained in Yellowstone; today's herd numbers around 2,500. Just some of the other mammals that live here include approximately 2,500 mule deer, 500 moose, 600 black bears, and 500 grizzlies. Gray wolves were re-introduced to the park in two releases in 1995 and 1996 after having been hunted and exterminated from Yellowstone during the late nineteenth and early twentieth centuries. There are now an estimated 160 here. Coyotes are common, and wild cats such as mountain lions, lynxes, and bobcats can be found, although they are not as common as coyotes. Small mammals such as hares, bats, shrews, chipmunks, and squirrels abound in the park, and more than 300 species of birds have been documented there to date.

Finally, there is the horse person's Yellowstone. And perhaps horseback riders, more than any other visitors, can truly experience all that the park has to offer as they travel its wild backcountry astride their horses, much as Native Americans did beginning four hundred years ago. In Yellowstone's backcountry, you'll find hundreds of miles of trails that meander through vast expanses of forest, wild rivers and streams, and

Yellowstone pack train

remote mountains. Yellowstone's designated backcountry campsite system
enables visitors and their horses to
share the extraordinary natural wonders of Yellowstone in overnight stays.

The park also offers the following
visitor centers: Albright Visitor Center
and Museum (at Mammoth Hot
Springs; 307-344-2263); Norris Geyser
Basin Visitor Facilities (307-344-2812),
Madison Area Visitor Facilities (307-
344-2821), Old Faithful Visitor Center
(307-545-2750), Grant Village Visitor
Facilities (307-242-265), Fishing Bridge
Visitor Facilities (307-242-245), Canyon
Area National Park Service Visitor
Facilities (307-242-2550), Tower-
Roosevelt Area Visitor Facilities (307-
344-2817), and the Public Lands Desk
at West Entrance (Forest Service and
National Park Service; 406-646-4403).

A gray wolf

SnapShot - Yellowstone National Park

Description: Most famous for Old Faithful and thousands of other geysers, Yellowstone also
includes spectacularly wild backcountry, with 1,000 miles of trails for horseback riders.
Primitive backcountry camping is allowed, and there are stabling options near the park,
but make your reservations well in advance. Guided day trips and overnight stock trips into
the backcountry (horse or llama) may be arranged with any of the stock outfitters licensed
to operate in Yellowstone: Mammoth Hot Springs, Roosevelt Lodge, and Canyon Village.
Call 307-344-7311 for more information. There are also a number of licensed conces-
sions, not located at these three corrals, that offer horseback riding and pack trips within
the park and outside of its borders in the surrounding area. Snack shops, cafeterias, and
fine dining are all available in the park.
Open: Year-round
Address: Backcountry Office, PO Box 168, Yellowstone National Park, WY 82190
Phone: 307-344-7381 (main number); 307-344-2160 (backcountry office)
Web site: http://www.nps.gov/yell or http://www.yellowstone.net
Getting there: To the North Entrance (open all year): Take Interstate Highway 89 to the gate-
way community of Gardner. To the West Entrance (open end of April through beginning of
November): Take I-287 from the north, I-20 from the south. The entrance is adjacent to the
town of West Yellowstone, Montana. To the South Entrance (open mid-May through early
November): Take I-191. The closest large town is Jackson, Wyoming. To the East Entrance
(open mid-May through early November): Take I-14. The closest large town is Cody,
Wyoming.
Fees/permits: Admission is $20 for a seven-day vehicle pass; $15 for campsite reservations
Horse rentals: Available in the park and locally
Horse camping: Available in the park
Trail conditions/level of difficulty: 30% easy, 55% moderate, 15% difficult

OTHER GREAT PLACES TO RIDE

Colorado

Arapaho and Roosevelt National Forests

12150 Centre Avenue, Building E,
Fort Collins, CO 80524
970-295-6700
http://www.fs.fed.us/r2/arnf
Located in north central Colorado, the combined
Arapaho and Roosevelt National forests make up
1.3 million acres. The forests are easily accessible
from Denver and other Front Range towns.

Chatfield State Park

11500 N. Roxborough Park Road, Littleton, CO 80125
303-791-7275
http://www.parks.state.co.us
This state park just outside the Denver metro area provides miles of trails for horse owners
as well as a livery for horse renters. Overnight horse corrals are available for campers in
the park.

San Juan National Forest

15 Burnett Court, Durango, CO 81301
970-247-4874
http://www.fs.fed.us/r2/sanjuan
Located in the southwestern part of the state, the San Juan National Forest stretches across
five counties and offers miles of trails. Bring your own horse, stay at a guest ranch, or ride
with one of several outfitters.

Idaho

Boise National Forest

1249 S. Vinnell Way, Boise, ID 83709
208-373-4300
http://www.fs.fed.us/r4/boise
Enjoy summer horseback riding on miles of shared-use trails.

Bruneau Dunes State Park

HC 85, Box 41, Mountain Home, ID 83647
208-366-7919
http://www.idahoparks.org/parks/bruneaudunes.html
This park contains the country's largest sand dune. Overnight horse facilities are available
in the park.

Montana

Bob Marshall Wilderness

Rocky Mountain Ranger District, 1102 Main Avenue, NW, PO Box 340,
Choteau, MT 59422
406-466-5341
http://www.wildernessranch.com
Spotted Bear Ranger District, 8975 Highway 2 East, PO Box 190340,
Columbia Falls, MT 59919

406-387-3800 October through May, 406-758-5376 June through September
http://www.wilderness.net
The Bob Marshall Wilderness offers horse packing in wild, untamed lands along the
Continental Divide.

Wyoming

Bighorn National Forest
2013 Eastside 2nd Street, Sheridan, WY 82801
307-674-2600
http://www.fs.fed.us/r2/bighorn
Riding in the Bighorn National Forest, sister range of the Rockies, will delight horse lovers.
Just a few places to ride include the Bucking Mule Falls National Recreation Trail, the Little
Horn Trail, and the Cloud Peak Wilderness area.

Shoshone National Forest
808 Meadow Lane, Cody, WY 82414
307-578-1200/307-527-6241
http://www.fs.fed.r2/shoshone
Shoshone National Forest, located in northwestern Wyoming, was the first national forest in the United States. Miles of riding trails are open to horses, and outfitters and dude
ranches are within its borders and nearby.

Yellowstone glacial boulder

WEST TRAVEL SECTION

IF YOU ARE TRAVELING WITHOUT YOUR HORSE, OR IF YOUR HORSE IS BOARDED SAFELY AT A STABLE, ENJOY THE SITES IN THE NEIGHBORING TOWNS. BELOW, YOU'LL FIND A MILEAGE CHART LISTING THE DISTANCES BETWEEN THE TRAILS AND ALL THE AREAS DISCUSSED IN THE FOLLOWING TRAVEL SECTION. THE AREAS CLOSEST TO THE TRAILS ARE INDICATED BY AN X. FOR AREAS WHERE NEITHER STABLING NOR HORSE RENTALS ARE AVAILABLE, NO SIGHTSEEING OPTIONS ARE LISTED.

COAST TO COAST	Castle Rocks State Park, Almo, Idaho	Colorado Springs, Colo.	Estes Park, Colo.	Jackson Hole, Wyo.	Kalispell, Mont.	Manitou Springs, Colo.	Yellowstone National Park, Wyo., Mont., and Idaho
City of Rocks National Reserve (Idaho)	**X** * miles	745 miles	660 miles	250 miles	590 miles	750 miles	300 miles
Glacier National Park (Mont.)	635 miles	1140 miles	1055 miles	575 miles	**X** 50 miles	1145 miles	485 miles
Grand Teton National Park (Wyo.)	270 miles	580 miles	500 miles	**X** 25 miles	505 miles	585 miles	100 miles
Pike National Forest (Colo.)	640 miles	**X** 135 miles	155 miles	530 miles	1120 miles	**X** 130 miles	695 miles
Rocky Mountain National Park (Colo.)	610 miles	175 miles	**X** 55 miles	480 miles	1060 miles	180 miles	535 miles
Yellowstone National Park (Wyo., Mont., and Idaho)	295 miles	660 miles	580 miles	115 miles	435 miles	665 miles	**X** * miles

*The area to visit is the same as or is within 10 miles of the trails.

MUST SEE / MUST DO

COLORADO

PIKE NATIONAL FOREST AREA

The red sandstone rock formations towering against a backdrop of the snow-capped Pikes Peak and brilliant blue skies could only be suitably named the **Garden of the Gods**.

Learn fascinating facts and lore regarding wildflowers, and learn about the geology, the rattlesnakes, and the gold seekers during the naturalist-led guided walks. Enjoy a leisurely lunch at the Garden Café, and then head off with your horse on one of the many trails for a closer encounter with the park's natural beauty and magnificent spires.

Garden of the Gods

Admission is free at the **Garden of the Gods Visitor & Nature Center** (1805 N. 30th Street at Gateway Road, Colorado Springs, CO 80904; 719-634-6666; http://www.gardenofgods.com). The center is open from 9:00 a.m. to 5:00 p.m. every day, and the hours are extended in the summer; it is closed on Thanksgiving, Christmas Day, and New Years Day. Free guided nature walks are offered daily at 10:00 a.m. and 2:00 p.m. In summer only, bus tours are available for $3.75 for adults and $2.50 for children. Private horse trailers can be parked and unloaded at South Spring Canyon Picnic area. Get a trail map from the Garden of the Gods Visitor & Nature Center.

Exploring the rock formations

The **Manitou and Pikes Peak Railway** (515 Ruxton Avenue, PO Box 351, Manitou Springs, CO 80829; 719-685-5401/Fax: 719-685-9033; http://www.cograilway.com) has taken passengers to the 14,110-foot summit of Pikes Peak since 1891. It claims several honors, including being the world's highest cog railroad, the highest Colorado railroad, and the highest train in the United States. It's open April through January, and online reservations are accepted at least five days in advance. Fees are $29 ($31 July 1 through August 21) for adults, and $16 ($16.50 July 1 through August 21) for children three through twelve; children under two are free (if held on a lap the entire trip). Group rates are available for groups of twenty-five or more if fees are paid in advance. Box lunches are available. But a note of warning: some people may suffer altitude sickness.

ROCKY MOUNTAIN NATIONAL PARK AREA

Once you have soaked up all the beauty and wilderness of Rocky Mountain National Park, you may want to learn more about the history of the area. The **Estes Park Museum** (200 4th Street, Estes Park, CO 80517; 970-586-6256; http://www.estesnet.com/museum) is here to help you do just that. The Estes Park/Rocky Mountain National Park area has seen its share of people passing through, including the Ute, the Arapaho, and the Cheyenne peoples; explorers and settlers to the area; and hunters and ranchers. The museum features a permanent exhibit, Tracks in Time, that details the history of the

Estes Park Museum

area, and four temporary exhibits per year. Temporary exhibits are housed in the original headquarters of Rocky Mountain National Park, which is at the museum. Admission is free and donations are appreciated. Hours are 10:00 a.m. to 5:00 p.m. Monday through Saturday and 1:00 p.m. to 5:00 p.m. on Sunday from May through October; 10:00 a.m. to 5:00 p.m. Friday and Saturday and 1:00 p.m. to 5:00 p.m. on Sunday from November through April.

IDAHO

CITY OF ROCKS NATIONAL RESERVE AREA

The nearby **Castle Rocks State Park** (3035 Elba Almo Road, Almo, ID 83312; 208-824-5519; http://www.idahoparks.org/parks/castle_rocks.html) features giant granite spires that some believe rival those at City of Rocks. The park is the most recent addition to the Idaho State Parks system. The National Park Service purchased Castle Rock Ranch in 2000 and then traded the 1,200-plus acres of land to the Idaho Park Service in exchange for other land. The exchange was completed in 2004. As this park is so new, some areas are still under development. The ranch land includes early twentieth-century ranching structures and irrigat-

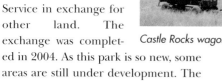
Castle Rocks wagon ride

ed pastureland. Recreational opportunities include riding the trails, rock climbing, bird watching, hiking, and viewing native cultures through archaeological sites. Hours are 7:00 a.m. to 10:00 p.m. There is a motor vehicle entry fee of $4.

MONTANA

GLACIER NATIONAL PARK AREA

Glacier Park Boat Co. (PO Box 5262, Kalispell, MT 59903; 406-257-2426;

A Glacier Alpine Lake

http://www.glacierparkboats.com) offers boat tours and rentals from June through September. You won't want to miss the opportunity to glide across the glasslike Alpine lakes nestled among the mountain peaks. Cruises are one hour and fifteen minutes long, and they depart from Many Glacier, Lake McDonald, St. Mary Lake, Two Medicine, and Apgar. They include narration about the area, photo stops, and optional half-day guided hikes, with hike participants returning on a later boat. Check destination locations for morning, afternoon, and evening departure schedules. Fares are $13.00 for adults and $6.50 for children (four through twelve); children under four are free.

There is no additional charge for the guided hikes. Reservations must be paid in full in advance. In addition to taking wooden boat tours, visitors can rent skiffs, rowboats, sea kayaks, and canoes. Rental boat availability varies by location, so check your destination for specifics. All boat rentals are priced for family affordability.

WYOMING

GRAND TETON NATIONAL PARK AREA

What trip to the Old West would be complete without witnessing a gunfight or experiencing travel via wagon train? You can do both near Grand Teton.

A favorite visitor attraction is the **mock gunfight** by the town square in Jackson Hole staged every summer evening at 7:00 p.m. This elaborate production lasts about twenty minutes and is well worth the time spent watching it. A cast of around a dozen people act out a stagecoach robbery, kidnapping, and final shoot-out with the sheriff.

Jackson gunslingers

The main street of town is closed off for the free event while hundreds of people watch, photograph, and videotape the action.

Or venture into the past and relive the experiences of the American West on the **Teton Covered Wagon Train and Horse Adventure** in Jackson Hole (PO Box 10307, Jackson Hole, WY 83002; 888-734-6101/307-734-6101/Fax: 435-789-5400; http://www.tetonwagontrain .com). Ride in modern versions of the old Conestoga Wagons as they encircle the Teton Mountain Range, and trek in country nestled very close to Yellowstone and Grand Teton National parks—or ride along on one of the ranch horses. Spend four days and three nights in new camps each day and experience visits from Indians, mountain men, and the pony express. Evenings are spent singing with the cowboys around the campfire, listening to yarns about the Old West, or

Cloudy skies at Teton

enjoying the western views of the stars and the northern lights, if you're lucky! Fees are $795 for adults, $695 for youths (ages nine through fourteen), and $645 for children (four through eight). Send correspondence to Teton Wagon Train & Horse Adventure, Double H Bar, Inc., PO Box 10307, Jackson Hole, Wyoming 83002-0307.

WYOMING, MONTANA, AND IDAHO

YELLOWSTONE NATIONAL PARK

When visiting Yellowstone, there is so much to see within its majestic boundaries, you won't want to go anywhere else. Here are the places you do not want to miss (courtesy of the National Park Service):

Old Faithful, in the Upper Geyser Basin, is the most popular attraction in Yellowstone. Don't miss seeing it erupt. Visit the Old Faithful Visitor Center next to the geyser for predicted eruption times for that day. The predicted eruption schedule is updated by park rangers daily.

The **Grand Canyon** of Yellowstone is smaller than the Grand Canyon in Arizona

Lower Falls

but equally breathtaking. The 308-foot-high Lower Falls is one of the most photographed features in Yellowstone.

Hayden Valley is a favorite place for wildlife spotting. Riding through this beautiful valley, you are likely to see herds of bison, possibly elk, and an occasional grizzly bear.

Mammoth Hot Springs is the site of the park headquarters (307-344-7381; http://www.yellowstoneparknet.com/mammoth_hot_springs/park_head quarters.php), and it features some of the oldest buildings in the park. It was chosen for the headquarters site because of its comparatively mild winters and year-round access. In the early years, the hot springs were commercialized to attract visitors seeking relief from ailments in the mineral waters.

Yellowstone Lake is the largest high-altitude lake in the lower forty-eight states. On windy days, oceanlike waves break onto the shore.

Norris Geyser Basin is one of Yellowstone's most popular geyser basins and home to Echinus (one of the park's most popular geysers) and Steamboat (the world's tallest geyser).

A must-see for serious wildlife lovers, the large and remote **Lamar Valley** is home to bison, elk, coyotes, grizzly bears, and wolves. Bison and elk are readily visible, and coyotes can often be spotted; bears and wolves may be seen early in the morning or at dusk.

Tower Falls is the second most popular waterfall in Yellowstone. It is located behind the Tower Falls General Store, and a short walk will take you to an overlook for a short (although steep) hike down to the waterfall's base. Tower Falls is located in the northern area of the park, closest to the North Entrance.

The **Lower Geyser Basin** and **Fountain Paint Pots** thermal areas feature erupting geysers, hot springs, and a mud pool.

West Thumb Geyser

Finally, **West Thumb Geyser Basin** has some interesting thermal features, including several that are in Yellowstone Lake itself.

Yellowstone Lake

WHERE TO STAY & STABLE

COLORADO

PIKE NATIONAL FOREST AREA

Horses and Riders

H-2 Ranch Horse Motel and Bed & Breakfast
6665 Walker Road
Colorado Springs, CO 80908
719-495-2338
http://www.H2stables.com
$75.00 per night for rooms, includes hot gourmet breakfast; $18.00 per night for 12 x 12–foot stalls, includes grass hay; $7.00 per night for camping with electric hookup

H-2 Stables, Horse Motel and Bed & Breakfast, is located on 40 acres, just 11 miles north of Colorado Springs. It's a short distance off I-25 (exit 161, east on Highway 105 across Highway 83, then east 3 miles on Walker Road) and only minutes from the Air Force Academy, Pikes Peak, Garden of the Gods, and Seven Falls. Two uniquely decorated bedrooms with adjoining baths make this an intimate and cozy place to stay. Evening meals are available but by reservation only. Horse accommodations are stalls with wood shavings for bedding, grass hay for meals, and a wash rack for bathing. Turnout is available to private paddocks or to a small pasture area. A round pen and large indoor and outdoor arenas are also available. Fox Run Regional Park, Black Forest Park, and the Air Force Academy are close by for excellent riding trails.

M-Lazy-C Ranch
PO Box 461
Lake George, CO 80827
800-289-4868
http://www.mlazyc.com
$65–$95 per night, $10 for each additional guest, breakfast included; $65–$105 per horse for overnight stabling

The M-Lazy-C Ranch is easily accessible from Highway 24 and is surrounded by thousands of acres of the Pike National Forest. Numerous ranch activities are available, and attractions such as Pikes Peak, Garden of the Gods, Cave of the Winds, and Cripple Creek are close by. There are twenty-five RV sites and a primitive camping area with teepees, wall tents, and RV sites. For more comfortable accommodations, cozy cabins, originally built for working cowboys, are also available. For equine guests, there are 16 x 16–foot stalls, a round pen, and an arena. Guests need to provide their own feed. Unlimited access to trails with a wide variety of terrain provides rewarding riding experiences throughout the National Forest. If you don't have your own horse, hourly horse rentals are available ($25 per person for the first hour; $20 per hour for each additional hour). You can also make reservations for a dinner or a breakfast ride. To enjoy more of the gorgeous surrounding country, take a one-, three-, or five-day guided pack trip into the Pike National Forest for $150 per person per day. The ranch provides the guide, horse, equipment, food cooked over an open fire, and cowboy teepees; or you can sleep under the Colorado star-studded sky. The ranch also offers cattle roundups and hayrides.

ROCKY MOUNTAIN NATIONAL PARK AREA

Horses and Riders

Peaceful Valley Ranch & Conference Center
475 Peaceful Valley Road
Lyons, CO 80540

800-955-6343
http://www.coloradodirectory.com/peacefulvalleyranch
$110–$220 per night, $750–$1,600 weekly in season (call for off-season rates); additional fee
or deposit for horses
Peaceful Valley Ranch is situated along a rushing stream and has pine-paneled lodge
rooms and cozy secluded cabins with fireplaces and hot tubs. Immediate access to
Rocky Mountain National Forest provides hiking and riding through wildflower valleys to Alpine lakes and waterfalls. Included are meals such as "breakfast on the
mountain," steak cookouts, and riverside lunches; and Western activities such as barn
dances, Old West nights, chili cook-offs, and rodeos are offered.

Rocky Mountain National Park Backcountry Camping
Located in the park
970-586-1242
http://www.nps.gov/romo
$20 in summer, free in winter
Rocky Mountain National Park hosts hundreds of backcountry sites, several of which
allow horses. Reservations are suggested and can be made by calling the Backcountry
Office. It can take a while to get through at times, so patience is required.

Winding River Ranch
PO Box 650, 1471 Country Road 49
Grand Lake, CO 80447
970-627-3251/Fax: 970-627-8558
http://www.windingriverresort.com
$95–$185 per night, double occupancy; $15 for single horse pen, $20 for double horse pen
Adjacent to the public lands of Rocky Mountain National Forest is Winding River
Ranch. Horse owners may bring their own horses. Open May through October, the
ranch offers private pens, riding arenas, a barn, and spectacular rides in the directly
accessible forests and Rocky Mountain National Park. While the horses graze in their
corrals after a long day in the wilderness, their riders may relax at the ranch's health
resort with its indoor pool, sauna, whirlpool, steam room, salon, and massage center.

Riders Only.

Aspenglen Campgrounds
Located in the park
970-586-1206
http://www.nps.gov/romo/visit/park/campgrounds.html
$20 per night
Available on a first-come, first-served basis only; no reservations are taken. No electric, water, or sewer hookups are available. Campgrounds feature RV sites and walk-
in (tent) sites located among shade trees. Open from mid-May to late September.

Glacier Basin Campgrounds
Located in the park
970-586-1206 for information, 800-365-2267 for reservations
http://www.nps.gov/romo/visit/park/campgrounds.html
$20 per night
The campground includes tent and RV sites as well as a group tent site. The site has
restrooms, water, and bear-proof food storage boxes. Open summers.

Longs Peak Campgrounds
Located in the park
970-586-1206
http://www.nps.gov/romo/visit/park/campgrounds.html
$20 per night in summer, $14 in fall, winter, and spring
Camping is available on a first-come, first-served basis, for tent camping only. There

is water during the summer season, but it is turned off from October through May. The grounds are open year-round.

Moraine Park Campgrounds

Located in the park
970-586-1206 for information, 800-365-CAMP for reservations
http://www.nps.gov/romo/visit/park/campgrounds.html
$20 per night in summer, $14 in fall, winter, and spring
The campgrounds offer RV and tent camping year-round. There is water during the summer months, but it is turned off from September to May. The campground also includes an amphitheater.

Timber Creek Campgrounds

Located in the park
970-586-1206
http://www.nps.gov/romo/visit/park/campgrounds.html
$20 per night during summer, $14 in fall, winter, and spring
Timber Creek has RV and tent camping. It is open year-round; however, water is turned off from October to May. No reservations are taken here.

IDAHO

CITY OF ROCKS NATIONAL RESERVE AREA

Horses and Riders

Juniper Group Site Horse Campground

Located in the park
208-824-5519
http://www.nps.gov/ciro
$6.00 per night per site reservation fee (reservations recommended); $7.00 per night for campsites
This small horse campground, located in the south end of City of Rocks, includes electric hookups. There is water for horses, but not potable water for people. There are no showers, but vault toilets are provided. Horse amenities include a corral, water troughs, feed stalls, and a hitching post.

Riders Only

The Marsh Creek Inn

386 South Main Street
Albion, ID 83311
208-673-6259
http://www.marshcreekinn.com
$54 and up per night, includes fresh breakfast muffin and hot beverage
The Marsh Creek Inn is located on Highway 77, the City of Rocks Backcountry Byway, in the beautiful and historic Albion Valley—just a short distance from Pomerelle Ski Resort and City of Rocks. The Marsh Creek Inn has a beautiful rustic lobby and breakfast area, and each room is air-conditioned and has a kitchenette. After a long day of riding, you are sure to enjoy a soak in the covered hot tub.

Old Homestead Bed and Breakfast

PO Box 186
Almo, ID 83312
208-824-5521
$45–$50 per night for a room, $100 per night for all rooms (group lodging; bring your own food)
The Old Homestead Bed and Breakfast is conveniently located in Almo and offers a comfortable spot to relax after a long day. It is open April through November.

MONTANA

GLACIER NATIONAL PARK AREA

Horses and Riders:

Devil Creek (U.S. Forest Service)
Flathead National Forest, 10 miles west of East Glacier on US Highway 2, Milepost 190
Hungry Horse, MT 59919
406-387-3800
http://www.fs.fed.us/r1/flathead
No camping fee
There is no camping with horses at the Devil Creek campground. Adjacent to the campground, however, is the Devil Creek trailhead. The trailhead has a trailer unloading ramp, hitch rails, and feed troughs. There is no official camping here, but riders can spend the night in their rigs. There is no fee for staying overnight at the trailhead.

Glacier National Park Backcountry Camping
Located in the park
Visitor centers: 866-646-0388; Bowman Lake Campground, Polebridge Ranger Station 406-888-7842
http://www.nps.gov/glac or http://www.nationalparkreservations.com/glacier_national_park
$20 per site for confirmed advance reservation, $4 additional per person per night (ages sixteen and under free)
Visitor centers are located in Apgar, Logan Pass, St. Mary, Many Glacier Ranger Station, and Two Medicine Ranger Station. The Apgar Visitor Center is open on weekends in the winter.

St. Mary-Glacier Park KOA
Located outside the park
North of St. Mary, on Lower St. Mary Lake
406-732-4122
http://www.goglacier.com
$27–$42 per night for RV sites; $23 per night for tent sites; $64 per night for single "kabins," $74 per night for double "kabins"; $155 per night for "kamping kottages"
This campground is central to most of the famous features of the park, including Going to the Sun Road, Many Glacier, Chief Mountain, Two Medicine, Lake McDonald, and Waterton. Each kabin has a picnic table, barbecue, and water spigot nearby. Bring your own bedding. The kottages are similar to the kabins but include a bath, a shower, and a fully stocked kitchen. Make reservations well in advance. The site also contains a playground and game room.

Riders Only:
Agpar Village Lodge
PO Box 410
West Glacier, MT 59936
406-888-5484
http://www.westglacier.com/lodge.html
$68–$232
This AAA-approved lodge features twenty motel rooms and twenty-eight cabins. All units have showers and heat and are nonsmoking. All but two of the cabins feature fully equipped kitchens. The lodge is located on the south end of Glacier's Lake McDonald.

Glacier Park Hotels and Lodges
Glacier Park, Inc., Central Reservations
PO Box 2025
Columbia Falls, MT 59912

406-892-2525/Fax: 406-892-1375
http://www.glacierparkinc.com
$68–$799 per night, depending on the hotel and the season
The lodges and inns located throughout Glacier National Park provide a range of accommodations steeped in history. From the various lodge sites you can hike, sightsee, shop, horseback ride, boat, golf, fish, or take numerous scenic and interpretive bus tours. Glacier Park Lodge features modern amenities such as a heated swimming pool, a nine-hole golf course, in-room telephones, a lounge, and the Great Northern Rib and Steak House. A total of one hundred rooms are available at Lake McDonald Lodge through a combination of lodge, cottage, and motel room accommodations. Located on picturesque Swiftcurrent Lake, Many Glacier Hotel, the largest hotel in the park with 208 rooms, is a favorite for its panoramic views of nearby Grinnell Point, Mount Henkel, and the shimmering lake waters. The regal Prince of Wales is worth a visit, if not for an overnight stay, at least for afternoon tea. Immense picture windows in the lobby behold the majestic views of Waterton Lakes National Park, in Alberta, Canada. Reservations should be made in advance and require a deposit.

WYOMING

GRAND TETON NATIONAL PARK AREA

Horses and Riders:

Grand Teton National Park Backcountry Camping
Backcountry Permits
PO Box 170
Moose, WY 83012
307-739-3300/Fax: 307-739-3438
http://www.nps.gov/grte
$15 for reservations
The five designated stock camps are Berry Creek, near Hechtman Creek; Death Canyon; North Fork of Granite Canyon; Paintbrush Canyon, below Holly Lake; and South Fork of Cascade Canyon. The site may be reserved by a written request to the Permits Office between January 1 and May 15. Sites that were not previously reserved are available on a first-come, first-served basis.

Luton's Teton Cabins
PO Box 48
Moran, WY 83013
307-543-2489
http://www.tetoncabins.com
$171–$342 per night, $1,092–$2,289 per week, depending on the date and the cabin
For Teton visitors who bring their horses and would like to explore the backcountry trails but prefer not to camp, Luton's Teton Cabins has boarding facilities for horses and personally crafted and fully furnished log cabins for their people. Located in the north part of Jackson Hole, with just a short drive to Grand Teton and Yellowstone National parks, Luton's Teton Cabins is surrounded by the Teton range and has spectacular scenic views of Bridger-Teton National Forest and Grand Teton National Park.

Riders Only:
Grand Teton National Park Hotels and Lodges
Grand Teton National Park Lodging and Dining Services
PO Drawer 170
Moose, WY 83012
307-543-2861
http://www.nps.gov/grte Prices vary
Lodging within the park is available through park concessionaires, and there are

various options in all price ranges. Jenny Lake Lodge offers the nicest and most expensive lodging and dining in the park. Flagg Ranch, Grand Teton Lodge Co, Signal Mountain Lodge Co, and Dornan's Spur Ranch Cabins also offer lodging within the park. Reservations recommended.

WYOMING, MONTANA, AND IDAHO

YELLOWSTONE NATIONAL PARK AREA

Horses and Riders:

Carriage House Ranch and Horse Hotel
771 Highway 191 North
Big Timber, MT 59011
406-932-5339/877-932-5339/Fax: 406-932-5863
$125 per night single, $150 per night double; call for current stabling rates
Carriage House Ranch specializes in overnight stabling and vacationing with your own horse and was named for the ranch's nineteenth-century Dutch carriage barn. Contact the ranch for Horse Hotel information suiting your needs. Recently renovated, Carriage House is a secluded guest ranch, bed-and-breakfast, and horse hotel that stands lone sentry over hayfields, Rattlesnake Butte (sacred to Native Americans), and a gently flowing mountain creek. Magnificent mountains, wide vistas, rolling hayfields, and a Native American buffalo jump are unforgettable experiences the Ranch offers its guests. Staying at this popular horse vacationing base camp, owners can venture with their horses into the wilderness areas for day or overnight trips. Barn stalls are 12 x 16 with rubber mats, Nelson automatic waterers, and attached 16 x 30 runouts. Outside paddocks are either pipe corrals or wood fence. Other amenities include a round pen, 100 x 225 lighted and heated indoor arena, hot and cold water wash rack with overhead heaters, and two large outdoor arenas, all with outstanding footing. Hookups for live-aboard horse trailers are available for guests who are boarding their horses at the ranch.

Montana Buffalo Company
50 Shooting Star Trail
Gardiner, MT 59030
406-848-7007/800-Corrall
http://www.MontanaBuffaloRanch.com
$75–$150 per night, depending on the season and the number of guests
No visit to Montana would be complete without staying in a secluded log cabin on a private mountain ranch with its own roaming herd of buffalo and other wildlife. Montana Buffalo Company provides this perfect Montana escape only 3 miles from Yellowstone Park by horseback (10 by car), making this site far enough away from the park's crowds yet close enough to enjoy its beauty. Contact the ranch to discuss rates and options if you're bringing your own horse.

Yellowstone National Park Backcountry Camping
Backcountry Office
PO Box 168
Yellowstone National Park, WY 82190
307-344-2160
http://www.nps.gov/yell or http://www.yellowstone.net
$20 per vehicle for a seven-day pass; a permit is required
Yellowstone has a designated backcountry campsite system: each designated campsite has a maximum limit for the number of people and stock allowed per night. The maximum stay per campsite varies from one to three nights per trip. Campfires are permitted only in established fire pits. A food storage pole is provided at most designated campsites so that food and other items attractive to bears may be secured.

Horses are not allowed overnight in the park during spring and early summer due to range readiness and or wet trail conditions. Horses are allowed beginning July 1.

Riders Only:

Xanterra Parks & Resorts
14001 E. Iliff, Suite 600
Aurora, CO 80014
303-297-2757/888-297-2757/Reservations: 307-344-7311/Fax: 303-297-3175 http://www.xanterra.com
Prices vary

All accommodations provided within Yellowstone's boundaries are through their park concessionaire, Xanterra Parks & Resorts. They offer a wide variety of lodging choices such as rustic cabins, lodge rooms, motel-style rooms, and elegant hotel rooms. Reservations can be made by calling them directly; be sure to make reservations well ahead.

Horses Only:

North Yellowstone Stables
34 Maiden Basin
Gardiner, MT 59030
406-848-9404
http://www.yellowstone.ws/yellowstonestables
$10 per night, $155 per month
North Yellowstone Stables is privately owned and operated by Sue Stormer, who provides facilities for horses at reasonable rates. She personally does all the feeding, keeps a close watch over the horses, and has contacts with local veterinarians and farriers. Sue can also point you toward the best rides in Yellowstone. Located on Highway 89 five miles north of Gardiner, Montana, at Yellowstone's northern gate.

WHERE TO WINE & DINE

COLORADO

PIKE NATIONAL FOREST AREA

Craftwood Inn Colorado Cuisine
404 El Paso Boulevard
Manitou Springs, CO 80829
719-685-9000/Fax: 719-685-9088
http://www.craftwood.com
$20–$44 for entrées
Built in 1912 by an English architect, the Craftwood Inn is a nice departure from the Colorado chuck wagon. Although many people think early Colorado was filled only with cowboys, cavalry, trappers, traders, and miners, artists and craftsmen of the arts and crafts movement went to Colorado seeking freedom and creativity in a natural setting, including English architect and builder Roland Bautwell. The results of Bautwell's creativity may be appreciated when dining in this beautiful inn. The Craftwood Inn not only boasts spectacular views and historic significance but also has hosted celebrities and dignitaries and has received awards for its creative cuisine and romantic ambience. The inn serves steak, seafood, elk, pheasant, venison, quail (occasionally), antelope, caribou, and vegetarian fare. It is open nightly from 5:30 p.m. Reservations are recommended.

Flying W Ranch
3330 Chuckwagon Road
Colorado Springs, CO 80919
800-232-FLYW
http://www.flyingw.com
Summer show: $19.50 for adults, $9.50 for children eight and under; includes admission to the Western town, supper, show, tax, and tip; Winter show: $24–$26, $12 for children eight and under, includes dinner and show at Winter Steak House
The Flying W Ranch is a working mountain cattle ranch that has specialized in Western food and entertainment since 1953. In summer (Friday before Memorial Day to Oct. 1), an authentic Western town and barbecued beef or chicken dinners highlight this unique Colorado dining experience. The Flying W Wranglers top the evening off with a Western stage show. The Western town opens at 4:30 p.m., supper is at 7:15, and the show is at 8:30 (hours vary) seven nights a week. Reservations are recommended. In winter, dine in the Winter Steak House while enjoying the show of the Flying W Wranglers. Open Friday and Saturday nights, October through mid-May.

Iron Springs Melodrama Dinner Theater
444 Ruxton Avenue
Manitou Springs, CO 80829
719-685-5104/719-685-5572
http://www.pikes-peak.com/attractions/theater
$24.00 for adults, $22.50 for seniors, $14.50 for children
For more than thirty-nine years, the Iron Springs Melodrama Dinner Theater has provided the Pikes Peak region with hilarious comedy and quality entertainment. The evening begins with a family-style dinner of oven fried chicken or barbecued beef and all the trimmings, with the melodrama immediately following (audience participation is strongly encouraged). After the melodrama, a foot-stomping sing-along and vaudeville olio full of song, dance, and comedy continues the fun throughout the evening. The dinner theater is open Friday and Saturday in April; Tuesday, Wednesday, Friday, and Saturday from May through September; and Tuesday, Wednesday, Friday, and Saturday in December. Closed in October and November.

ROCKY MOUNTAIN NATIONAL PARK AREA

The Rapids
PO Box 1400
Grand Lake, CO 80447
970-627-3707
http://www.rapidslodge.com
$21–$35
Dine in a beautiful rustic atmosphere overlooking the roaring Tonahutu River. This award-winning, fine-dining restaurant features American regional cuisine and has an extensive wine list. Open daily in summer from 5:00 pm; open Wednesday through Sunday in winter from 5:00 p.m.

IDAHO

CITY OF ROCKS NATIONAL RESERVE AREA

Albion Café and Annie's Saloon
228 West North Street
Albion, ID 83311
208-673-5404
$8.75–$19.95 for dinner; less for breakfast and lunch
The Albion Café serves breakfast, lunch, and dinner seven days a week, year-round.

Dinner entrées include prime rib, seafood, and more. Hours are 7:00 a.m. to 9:00 p.m. Monday through Thursday, 7:00 a.m. to 10:00 p.m. Friday and Saturday, and 8:00 a.m. to 8:00 p.m. on Sunday. Annie's Saloon serves wine and mixed drinks. The attached Albion Village Gas and Grocery (248 West North Street; 208-673-6614) provides grocery and snack items as well as gasoline and diesel fuel.

Sage Mountain Grill
241 West North Street
Albion, ID 83311
208-673-6696
$3–$7 for breakfast, $5–$8 for sandwiches, $18–$23 for gourmet dinners
Sage Mountain Grill is owned by an avid equestrian, Ina Digrazia, who is happy to provide advice on area trails to riders, so be sure to try to stop here for a meal. The restaurant serves dinner items such as New York steak, salmon, and grilled rib eye as well as pizza, Chinese chicken salad, and more. There is a full bar and a wine list. Hours are 8:00 a.m. to 9:00 p.m., Sunday through Thursday; open until 10 p.m. on Friday and Saturday.

MONTANA

GLACIER NATIONAL PARK AREA

Ptarmigan Dining Room
Many Glacier Hotel, located in the park
406-892-2525/Fax: 406-892-1375
http://www.manyglacierhotel.com
$9 for breakfast buffet; $4–$14 for lunch; $17–$27 for dinner
Picture windows with a view of Many Glacier's towering peaks add a Swiss Alps atmosphere to this dining room. Entertainment often accompanies the meal. Dress is casual, and reservations are not accepted for groups of fewer than twelve people. The restaurant serves continental and American cuisine, full breakfast buffet, lunch, and dinner. Open 7:00 a.m. to 9:30 p.m. in season.

Royal Stewart Dining Room
Prince of Wales Hotel
Located in the park
406-892-2525/Fax: 406-892-1375
http://www.princeofwaleswaterton.com
$12 for breakfast; $16 for lunch; $30 for dinner (Canadian currency)
With a dramatic lake view, the Royal Stewart Dining Room is the perfect spot for a break from roughing it in the wilderness. The dining room offers a buffet breakfast and traditional English fare as well as continental cuisine for lunch and dinner. Although the surroundings are majestic, casual dress is acceptable. Open 7:00 a.m. to 9:30 p.m.

WYOMING

GRAND TETON NATIONAL PARK AREA

Grand Teton National Park Restaurants
Grand Teton National Park Services, PO Drawer 170
Moose, WY 83012
800-443-2311/307-739-3300
http://www.nps.gov/grte
Range of prices

There are several restaurants inside the park that offer a variety of fare, including modest buffet and counter service, family dining, and full-service elegant dining. Restaurants are located at the Jenny Lake Lodge, Signal Mountain Lodge, Jackson Lake Lodge, and Flagg Ranch. Buffet and snack bar services are available at Signal Mountain Lodge, Jackson Lake Lodge, Colter Bay, and Flagg Ranch. Dornan's offers a full meal service, soup and sandwich delicatessen, or outdoor barbecue. Camper stores are available at Dornan's, South Jenny Lake, Signal Mountain, Colter Bay, and Flagg Ranch.

Horse Creek Station
Highway 89 at Horse Creek
10 miles south of Jackson
307-733-0810
$7.95–$17.95
"Doing the Wyoming thing" is what the Horse Creek Station does best. It specializes in Wyoming's finest smokehouse foods, plus it offers a wide range of steaks, seafood, and nightly specials. Nestled in the woods at the mouth of Horse Creek Canyon, the Horse Creek Station has a quiet, relaxing atmosphere. Famous smokehouse specialties served are "Wyoming's finest Bar-B-Que," Charlie's beans, baby back pork ribs, smoked prime rib, and more.

Solitude Cabin Dinner Sleigh Rides and Buffet Lunch
Teton Village, WY 83025-0290
307-739-2603
$66.95 for adults, $36.95 for children four to ten, $14.94 for children three and under for a sleigh ride and dinner, including tax; $19.95 for a buffet lunch, including salad, soup, fruit, cookies, and beverages
Wrap up in cozy lap robes and enjoy a memorable ride by horse-drawn sleigh along an Alpine trail at Teton Village. When you arrive at Solitude Cabin, live entertainment and a hearty four-course dinner of your choice of prime rib or broiled salmon with beer or wine await you on this special evening out. Dinner served daily at 5:00 p.m. and 7:30 p.m. Reservations and full payment in advance are required.

WYOMING, MONTANA, AND IDAHO

YELLOWSTONE NATIONAL PARK AREA

Lone Mountain Ranch Sleigh Ride Dinners
Box 160069
Big Sky, MT 59716
800-514-4644/406-995-2783/Fax: 406-995-4670
http://www.lmranch.com
$69 for adults, $64 for children four through twelve (higher holiday rates apply)
Big Sky's original sleigh-ride dinner is a magical way to spend an evening. Be sure to book your reservations well in advance. Lone Mountain's horse-drawn sleigh takes guests out to a remote North Fork cabin for a family-style prime rib dinner cooked on an old-fashioned wood-fired stove. The dining room is delightfully lit with kerosene lamps and filled with live entertainment.

Yellowstone Park Restaurants
Xanterra Parks & Resorts
14001 E. Iliff, Suite 600
Aurora, CO 80014
303-297-2757/888-297-2757/Reservations: 307-344-7311/Fax: 303-297-3175
http://www.xanterra.com
Range of prices

Xanterra Parks & Resorts manages all the dining facilities that are available throughout the park, ranging from fine dining to snack shops and cafeterias. Call Xanterra ahead for reservations at the fine-dining restaurants or inquire at any lodging's front desk when you arrive at the park. There are also many excellent options just outside the park in the gateway communities.

Mammoth Hot Springs dining

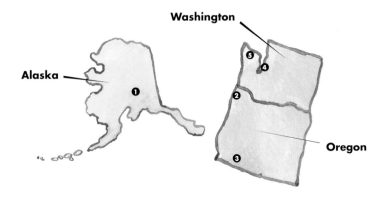

PACIFIC NORTHWEST MAP LEGEND

Alaska
❶ Denali National Park

Oregon
❷ Nehalem Bay State Park

❸ Rogue River-Siskiyou
National Forest

Washington
❹ Mount Rainier
National Park

❺ Olympic National
Park

THE PACIFIC NORTHWEST

G lacier-covered mountains, lush rain forests, rugged coastlines, sandy beaches, gray days, brilliant blue skies, endless drizzle, forever vistas, grizzly bears, killer whales, fresh salmon, aromatic coffee, delicious wine, dog sledding, mountain climbing, fly-fishing, Mount McKinley, Mount St. Helen, Mount Hood, the Cascades, the Columbia, Anchorage, Seattle, Portland. . . Trying to record all that characterizes the Pacific Northwest would be a never-ending task. This dramatic, beautiful area of the country is, and always has been, many different things to many different people.

To its first native inhabitants, the Pacific Northwest was a land of plenty. To early Spanish visitors, it was a place of myth and dreams where they might find the fabled Seven Cities of Gold or discover the rumored Northwest Passage. Later Europeans came to plunder the region's wealth and claim the land for their countries. The Russians came in search of fur and nearly decimated sea otter and other animal populations. The first Americans came for exploration, trade, and, finally, occupation. Gold seekers came hoping for riches, and pioneers from the East arrived.

Today, people are still coming, some to stay, and many more just to visit. Equestrians will enjoy exploring the rugged mountain trails, dense rain forests, and trailless wilderness. There are smooth beaches, peaceful meadows, and flat canyon floors on which to canter. Whatever type of trail riding you are looking for, you will find it here in the bounteous Pacific Northwest.

ALASKA

DENALI NATIONAL PARK

Denali National Park (and Preserve) features North America's highest mountain, the towering 20,320-foot-tall Mount McKinley. Its peak, covered with ice and snow and devoid of trees, reigns over the Alaskan Range, a 600-mile arc of mountains that divides south central Alaska from the interior plateau. The giant mountain was named Denali by native peoples, and it translates to "the great one" or "the tall one." In 1896, it was officially named Mount McKinley after the president at the time, William McKinley.

Alaskan wolf

Tanana, Koyukon, Ahtna, and Athabascan tribes were among the many native peoples who lived in Denali long before nonnatives came into the area. In fact, this raw and untamed land wasn't explored until relatively recently by people other than native Alaskans. In 1897, newspapers touted the mountain's "discovery," calling it "America's rival to Everest." And where tall mountains are, there will always be people wanting to climb them. Although many tried throughout the early 1900s to "conquer" McKinley, Harry Karsten, a packer and guide who had come to Alaska chasing gold in the Klondike gold fields, made the first successful ascent of McKinley's south peak in 1913. Karsten later became the first superintendent of the park.

Contrary to what some people may believe, this beautiful wild area was not designated a national park because of Mount McKinley. Rather, the park was established to protect its many large mammals. A naturalist, hunter, and conservationist named Charles Sheldon (who was guided by Harry Karsten) conceived and studied the idea of turning the area into a national park during visits in 1906 and 1907. A year later, Sheldon launched a campaign to establish a national park through an organization of which he was chairman, the Game Committee of the Boone and Crockett Club. He was successful, and Mount McKinley National Park was established in 1917. Although Sheldon wanted to call the park Denali, this designation of the park would not occur until 1980, when the boundary was enlarged by 4 million acres and President Jimmy Carter signed the bill that established Denali National Park and Preserve.

Denali National Park

A Denali sunset

Although the sheer magnitude of Mount McKinley defines Denali, the Alaska Range also includes countless other spectacular mountains and many large glaciers. Some of these are the peaks of Foraker, Mather, Hunter, and Cathedral Spires. Denali's more than 6 million acres (about the size of Massachusetts) also encompass a complete subarctic ecosystem with large mammals such as caribou, grizzly bears, wolves, Dall sheep, and moose as well as smaller critters such as hoary marmots, pikas, snowshoe hare, and ground squirrels.

To preserve the park's wilderness and prevent disturbing its wildlife, access to the park is limited to a shuttle and tour bus system, bicycles, and foot traffic. There are very few trails in the park as Denali is truly a wilderness area. Buses and bicycles travel along the Denali Park Road, and hikers can enjoy walks, day hikes on short trails, or plunge into the trail-free backcountry, with a permit, for overnight excursions. Many surrounding areas, however, allow horseback riders to bathe in the magnificence of Mount McKinley and Denali. Although the winters are long and harsh, lasting six to nine months, summers feature twenty-four hours of daylight for visitors to enjoy.

SNAPSHOT - DENALI NATIONAL PARK

Description: The vast wilderness of Alaska with the massive Mount McKinley as its backdrop beckons to be explored on horseback. Areas around Denali National Park abound in scenic opportunities either to ride your own horse or to take advantage of a guided horse tour. Horse outfitters include Denali Saddle Safaris (PO Box 435, Healy, AK 99743; 907-683-1200; http://www.denalisaddlesafaris.com) and Tumbling B Ranch (PO Box 114, Healy, AK; 907-683-6000; http://www.alaskan.com/snotrek/tumblingb/index.htm). Or you can stay and ride at Adventures Unlimited Denali Country Ranch (14901 Wildien Drive, Anchorage, AK 99516; 907-345-3083; http://www.saddletrailsnorth.com).

Open: May 1 to September 15
Address: PO Box 9, Denali Park, AK 99755
Phone: 907-683-2294
Web site: http://www.nps.gov/dena
Getting there: Headquarters is located along Alaska Route 3, the George Parks Highway, approximately 240 miles north of Anchorage, 125 miles south of Fairbanks, and 12 miles south of Healy.
Fees/permits: Admission is $5 for a seven-day individual pass, $10 for a family pass
Horse rentals: Available near the park
Horse camping: Not available
Trail conditions/level of difficulty: Easy to moderate trailless wilderness area

OREGON

NEHALEM BAY STATE PARK

Nehalem is a Native American word from a northwestern tribe that means "where the people live." And although you can't live at Nehalem Bay State Park, you'll certainly enjoy visiting and will want to come back time and time again. This popular location for horseback riders and others seeking outdoor recreation is located in northwest Oregon,

Smelling the salt air

nestled on the coast near the tiny towns of Manzanita, Nehalem, and Wheeler.

All three of these communities offer services to park visitors and are worth visiting for their quaint coastal ambiance. With nearly 800 inhabitants, Manzanita is the largest of the three towns; Nehalem is the smallest with a population of approximately 250.

The 890-acre park, which opened in 1970, sits on a 4-mile-long sand spit with Nehalem Bay on one side and the Pacific Ocean on the other. The park's camping area is separated from the ocean beach by sandy dunes, and the bay side offers a quiet and peaceful sanctuary. North of the park and Manzanita, offering a picturesque skyline to park visitors, is Neahkahnie Mountain.

The dramatic mountain rises 1,600 feet above the beach and plunges into the ocean at the north end of Manzanita Beach. According to Native American legend, the mountain was thought

Stately driftwood

to be a sleeping giant, waiting to be awakened from his slumber. It was also the location of a shipwreck early in the twentieth century, when the *Glenesslin*, built in Liverpool in 1885 and commanded by a young captain who was found to have been negligent in his duties, drifted into the rocks at the mountain's base. Another shipwreck, purportedly a Spanish merchant ship carrying beeswax, occurred on Nehalem Beach in the 1500s. Visitors to the park today still find chunks of beeswax when beachcombing.

In addition to walking the beaches looking for mementos from a time long ago, you'll find many activities to keep you occupied. Kayaking on the bay as well as crabbing and fishing are popular activities. Walking and biking the 1.75-mile trail that circles the park's airstrip is popular with visitors. The airstrip itself serves the surrounding communities as well as visitors seeking to camp.

Horse riders will enjoy the trail all the way out to the end of the spit as well as rides along the beach. Expect to see deer, elk, plenty of squirrels, and even coyotes as you explore the park. At the end of the spit, you'll be welcomed by an abundance of seals hanging out at the north jetty. The park, which is very popular with horse people, offers seventeen campsites for horses, each with two stalls.

ROGUE RIVER-SISKIYOU NATIONAL FOREST

Located mainly in southwestern Oregon, with portions dipping into California, the nearly 1.8-million-acre Rogue River-Siskiyou National Forest provides a rich diversity of scenery suitable for horseback exploration. Hundreds of miles of trails take you through open oak woodlands; dense conifer forests; narrow canyons; and barren, rocky ridgetops. Vividly clear lakes reflect the rich green forested walls of mountains, and riders will also appreciate the beauty of the more than 200 miles of rivers in the forest.

Showing off the hackamore

The Rogue River-Siskiyou National Forest, previously two separate forests that were

On a forest trail

administratively combined in 2004, ranges from the crest of the Cascade Mountains, west into the Siskiyou Mountains (a range of the Klamath Mountains) reaching toward the Pacific. The forests were established by Theodore Roosevelt in the early 1900s. Rogue River, initially called Crater National Forest, was renamed in 1932 for the Takelma Indians, early inhabitants of the area. The Takelma's defense of their homeland from outsiders led early French-Canadian trappers to call them *les Croquins*, or "the Rogues." French Canadians can also be thanked for naming the Siskiyou. Workers for the Hudson Bay

SNAPSHOT - NEHALEM BAY STATE PARK

Description: At Nehalem Bay State Park you can hike, bike, look for deer and elk, or ride horses, of course. There is a horse camp for people traveling with their own horses, and horse rentals are available during spring break and summer. This park is popular, and accommodations and activities fill up fast during the summer high season, so be sure to reserve ahead. If you don't bring your own horse, Northwest Equine Outfitters offers guided beach and trail rides. This concession is open during spring break and from Memorial Day to Labor Day (Nehalem Bay State Park Day Use Area, 503-801-RIDE).

Open: Year-round
Address: 9500 Sandpiper Lane, PO Box 366, Nehalem, OR 97131
Phone: 800-551-6949/503-368-5154
Web site: http://www.oregonstateparks.org
Getting there: Located off Highway 101, 3 miles south of Manzanita Junction
Fees/permits: Daily admission is $3 per vehicle
Horse rentals: Available in the park
Horse camping: Available in the park
Trail conditions/level of difficulty: Easy

Rogue River National Forest

1950s found that plant diversity in the Siskiyous is rivaled only by the Great Smoky Mountains in North Carolina. This abundance of plant variety is attributed to the position, orientation, and geologic complexity of the mountain range.

Riding trails throughout the forest range from easy to very difficult. A list of all the trails is available by visiting the Rogue River-Siskiyou National Forest Web site or by contacting one of the nine ranger districts that oversee the

Company bestowed the area with the name Siskiyou, which is a Cree word for "bobtail horse."

Mount McLoughlin, in the southern portion of the Oregon Cascade Range, is the highest point in the forest at 9,495 feet. It is one of the major volcanic cones in these mountains, which are a relatively young range at 60 million years old. Much more ancient are the Siskiyou Mountains, claiming a legacy reaching back nearly 200 million years. The summit of the Siskiyou's Mount Ashland, at 7,533 feet, is the highest point in Oregon west of the Cascades. Geologic studies during the

Taking a quiet walk

SNAPSHOT - ROGUE RIVER-SISKIYOU NATIONAL FOREST

Description: Natural diversity in every aspect describes Rogue River-Siskiyou National Forest. Horseback riders can ride through dense conifer forests; across wildflower-filled meadows; or down deep, rock-walled canyons. They can enjoy the peacefulness of the low elevation headwaters of the Applegate River or climb upward to view magnificent vistas. Riders can go deep into mountainous backcountry or ride trails overlooking the Pacific Ocean. Some trails allow bicycles; others are only for horses and hikers. Horse campsites are available.

Open: Year-round; some trails may close during inclement weather

Address: 333 W 8th Street, Medford, OR 97501

Phone: 541-858-2200

Web site: http://www.fs.fed.us/r6/rogue-siskiyou

Getting there: Forest area: Can be reached from I-5; Siskiyou National Forest area towns of Port Orford, Gold Beach, and Brookings: Can be reached from Highway 101, west of the forest; Grants Pass: East of the forest along I-5

Fees/permits: None

Horse rentals: None

Horse camping: Available in the forest

Trail conditions/level of difficulty: Easy to very difficult

forest and its various trails. These include the Applegate, Ashland, Butte Falls, and Prospect ranger districts in the Rogue River forest area, and the Chetco, Galice, Gold Beach, Illinois Valley, and Powers districts in the Siskiyou forest area.

WASHINGTON

MOUNT RAINIER NATIONAL PARK

Mount Rainier National Park is located in west central Washington, 45 miles southeast of Seattle and 75 miles northeast of Portland, Oregon. This fifth oldest national park in the country is dominated by the 14,411-foot Mount Rainier, the highest of the volcanoes in Washington's Cascade Mountain Range. Shooting almost 3 miles above sea level into the sky, it dominates the skyline on clear days, welcoming you for 100 miles before you actually set foot in the park. The behemoth volcano, shaped by fire and ice, dwarfs everything around it, including other mountains, glaciers,

A trail beneath the peak

steep-walled valleys, and subalpine meadows. Geographically, the 26 glaciers covering the mountain make it the largest remnant of the Ice Age to be found on one mountain in the world. Further marking its place in the world of volcanoes is its status as one of sixteen volcanoes worldwide to be designated a "Decade Volcano" in a United Nations program aimed at better using science and emergency management to reduce the severity of natural disasters.

Mount Rainier

Lupine and paintbrush

At only one million years old, Mount Rainier is a relatively young volcano, and although it is near and dear to the hearts of the locals and visitors who marvel at its stark beauty, it is considered the most dangerous volcano in the range. An eruption could affect the large number of people living in its shadow, sending Rainier's huge volume of ice, snow, and earth into the area. The last severe volcanic eruption of Mount Rainier occurred about 2,500 years ago, and the mountain and its major volcanic outbursts seem to occur in a 3,000-year cycle. People should not breathe easily when the mountain appears inactive. During its inactive period, Rainier also

SNAPSHOT - MOUNT RAINIER NATIONAL PARK

Description: Ride in the shadow of the majestic Mount Rainier. The park offers 100 miles of horse trails for intermediate to advanced riders, and four horse campgrounds. Contact area ranger stations for information on trail conditions and which trails are open to horses. If you're not bringing your own horse, area outfitters provide guided hourly trail rides and multiday pack trips. Circle C Outfitters (PO Box 1676, Eatonville, WA 98328; 360-663-0148 July 1–September 2/360-832-4430 September–June; http://www.circle coutfitters.com) has horses for rent for 2-hour to full-day rides. In the spring and fall, you can go riding with Chinook Pass Outfitters (10821 Old Naches Highway, Naches, WA 98937; 800-726-3631/509-653-2633; http://www.chinookpass.com), about a forty-five-minute scenic drive away.

Open: Year-round; all locations and facilities open from July 1 through Labor Day; most locations are accessible from Memorial Day into early October; snow limits access

Address: Tahoma Woods Star Route, Ashford, WA 98304

Phone: 360-569-2211; extension 3314 for Longmire Museum & Information Center, extension 2328 for Paradise Visitor Center (limited winter hours), extension 2352 for Ohanapecosh Visitor Center (summer only), extension 2357 for Sunrise Visitor Center (summer only)

Web site: http://www.nps.gov/mora; http://www.mount.rainier.national-park.com

Getting there: From Seattle to Paradise: South on I-5 to SR 512 (exit 127), east on SR 512 to SR 7, south on SR 7 to SR 706 in Elbe, east on SR 706 through Ashford to the Nisqually Entrance, Longmire, and Paradise. From Seattle to Sunrise: South on I-5 to I-405 (exit 156), east on I-405 to SR 167, south on SR 167 to SR 410, east on SR 410 to the White River Entrance, White River, and the Sunrise turnoff (summer only)

Fees/permits: Admission is $10.00 for a seven-day pass for people traveling in one private, noncommercial vehicle, $5.00 for individuals traveling on foot, bicycle, horseback, motorcycle, or in a vehicle owned by a nonprofit organization; no individual fee for people with a disability, people with a valid pass, or children sixteen years of age or younger; free permits are required for parties camping overnight in the backcountry

Horse rentals: Available locally

Horse camping: Available in the park

Trail conditions/level of difficulty: Moderate to difficult; can be steep and tiring

Fit horses tackle the terrain.

MOUNT RAINIER NATURE NOTES

Mount Rainier National Park, established on March 2, 1899, was one of the first parks in the National Park Service to employ naturalists. From 1923 through 1939, Mount Rainier's naturalists—assisted by seasonal nature guides, rangers, and the park superintendent—published a series of informative notes about the park for visitors to read and enjoy. The notes discussed wildlife, plants, road and trail conditions, park regulations and safety, history, and more. Although one of the first, Mount Rainier was not the only national park to publish nature notes; Acadia, Bryce-Zion, Crater Lake, Glacier, Grand Canyon, Hawaii, Hot Springs, Lassen, Mesa Verde, Rocky Mountain, Yellowstone, and Yosemite also produced their own versions.

Mount Rainier National Park

One interesting story relayed in the *Mount Rainier Nature Notes,* Vol. XI, September—1933, No. 7, tells of Fay Fuller, the first woman to climb Mount Rainier. She made her ascent up the steep mountain in 1890. As a woman, Fay Fuller was ahead of her time. She not only was a pioneer where mountain climbing was concerned but also rode astride her horse like a man, rather than sidesaddle, which was the accepted style for women riders of the era. This behavior and her mode of dress while horseback riding and mountain climbing shocked the locals. She wore an outfit she had fashioned herself that consisted of baggy bloomers fastened at the ankles and covered by a skirt that ended several inches above the ground. According to the notes, Fay Fuller was also the first female harbor master in the world, overseeing harbor operations in Seattle.

An earlier version of the notes, from September 1931, discusses a six-day horseback trip made in the park. There were so many members of the packing party, that "the party almost completely encircled 'The Mountain' on the Wonderland Trail." On the horseback trip, participants took photographs of magnificent vistas and hoped to get "photos of that most interesting mammal, the Mountain Goat," which, unfortunately, did not happen.

The 93-mile Wonderland Trail is still a popular and distinguishing feature of the park (though no longer open to horses) as it winds its way up Mount Rainier. Established at the turn of the century to promote park visitation, it was later used by park rangers on patrol beat. Original cabins used by the rangers are still in use. The oldest was built in 1915.

presents the hazard of avalanches and debris flows. A mud flow caused by steam explosions about 5,700 years ago was one of the largest known in the world. This eruption reduced the height of the massive mountain by more than 1,500 feet, turning its volcanic cone-shaped top into a broad dome and sending a 100-foot-high wall of mud cascading like a river of wet cement as far as the waters of Puget Sound.

When not staring in awe at the spectacular presence of Mount Rainier, visitors can enjoy the more than 300 miles of trails in the park that are usually free of snow from mid-July through September. Trails range from short walks near visitor centers to the 93-mile Wonderland Trail that completely encircles the mountain. As you visit the park, be on the lookout for black-tailed deer and their fawns, a frequent sight along the park's trails and roads in the quiet morning and evening hours of early summer. You are not likely to encounter black bears and mountain lions, but they are common in the park, so keep your eyes open for them. Look to the ground and hillsides in July and August to marvel at the display of colorful wildflowers that are at their best then.

Horses are allowed on 100 miles of the park's trails, and there are four trailside camps allowing them. It is smart to plan ahead for your visit if bringing your horse to the park. Snow depth limits trail access from late July through late September, and even during the summer months the trails can be extremely challenging, so be prepared. Some trails have glacial rivers to cross, and by midday in the summer these rivers may be raging torrents complete with tumbling boulders. The park trails are also rarely level, climbing and descending steeply, and can be exhausting to both horses and people who are not conditioned for them.

OLYMPIC NATIONAL PARK

Located on the rugged Olympic Peninsula in northwestern Washington State and partially surrounded by the smaller Olympic National Forest, the nearly 1-million-acre park is an oasis of temperate rain forests, wild Pacific coast, and glacier-covered mountains. It received its moniker indirectly from English Captain John Meares, who named the area's highest mountain Mount Olympus in 1788. (Ten years earlier, another English explorer,

Rugged Olympic

Captain James Cook, had named the northwestern tip of the Olympic Peninsula Cape Flattery because an opening along the peninsula's coast had "flattered" Cook into believing he would find safe harbor there.)

Mount Olympus, the tallest mountain in the Olympic range, is not a huge mountain at just under 8,000 feet, but the glacier-covered mountain is distinctive. Olympus and the other mountains rise almost from the water's edge and are thought to have arisen over the eons from the sea. The Olympic Peninsula is surrounded on three sides by the

A local banana slug

salt waters of the Pacific Ocean, the Strait of Juan de Fuca, and the Hood Canal. The park encompasses more than 60 miles of coastline within its boundaries. Animals and plants that are found nowhere else in the world exist here, attributed to the genetic diversification that occurs in geographically isolated regions. There are fifteen animal and insect species and eight plant species that are endemic to the area;

just a few include the Olympic marmot, the Olympic torrent salamander, Mann's gazelle beetle, the Olympic Mountain dandelion, and Flett's violet.

Parts of the peninsula receive from 135 to more than 200 inches of precipitation each year in the form of rain or snow. The combination of ocean storm clouds meeting the coastal mountains can be thanked for this moisture. And thank it, we should. This meeting of nature's elements is what blesses the park with everything from its magnificent stands of tall old-growth forests—there are several record-setting trees in the park—to its underappreciated banana slug—that yellow-and-black-striped creature that leaves its slimy trail on the floors of the park's damp forests.

The majority of the park's acreage consists of rugged backcountry; in fact, almost 95 percent of the park is designated wilderness. There are no roads crisscrossing the park and only a few that make forays into it. Although

Olympic National Park

Tacking up

visitors by automobile can get a good impression of the park by visiting one of its more popular spots such as Hurricane Ridge, Marymere Falls, or the Hoh Rain Forest, to truly appreciate its wilderness, horseback riding or hiking are the only ways to go. Nearly 200 miles of trails in Olympic National Park are maintained for stock use, and there are accommodations such as holding

Wildflower at Olympic

corrals, hitch rails, trailer ramps, and horse camps at several of the ranger stations and trails. Olympic National Park is not a place for novice riders, and there are no rental horses in the park. Stock trails range from those for experienced users, such as the Hoh Lake Trail and the Wolf Creek Trail, to trails for

very experienced riders, such as the Queets River Trail and the Duckabush River Trail.

See the Where to Stay & Stable section for information on campsites. Complete information on horse trails and facilities is available at the Olympic National Park Web site and by contacting the rangers at Olympic National Park (http://www.nps .gov/olym/wic/stock.htm).

In addition to trails in Olympic National Park, the Olympic National Forest (1835 Black Lake Boulevard SW, Olympia, WA 98512; 360-956-2402; http://www.travelingusa.com/arti cles/horsetravelolympicpeninsula trails) features trails and horse facilities. Just some of the trails include the Mount Zion Trail, which is a 2-mile ride to the summit of Mount Zion and offers beautiful views of Puget Sound; Mount Baker; Mount Rainier; the Cascades; the Colonel Bob Trail, which is 6.3

A park deer

miles long and offers steeper terrain as it meanders through an old-growth forest wilderness area; and the relatively flat South Fork Skokomish Trail, ideal for horses, which parallels the Skokomish River for 15.2 miles to the Olympic National Park boundary.

Be aware when you ride in this area that trails may lead from the forest into the park or vice versa, and that there may be differing permit requirements depending upon which agency is managing the trail.

Olympic in winter

SNAPSHOT - OLYMPIC NATIONAL PARK

Description: From lush rain forests to deep canyons to high mountain ridges, the wilderness that is Olympic National Park on Washington's Olympic Peninsula is yours to enjoy. With holding corrals, loading ramps, hitch rails, and camps for stock use, this park is a haven for experienced riders. Don't forget your rain gear, as rain is always a possibility no matter what time of year. Food is available in the park, but there are no horse rentals.

Open: Year-round, twenty-four hours a day, although some trails may be closed during inclement weather

Address: 600 East Park Avenue, Port Angeles, WA 98362

Phone: 360-565-3130/360-565-3131

Web site: http://www.nps.gov/olym

Getting there: All park destinations can be reached from US Highway 101, the only highway that rings the peninsula.

Fees/permits: Admission is $10 per vehicle for a seven-day pass, $5 per horseback rider for a seven-day pass; permits are required for all overnight trips into the backcountry (fees vary depending on type of permit, whether single person or group, and number of people in party); no extra charge for horses

Horse rentals: None

Horse camping: Available in the park

Trail conditions/level of difficulty: Moderate to difficult (steep); for experienced horseback riders only

OTHER GREAT PLACES TO RIDE

Alaska

Chugach State Park
Potter Section House, Mile 115 Seward Highway; send correspondence to HC 52, Box 8999, Indian, AK 99540
907-345-5014
http://www.dnr.state.ak.us/parks/units/chugach/index.htm
This is the third largest state park in America, conveniently located near Anchorage, with .5 million acres of trails.

Oregon

Eagle Cap Wilderness
88401 Highway 82, Enterprise, OR 97828
541-426-5546
http://www.fs.fed.us/r6/w-w/recreation/wilderness/ecwild.shtml#intro
Horseback riders can choose from miles of trails with access to trailheads from three counties. Several horse rentals and outfitters are available.

Hells Canyon National Recreation Area
1550 Dewey Avenue, PO Box 907, Baker City, OR 97814
541-523-6391
http://www.fs.fed.us/hellscanyon
More than 900 miles of shared-use trails wind through the scenic Hells Canyon NRA, which straddles the Snake River that divides Oregon and Idaho. Horse camping and outfitters are available.

Siuslaw National Forest
4077 S.W. Research Way, PO Box 1148, Corvallis, OR 97339
541-750-7000
http://www.fs.fed.us/r6/siuslaw/index.shtml
The Siuslaw National Forest is located along the central Oregon coast. It offers riding on the beach, riding on miles of horse trails, and camping at the Wild Mare or Horse Creek campgrounds.

Williamette Mission State Park
Oregon Parks and Recreation Department, State Parks, 725 Summer Street NE, Suite C, Salem, OR 97301
800-452-5687
http://www.oregonstateparks.org/park_139.php
This park offers riding on miles of trails along the Williamette River. There are four day-use horse camps.

Washington

Bridle Trails State Park
Washington State Parks and Recreation Commission, 7150 Cleanwater Lane, PO Box 42650, Olympia, WA 98504
360-902-8844
http://www.parks.wa.gov
This 482-acre day-use forested park is on the northeast edge of metropolitan Seattle. Picnic facilities, water, and restrooms are available; horse rentals are not available.

Gifford Pinchot National Forest (above)
10600 N.E. 51st Circle,
Vancouver, WA 98682
360-891-5000
http://www.fs.fed.us/gpnf/index.shtml
Ride in the shadow of the famous volcano Mount St. Helens or beneath Mount Adams, the second highest peak in the state. Several horse camps are available in Gifford Pinchot National Forest.

North Cascades National Park (right)
810 State Route 20,
Sedro-Woolley, WA 98284
360-856-5700
http://www.nps.gov/noca/index.htm
Ride in the rugged majesty of the North Cascades with its jagged peaks, cascading waterfalls, and dipping valleys. Backcountry horse camping is available in the park.

PACIFIC NORTHWEST TRAVEL

IF YOU ARE TRAVELING WITHOUT YOUR HORSE, OR IF YOUR HORSE IS BOARDED SAFELY AT A STABLE, ENJOY THE SITES IN THE NEIGHBORING TOWNS. BELOW, YOU'LL FIND A MILEAGE CHART LISTING THE DISTANCES BETWEEN THE TRAILS AND ALL THE AREAS DISCUSSED IN THE FOLLOWING TRAVEL SECTION. THE AREAS CLOSEST TO THE TRAILS ARE INDICATED BY AN **X**. FOR AREAS WHERE NEITHER STABLING NOR HORSE RENTALS ARE AVAILABLE, NO SIGHTSEEING OPTIONS ARE LISTED.

COAST TO COAST	Ashland, Ore.	Elbe, Wash.	Manzanita, Ore.	Nehalem, Ore.	Port Angeles, Wash.	Sequim, Wash.	Talkeetna, Alaska	Victoria, B.C., Canada	Wasilla, Alaska	Wheeler, Ore.	Merlin, Ore.
Denali National Park (Alaska)	2840 miles	2425 miles	2605 miles	2605 miles	2385 miles	2415 miles	**X** 165 miles	2335 miles	210 miles	2610 miles	2795 miles
Mount Rainier National Park (Wash.)	460 miles	**X** 70 miles	220 miles	215 miles	175 miles	140 miles	2485 miles	200 miles	2440 miles	215 miles	415 miles
Nehalem Bay State Park (Ore.)	345 miles	175 miles	**X** * miles	**X** * miles	255 miles	240 miles	2650 miles	275 miles	2580 miles	**X** * miles	300 miles
Olympic National Park (Wash.)	570 miles	230 miles	260 miles	260 miles	**X** 80 miles	100 miles	2510 miles	105 miles	2440 miles	260 miles	525 miles
Rogue River-Siskiyou National Forest (Ore.)	**X** 70 miles	440 miles	375 miles	375 miles	550 miles	485 miles	2920 miles	575 miles	2850 miles	370 miles	**X** 85 miles

*The area to visit is the same as or is within 10 miles of the trails.

MUST SEE / MUST DO

ALASKA

DENALI NATIONAL PARK AREA

When you're in the park, the **park shuttle** (PO Box 9, Denali Park, AK 99755; 800-622-7275; http://www.nps.gov/dena), which leaves from the visitor center, is the primary means of entering the backcountry. From mid-May to mid-September, you may take a round-trip day trip to any of its destinations, or you may use the shuttle to reach campgrounds. Various passes are available at varying rates. Reservations are required for all outbound travel.

Denali sled dogs

You can't visit the park without stopping by the **Husky Kennels at Denali National Park and Preserve** (PO Box 9, Denali Park, AK 99755; 907-683-2294; http://www.nps.gov/dena). The sled dogs of Denali have been important to the park for so long that they have become a cultural tradition worthy of protection. The dogs and the kennels where they live represent important pieces of American history and have cultural and native significance. These are the only sled dogs in the United States who help protect a national park

A flightseeing plane

and the wildlife, scenery, and wilderness therein. The kennels are open to visitors daily at 10:00 p.m., 2:00 p.m., and 4:00 p.m. and are accessible from the green shuttle at the Railroad/Visitor Complex at the park entrance. The shuttle departs 20 minutes prior to demonstration times, and rides are free. Admission to the kennels is free.

A sled awaits winter

"Flightseeing" over Alaska's wilderness gives an entirely different perspective of the park than one gets from the ground. Contact **Fly Denali** (PO Box 1152, Talkeetna, AK 99676; 907-733-7768/866-733-7768/907-733-7767; http://www.flydenali.net) to experience a flightseeing adventure. Enjoy sights from above, and then land on a glacier in Denali National Park! Call for rates and reservations.

Alaska's Trails and Tails Dog Sled Tours and B&B (PO Box 874293, Wasilla, AK 99687; 907-373-1408/888-300-MUSH; http://www. dogsledtours .com) offers mushing adventures, rides, and family fun on the Iditarod Trail and in Denali National Park. Overnight trips and hour rides are available. Call for current rates. Bed-and-breakfast lodging is available there as well.

OREGON

NEHALEM BAY STATE PARK AREA

While you are in the area, take a drive to the three quaint coastal villages near the state park. They can all be accessed from Highway 101. **Manzanita**, which means "Little Apple" in Spanish, is the largest of the three towns. It was incorporated in 1946. You can marvel at **Neahkahnie Mountain**, which comes right down to the ocean and bisects the beach. On the south side of the mountain is **Manzanita Beach**, where you can walk to the jetty and observe the seals. When visiting all the villages, you can enjoy shopping for antiques, admiring artwork, and perusing the unique stores in each of the towns.

Nehalem is the smallest of the villages with a population of approximately 250. It is located on the Nehalem River, which empties into Nehalem Bay, and offers excellent fishing. You can relax on the benches at **Nehalem Dock** and enjoy the river's peacefulness.

Wheeler, spread out on the hillside overlooking Highway 101, has a population of approximately 400. It overlooks Nehalem Bay at the mouth of the Nehalem River. From Wheeler, you can take an **Oregon Coast Explorer Train** on special excursions around the area (503-842-8206; http://www.potb.org/oregoncoastexplorer.htm). Rates and schedules vary.

ROGUE RIVER-SISKIYOU NATIONAL FOREST AREA

If your horse is securely stabled at the Wells Ranch House Bed and Barn (see Where to Stay & Stable) or you've found other horse-friendly accommodations in the area, you may want to explore this region via the water. The excitement of a river-rafting journey through the most beautiful and scenic part of the Rogue River shouldn't be missed. **Rogue River Raft Trips, Inc.** (8500 Galice Road, Merlin, OR 97532; 800-826-1963/541-476-3825/Fax: 541-476-4953; http://www.morrisonslodge .com) offers trips from May through September. Call to arrange to spend one or more days on the river for a thrilling and nature-filled escapade. Day trips are $75; three-day camp or lodge trips are $660–$735.

A variety of award-winning wines have originated from three distinct wine-growing areas along the Rogue River. Bear Creek Valley, Applegate Valley, and the Illinois Valley all host wineries open to the public for wine tasting and tours. **Weisingers Winery** (3150 Siskiyou Boulevard, Ashland, OR 97520; 800-551-WINE (9463)/541-488-5989/Fax: 541-488-5989; http://www.weisingers.com), featuring wines made from Rogue Valley grapes, is the closest to the national forest. (Other area wineries can be found at the Southern Oregon Winery Association Web site at http://www.sorwa.org.)

Rogue River National Forest

The winery is open daily in spring and summer from 11:00 a.m. to 5:00 p.m. Tours, by appointment only, are offered daily at 2:00 p.m. in spring and summer and from 11:00 a.m. to 5:00 p.m. on Wednesday through Sunday throughout fall and winter.

WASHINGTON

MOUNT RAINIER NATIONAL PARK AREA

Climb aboard the **Mt. Rainier Scenic Railroad** (54124 Mountain Highway E., also known as State Highway 7, PO Box 921, Elbe, WA 98330; 360-569-2351/888-STEAM11; http://www.mrsr .com) to experience the Golden Age of Steam. Ride in a vintage steam locomotive, chugging across spectacular bridges and through lush, tall forests with the majestic Mount Rainier as a backdrop. This scenic ninety-minute, 14-mile round-trip ride through the foothills of Mount Rainier stops at Mineral Lake, where you can picnic and explore. Snacks are available at the gift shop; scheduled special events feature barbecues. The railroad operates every day in the summer until Labor Day, with three trains per day. Check for other seasonal schedules and activities.

Mount Rainier Scenic Railroad

Fares are $12.50 for adults, $11.50 for seniors, and $8.50 for children under twelve (children under three are free). Group discounts are available.

OLYMPIC NATIONAL PARK AREA

From Port Angeles, the gateway town in the area, you can visit **Victoria, British Columbia**, for the day or overnight via ferry. Contact the **Coho Ferry** (101 E. Railroad Avenue, Port Angeles, WA 98362; 360-457-4491; http://www.coho ferry.com) or **Victoria Express** (115 E. Railroad Avenue 36, Port Angeles, WA 98362; 360-452-8088; http://www.victo riaexpress.com) for schedules and rates. Once in Victoria, don't miss **Butchart Garden**s, a very popular attraction (800 Benvenuto Avenue, Brentwood Bay, BC, Canada V8M 1J8; 866-652-4422; http://www.butchartgar

Washington ferry

dens.com). Hours vary throughout the year, and admission prices vary seasonally, ranging from $12–$23.

When you are off the ferry and back in the United States, you can quench your thirst for the grape by visiting the four area wineries: **Black Diamond Winery** (2976 Black Diamond Road, Port Angeles, WA 98363; 360-457-0748; http://www.home.wave cable.com/~bdwinery), open February through December, Thursday through Saturday from 10:00 a.m. to 5:00 p.m. and Sunday and Monday from 11:00 a.m. to 4:00 p.m.; **Camaraderie Cellars** (334 Benson Road, Port Angeles, WA 98363; 360-417-3564; http://www.cama

raderiecellars.com), open May through October, weekends from 11:00 a.m. to 5:00 p.m., or by appointment; **Lost Mountain Winery** (3174 Lost Mountain Road, Sequim, WA 98382; 360-683-5229; http://www.lostmountain .com/home.html), call for hours, which vary throughout the year; and **Olympic Cellars Winery** (255410 Highway 101, Port Angeles, WA 98362; 360-452-0160; http://www.olympiccel lars.com), open May through October from 11:00 a.m. to 6:00 p.m.; and November through April, Monday through Saturday from 11:00 a.m. to 5:00 p.m.; and Sunday from 12:00 p.m. to 5:00 p.m.

WHERE TO STAY & STABLE

ALASKA

DENALI NATIONAL PARK AREA

Horses and Riders:
Adventures Unlimited Denali Country Ranch
14901 Wildien Drive
Anchorage, AK 99516
907-345-3083/Fax: 907-348-0514
http://www.saddletrailsnorth.com
$2,000 per person, double occupancy, five nights, 6 days minimum stay; $2,500 per person for the guided adventure package; call for private horse accommodations
Denali Country Ranch is a self-sufficient outpost on the last frontier. Located in the heart of wild Alaska in Denali County, you'll find the simple pleasures of the past at this ranch. There are no radios, televisions, newspapers, or phones to jar you back into the hustle and bustle of the twenty-first century. Duplex apartment units are situated behind the main ranch facility, located on the edge of a small creek, and the horses are pastured directly behind the guest units. In addition, a sauna and a campfire site are situated only a few steps from the guest units. Family-style meals and packed lunches are provided.

Stage Stop Bed & Breakfast
Box 69
Tok, AK 99780
907-883-5338/907-883-5242/In Alaska only: 800-478-5369
http://www.akpub.com/akbbrv/stage.html
$45–$70 per night per couple for rooms, $12.50 per additional person; $10 for a corral, up to five horses; $15 for barn stalls
The Stage Stop Bed & Breakfast can provide a safe place on the road for you and your horse as you travel toward Denali National Park from the east. Denali is approximately 325 miles from Tok. There is a log barn with two stalls and three extra-large pole corrals with no barbed wire. Three rooms and one cabin are available for human guests.

Riders Only:
Denali Bluffs Hotel
241 W. Ship Creek Avenue
Anchorage, AK 99501
907-683-8500
http://www.denalialaska.com/bluffs_contact.html
$219–$259 per night
The Denali Bluffs is the closest hotel to the park entrance. All 112 rooms in the hotel are decorated with an Alaskan theme. Many rooms have private balconies, and most have views of the surrounding mountains.

National Park Campgrounds
Located in the park
800-622-7275
http://www.nps.gov/dena/home/visitorinfo/camping/index.html
$9–$40 per night
There are five established campgrounds in the park. They have various amenities, some with flush toilets and water, and some with vault toilets and no water. There is one group campground among the camps.

OREGON

NEHALEM BAY STATE PARK AREA

Horses and Riders:
Nehalem Bay State Park Horse Camp
Located in the park
503-368-5154/Reservations: 800-452-5687
http://www.oregonstateparks.org
$16 per night May 1 through September 30, $12 per night October 1 through April 30
The primitive horse campground has seventeen campsites, each with two stalls, a picnic table, and a fire ring. There is water available in the camp. Four horses are allowed per campsite. It is open year-round. This is a very popular horse camping location, so reservations are highly recommended.

Riders Only:
Nehalem Bay State Park Campsites
Located in the park
503-368-5154/Reservations: 800-452-5687
http://www.oregonstateparks.org
$20 per night May 1 through September 30, $16 per night October 1 through April 30 for campsites with electricity; $27–$30 per night year-round for yurts; $4 per night year-round for hiker/biker camp; $3 year-round for fly-in camp
The park has 267 campsites suitable for RVs, with electrical hookups, hot showers, restrooms, and yurts—domed tents with wooden floors, lockable doors, lights, heating, and beds with mattresses. The hiker/biker camp offers more primitive camping for those on the move, and the primitive fly-in camp is for pilots and their passengers only. It is adjacent to the Nehalem Bay State Airport, located in the park. Open year-round; reservations are highly recommended.

ROGUE RIVER-SISKIYOU NATIONAL FOREST AREA

Horses and Riders:
Sturgis Fork Horse Camp
Applegate Ranger District, 6941 Upper Applegate Road
Jacksonville, OR 97530

541-899-3800/Fax: 541-899-3888
http://www.naturenw.org/hc-rogue.htm
$5 Northwest Forest Pass required; no camping fees

The Sturgis Fork Trail, named after local miner Albert Sturgis, is a popular feeder trail accessing the Boundary Trail #1207. Passing uphill through virgin timber stands of the Craggy Mountain Scenic Area, the Sturgis Fork Trail is the shortest route to the Oregon Caves National Monument from the Rogue River National Forest. The trailhead has been designed to accommodate horse trailers with three parking spurs, a small corral (10 x 10), and high line areas. A day-use parking area is located closer to the trailhead. There are rock fire pits. No reservations required.

Wells Ranch House Bed and Barn

126 Hamilton Road
Jacksonville, OR 97530
541-899-1472
http://www.bbonline.com/or/wellsranch
$95 per night, continental breakfast included (special rates for extended stays); $20 for horse stall or pasture

The friendly Wells family is very flexible in their accommodations, offering one guest room with an adjoining den as well as camping in their pasture in good weather. Horses, dogs, and even cows, sheep, goats, and other creatures can be accommodated on this cattle ranch. Call with questions for your particular accommodation needs. It's located in the Applegate area near the forest.

Willow Prairie Cabin

Butte Falls Ranger District
47201 Highway 62
Prospect, OR 97536
541-865-2700
http://www.fs.fed.us/r6/rogue-siskiyou/recreation/camping/index.shtml
$15 per night

Willow Prairie Cabin is adjacent to the Willow Prairie Horse Camp. The setting is rustic Old West. It is a historic one-room cabin with two shutter-style windows (no glass), one door, a wood stove, some rustic furniture, and a couple of sleeping cots. There are corrals and a water trough for up to four horses. Firewood is provided at times, but you are encouraged to bring your own or an alternative heat source. A splitting maul is provided. The Willow Prairie Cabin is a U.S. government–owned building and listed on the National Register of Historic Places, so the signing of a rental agreement and special use permit are required to rent the cabin.

Willow Prairie Horse Campground

Butte Falls Ranger District
47201 Highway 62
Prospect, OR 97536
541-865-2700
http://www.fs.fed.us/r6/rogue-siskiyou/recreation/camping/index.shtml
$8 per night for first vehicle, $4 for second vehicle for camping; $5 Northwest Forest Pass required for day use

Willow Prairie Horse Camp is located on Forest Road 3735 in the Butte Falls Ranger District. The campground has ten campsites with four corrals each for two to four horses, vault toilets, and potable water. The Willow Prairie Trail System is the closest trail system to the campground and provides several loop opportunities. This trail system also ties in with the Willow Lake and Rye Springs trail systems. All three trail systems begin from the campground. No reservations are required for the campsites.

Horses and Riders:
Oak Flat Campground
Gold Beach Ranger District, 29279 Ellensburg Avenue
Gold Beach, OR 97444
541-247-3600
http://www.fs.fed.us/r6/rogue-siskiyou/recreation/camping/index.shtml
Free camping
The Oak Flat Campground, with access to Illinois River Trail #1161, features horse corrals and pit toilets. It receives moderate use and is open May to November.

Sam Brown Horse Camp
Galice Ranger District
2164 N.E. Spalding Avenue
Grants Pass, OR 97526
541-471-6500
http://www.fs.fed.us/r6/rogue-siskiyou/recreation/camping/index.shtml
$5 per night
The Sam Brown Horse Camp is adjacent to the Sam Brown Campground. It features water, corrals, picnic tables, and toilets, and it accesses the 9.5-mile Briggs Creek Trail #1132. Riding is easy to moderate with some meadows and swimming holes along the way.

WASHINGTON

MOUNT RAINIER NATIONAL PARK AREA

Horses and Riders:
Mount Rainier National Park Campsites
Wilderness Information Center, Tahoma Woods, Star Route
Ashford, WA 98304
360-569-2211; ext. 3314 for Longmire Museum & Information Center; ext. 2328 for Paradise Visitor Center (limited winter hours); ext. 2352 for Ohanapecosh Visitor Center (summer only); ext. 2357 for Sunrise Visitor Center (summer only)
http://www.nps.gov/mora or http://www.mount.rainier.national-park.com
Free wilderness camping permit required
Horse campsites are at Deer Creek, Mowich River, North Puyallup River, and Three Lakes. The camps all have toilet facilities, marked sites, and a nearby water source.

Riders Only:
The Hobo Inn
54104 Mountain Highway East
PO Box 921
Elbe, WA 98330
360-569-2500
$70–$85 per night double occupancy May through September; $50–$60 per night double occupancy October through April
For an out-of-the-ordinary experience, The Hobo Inn provides the opportunity to spend the night in your own remodeled caboose. The oldest of the cars dates from 1916, and each of the eight cabooses has been uniquely outfitted with comfortable beds and bathrooms—one with its own private hot tub. Some have bay windows, whereas others have cupolas. Make your reservations well in advance. For the total railroad experience, you can dine in the adjacent Mount Rainier Dining Co. dining car restaurant and go for a ride on the Mount Rainier Scenic Railroad.

National Park Inn, Longmire
Southwest (Nisqually) entrance to park
PO Box 108

Ashford, WA 98304
360-569-2275/Fax: 360-569-2770
http://www.guestservices.com/rainier
$98–$181 per night; $15 for crib and each additional person; $15 for reservation changes or cancellations

The National Park Inn at Longmire offers twenty-five rooms, a full-service restaurant, and a gift shop. An oversized stone fireplace provides guests with a cozy lounge area. The veranda has a stunning view of Mount Rainier, and the wooded surroundings are resplendent with flora and fauna. A vintage 1911 log cabin near the inn houses a general store. This is the only park accommodation open year-round. There are guided tours on weekends and holidays (seasonal). The inn is operated as a bed-and-breakfast from late October through late April.

Paradise Inn

19 miles inside the southwest (Nisqually) entrance of Mount Rainier National Park
PO Box 108
Ashford, WA 98304
360-569-2275/Fax: 360-569-2770
http://www.guestservices.com/rainier
$92–$211 per night; $15 for crib and each additional person; $15 for reservation changes or cancellations; early season rates are available

Built in 1917 using Alaskan Cedar charred by a fire in the nearby Silver Forest, the Paradise Inn provides a rustic and historic retreat within the boundaries of Mount Rainier National Park. The lobby is still graced with hand-hewn furniture, tables, a piano, and an enormous grandfather clock designed and built in 1919 by Hans Fraehnke, a German carpenter. This official National Historic Landmark inn features 117 guest rooms, a dining room, a lounge, and a gift shop offering Native American crafts. The inn is open only from May through October.

OLYMPIC NATIONAL PARK AREA

Horses and Riders:
Olympic National Park

600 East Park Avenue
Port Angeles, WA 98362
360-565-3130/360-565-3131
http://www.nps.gov/olym
$15 per day per vehicle for a seven-day pass; $5 per horseback rider for a seven-day pass; wilderness use permits are required for all overnight trips into the backcountry (fees vary depending on type of permit, whether single person or group, and number of people in party; no extra charge for horses)

An overnight holding corral is available at the Hoh and Staircase ranger stations. The "barn site," .25 mile from the Eagle Ranger Station, is available for overnight holding of stock; reservations are required. Elwha (Whiskey Bend) has a small corral with two campsites and an unloading ramp. Sol Duc also has an unloading ramp, and there are hitch rails at the following trailhead locations: Dosewallips, Whiskey Bend (Elwha), Sol Duc, Hoh, and North Fork Quinault. The following primitive campgrounds are available along the trails: Ten Mile Camp; Upper Duckabush, on the Duckabush River Trail; Deception Creek; Bear Camp; Big Timber; Diamond Meadows, on the Dosewallips River Trails; Elkhorn, on the Elwha River Trail; 5-mile Island; Lewis Meadow; Martin Creek, on the Hoh River Trail; Nine Stream; Camp Pleasant, on the North Fork Skokomish River Trail; and Horse Head, in the Sol Duc area.

Riders Only:
Lake Crescent Lodge

416 Lake Crescent Road
Port Angeles, WA 98363

360-928-3211
http://www.lakecrescentlodge.com
$68–$211 per night
This charming, turn-of-the-century lodge sits among giant hemlock and fir trees on Lake Crescent's shore in the shadow of Mount Storm King. The main lodge was built in 1916 as Singer's Tavern. President Franklin D. Roosevelt stayed here in 1937. There are five rooms in the main lodge, all with lake views but no private baths. In addition, guests have their choice of thirty modern guest rooms and seventeen cottages. Four cottages built in the 1930s have fireplaces and a rustic ambience. The lodge has a dining room, a cocktail lounge, a gift shop, and rowboat rentals. Open mid-May to mid-October.

Red Caboose Getaway
24 Old Coyote Way
Sequim, WA 98382
360-683-7350/Fax: 360-683-7364
http://www.redcaboosegetaway.com
$100–$180 per night
Nestled in the shadow of the majestic Olympic Mountains and close to both Victorian Port Townsend and Port Angeles, the Red Caboose Getaway invites guests to stay in their own themed cabooses. The Casey Jones features a conductor's desk and chair as well as the cupola intercom; the elegant Orient Express offers high-class amenities such as a two-person whirlpool bath, a gas fireplace, a queen feather bed, and a TV/VCR. Other themes include a Western caboose and a circus caboose. A 1937 dining car, The Silver Eagle, serves gourmet breakfast.

Sol Duc Hot Springs Resort
PO Box 2169
Port Angeles, WA 98362
866-4SOLDUC/Fax: 360-327-3593
http://www.northolympic.com/solduc
$139 per night double occupancy for cabin with kitchen, $119 without kitchen, $20 per additional person over age four (maximum number: four per cabin); $20.00 for RV sites/hookups
After a day riding in the park, check out Sol Duc Hot Springs Resort in the Sol Duc River Valley. Soak in any of three mineral pools with water temperatures ranging from 100–105 degrees Fahrenheit, or relax with a professional massage. Located at the site of natural hot mineral springs, the present lodge was built in 1966, but there's been a resort here since 1912. The resort has thirty-two cabins, all with private baths, and six have full kitchens. Grounds include a swimming pool and three hot springs pools; massage therapy; phones in the lobby; a dining room; a snack bar; a gift shop and grocery store with fishing tackle, camping supplies, curios, and gifts. There are no TVs. Open mid-May to late September.

Horses Only

Hunter's Pony Farm
3940 Leland Valley Road West
Quilcene, WA 98376
360-765-0130
http://www.huntersponyfarm.com/vacationstabling.html
$10 per day per tent or camper for campsites; $20 per day for large RVs; $25 per day per horse for horse camps; $25 per day for stalls; $40 per day for large paddock (three to five horses), $20 per day for small paddock (one or two horses); $2.00 for trailer parking; $5 per day for electric hookup (not available at all campsites)
Horse safety is the prime concern for the owners of Hunter's Pony Farm, and the Hunter family takes great pride in providing a vacation stable for those needing one while exploring the national park and forest. There are indoor and outdoor arenas and a barn featuring six large box stalls with mats, a spacious aisle, a large tack room, a work area, and hay storage. You feed your horse, they water. A large paddock is also

available. Ride in the Olympic National Park or Forest, or stable your horses for a day for other Olympic Peninsula sightseeing. No stallions, please. Dog kenneling is available by request for $5.00 per day; you feed, they water.

Nodaway Farm

226 Sofie Road
Sequim, WA 98382; send correspondence to PO Box 2406, Sequim, WA 98382
360-582-9514
http://www.nodawayfarm.com
$11.00 per day for pasture with field shelter; $15.00 per day for stall and turnout
Nodaway Farm is located in sunny Sequim. Miles of scenic backcountry trails await you with access from and near Nodaway Farm. Your horse will be well cared for if you should decide to take day trips to Victoria, British Columbia; Hoh Rain Forest; Hurricane Ridge; or romantic, historic Lake Crescent Lodge. Basic board services include daily stall cleaning; field mowing and dragging of pasture; daily fence checks; twice daily hay, feed, and water; free-choice salt block; blanket and unblanket service for stalled horses; turn ins and outs; and feed supplements as provided by owner or veterinarian. (Lunch feeding is available for an additional fee.)

WHERE TO WINE & DINE

ALASKA

DENALI NATIONAL PARK AREA

Denali Smoke Shack

Mile 238.5 Parks Highway
Denali National Park
907-683-7665
http://www.nps.gov/dena
$14–$25
The Denali Smoke Shack is located within the national park. It serves barbecue, king crab legs, and vegetarian dishes. Open daily; no reservations needed.

McKinley Denali Salmon Bake

Mile 238.5 Parks Highway
Denali National Park
907-683-2733
http:// www.denaliparksalmonbake.com
$9–$21
Established in 1984, McKinley Denali Salmon Bake is one of the last locally owned restaurants in the Denali Park area. They serve a wide range of home-cooked meals, from burgers and fish tacos to their famous surf and turf. They offer live entertainment many times a week and a full bar with billiards for those who enjoy a little night life. They also have some of the most economical cabin rates in the area, with cabins starting at $69.

The Overlook Bar & Grill (at the Crow's Nest)

Mile 238.5 Parks Highway, PO Box 70
Denali National Park, AK 99755
907-683-2723
http://www.denalicrowsnet.com
$9–$15 for lunch; $16–$30 for dinner
The Overlook Bar & Grill is located on Sugarloaf Mountain in the Alaska Range at the Crow's Nest Cabins. It is 1 mile north of the Denali National Park entrance and

offers a spectacular view of the area. The grill features seafood, steaks, burgers, and pastas. Open daily; reservations are requested.

OREGON

NEHALEM BAY STATE PARK AREA

The Bunkhouse Restaurant
36315 Highway 101 North
Nehalem, OR 97131
503-368-5424
Under $5
The Bunkhouse offers casual dining with traditional American breakfast fare and burger items. They serve large portions. Breakfast is available all day, featuring biscuits and country-style gravy.

Wanda's Café and Bakery
12870 US 101 North
Nehalem, OR 97147
503-368-8100
$6.50–$10.00
In addition to breakfast and lunch, Wanda's offers baked items to go. This is a very popular breakfast location, so get there early. Open Thursday through Tuesday from 8:00 a.m. to 2:00 p.m.

ROGUE RIVER-SISKIYOU NATIONAL FOREST AREA

Jacksonville Inn
175 East California Street
Jacksonville, OR 97530
800-321-9344/541-899-1900
http://www.jacksonvilleinn.com
$14.95–$31.95
This upscale restaurant features an array of menu choices including pastas, pork, steaks, and seafood. There are more than two thousand wines available. The inn and restaurant is housed in an early structure from the gold rush era. President George W. Bush and First Lady Laura Bush have stayed at this historic inn.

Prospect Hotel Dinner House
391 Mill Creek Drive
Prospect, OR 97536
800-944-6490/541-560-3664/Fax: 541-560-3825
http://www.prospecthotel.com
$7–$27; $19–$23 for fixed price menu, includes appetizer, salad, entrée, and dessert
The Prospect Hotel Dinner House offers dining in a historic stagecoach stop. *Sunset* magazine rated the Dinner House as "the best dinner house between Crater Lake and Medford." Local Oregon wine accompanies a variety of fresh dinner choices, such as lemon-dill roasted salmon and wild mushroom linguine, and dinner is served with freshly baked breads and just-picked garden salads. Open Friday and Saturday only from 5:30 p.m. to 8:30 p.m. in May and October; open seven days a week June through September. Reservations are recommended. For riders who are stabling nearby, the dinner house will arrange to pick up and drop off diners.

WASHINGTON

MOUNT RAINIER NATIONAL PARK AREA

Alexander's Restaurant
37515 State Road 706 E.
Ashford, WA 98304
800-654-7615/360-569-2300
http://www.alexanderscountryinn.com
$4.95–$11.95 for breakfast; $5.95–9.95 for lunch; $7.95–$22.95 for dinner
Located in Alexander's Country Inn, 1 mile from the Nisqually entrance to Mount Rainier National Park, Alexander's Restaurant is known for its icy pond-fresh steelhead trout, hearty homemade breads, and freshly baked blackberry pie; it is considered to be the number one place in the Mount Rainier area for breakfast, lunch, and dinner. Alexander's wine list features northwestern wines as well as selections from California and Europe. A variety of northwestern microbrew beers complete its friendly menu. Families are welcome, and a special children's menu is provided. Box lunches are offered for riders and others on the go.

National Park Inn Dining Room
PO Box 108
Ashford, WA 98304-0108
360-569-2275/Fax: 360-569-2770
http://www.guestservices.com/rainier
$7–$11 for breakfast; $6–$11 for lunch; $11–$24 for dinner
Located at the southwest (Nisqually) entrance to Mount Rainier National Park, National Park Inn's family-style dining room offers hearty meal selections in a casual setting. Breakfast, lunch, and dinner are served. During the summer, you can enjoy beverages and ice cream from a take-out window. Open year-round.

OLYMPIC NATIONAL PARK AREA

Kalaloch Lodge Restaurant
Located in the park
157151 Highway 101
Forks, WA 98331
866/525-2562/Fax: 360-962-3391
http://www.visitkalaloch.com
$5–$12 for lunch; $9–$24 for dinner
Cinnamon crunchy French toast, lodge burger, wild mushroom Wellington, marionberry chicken, and tuxedo moose truffle are just a few of the mouthwatering menu items at Kalaloch Lodge Restaurant, perched on a bluff overlooking Kalaloch Creek and the Pacific Ocean. Open for breakfast, lunch, and dinner; children's menu is available. Open for limited hours in the off-season. Reservations are recommended.

The Three Crabs
11 Three Crabs Road
Sequim, WA 98382
360-683-4264
http://www.the3crabs.com
$6.95–$21.95
Recognized as one of the "ten great places to eat seafood by the seashore" by *USA Today*, The Three Crabs has welcomed hungry people for more than forty-six years. Serving fresh seafood and steaks, the restaurant has a view of the nearby Dungeness Spit and its lighthouse. Open for lunch and dinner. Reservations are recommended.

Changing seasons in the high country

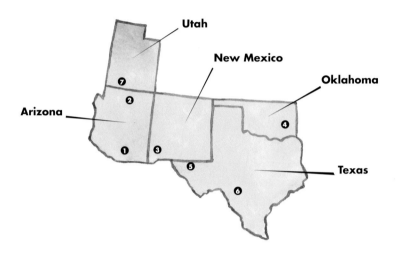

Utah

New Mexico

Oklahoma

Arizona

Texas

SOUTHWEST MAP LEGEND

Arizona
❶ Catalina State Park

❷ Grand Canyon
National Park

New Mexico
❸ Gila National Forest

Oklahoma
❹ Robbers Cave State Park

Texas
❺ Guadalupe Mountains
National Park

❻ Hill Country State
Natural Area

Utah
❼ Zion National Park

THE SOUTHWEST

*T*he American Southwest is a land of distinctive cultures and ecosystems. Its foods, architecture, languages, and traditions reflect its past and present peoples, including the Native Americans, who were the first inhabitants of the region and who still have a major presence and cultural influence today; the Spanish, who hundreds of years ago made the Southwest an outpost of their European empire; and the Mexicans and Anglos, who once fought bitterly for ownership and control of parts of this land. When visiting here, you're sure to see, hear, feel, taste, and smell the uniqueness of this land that is the Southwest.

You'll also notice the uniqueness in the landscape itself. Although you may imagine the Southwest as a place of hot, parched desert, its land is actually as varied as its peoples and cultures: there are also high mountains, deep canyons, dense forests, lush grasslands, meandering streams, and much more.

A wide variety of differing ecosystems can be found in the Southwest, which includes for the purposes of this book Arizona, New Mexico, Oklahoma, Texas, and Utah. And the landscape doesn't differ only among the states; it also can differ dramatically within a particular area. Just one example of this is found in Guadalupe Mountains National Park, where some scientists believe four different ecosystems exist within the park.

Wherever you ride in the Southwest, you're sure to enjoy the uniqueness and beauty of its land, its cultures, and its people.

ARIZONA

CATALINA STATE PARK

The nearly 5,500 acre Catalina State Park is located in the northwestern foothills of the Santa Catalina Mountains, which is one of five ranges surrounding the city of Tucson. (Tucson, Arizona's second-largest city, was originally a Native American village called *Stookzone*, which means "water at the foot of black mountain.") The Santa Catalinas are the area's highest mountains, boasting the 9,157-foot Mount Lemmon, scene of a devastating wildfire in 2003. The park is located within the Coronado National Forest, which covers 1,780,000 acres of southeastern Arizona and southwestern New Mexico. At its altitude of 2,650 feet, Catalina State Park is considered a high desert park. Average daytime temperatures range from the high 50s in December and January to the low 90s in June and July. Visitors will enjoy the park's mountain vistas as well as its

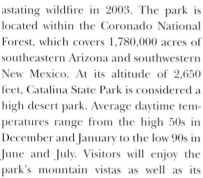
Saguaro cactus at Catalina

views of the large Sonoran Desert, which stretches across southwestern Arizona and into Mexico and southeastern California.

The park contains a wide variety of desert plants and wildlife. Mesquite, palo verde, and acacia trees as well as cholla, prickly pear, crucifixion thorn, and giant saguaro cacti in magnificent cactus forests are found here. Animals roaming its land include mule deer, javelinas, coyotes, jack and cottontail rabbits, and many lizards and snakes. It is a popular spot for bird watching as more than 150 species of birds live in the park. Hikers, mountain bikers, and horseback riders will find trails that wind through the park and continue into the adjoining national forest.

The park's eight trails vary in length and difficulty; they can be extremely difficult in mountainous (high altitude) areas, and they can be rocky. Five of the trails are open to horses. An equestrian center within the park offers a staging area for day riders as well as facilities for overnight camping with horses. The 1.4-

View of the Santa Catalinas

mile Bridle Trail, the only completely flat trail in the park, connects the equestrian center to the main trailhead. The 50-Year Trail is a popular trail for riders, but be aware that this 7.8-mile trail is also popular with mountain bikers. The other trails open to horses include the 10.5-mile Sutherland Trail, the 7.2-mile Romero Canyon Trail, and the 2.3-mile Canyon Loop Trail. Although the Romero Ruin Interpretive Trail is not open to horses, the .75-mile trail is worth hiking if you want to learn more about the fascinating native history of the area. The trail meanders through the ruins of a Hohokam village site that is more than 1,000 years old. The Hohokam inhabited southern Arizona for more than 1,100 years until their culture died out around 1,500 AD, which is about the time that Romero Ruin was abandoned. It is one of several large Hohokam villages in the Tucson area. It features trash mounds, ball courts, and the remains of stone structures and an agri-

Catalina entrance road

cultural field system. In addition to Romero Ruin, dozens of smaller archeological sites have been found within the park's boundaries.

Riders and other visitors to Catalina State Park can enjoy many other trails near Tucson. Other places to ride and hike include Coronado National Forest; Saguaro National Park, west of Tucson; and Oracle State Park, also at the base of the Santa Catalina Mountains.

Southwestern flora

SnapShot - Catalina State Park

Description: Ride through the high desert of southern Arizona at Catalina State Park. Camping is available in the park, and accommodations for horses and riders are available nearby. Horseless riders can enjoy the trails by renting mounts for guided rides from Pusch Ridge Stables (13700 N. Oracle Road, Tucson, AZ 85739; 520-825-1664; http://www.puschridgestables.com) or Walking Winds Stables (10000 N. Oracle Road, Tucson, AZ 85737; 520-742-4422). Other than bottled water, there are no supplies or food available in Catalina State Park, but riders can find hundreds of grocery stores and restaurants in nearby Tucson.

Open: Year-round, twenty-four hours a day; day-use hours are 5:00 a.m.–10:00 p.m.; Visitor Center hours are 8:00 a.m.–5:00 p.m.

Address: PO Box 36986, Tucson, AZ 85740

Phone: 520-628-5798

Web site: http://www.pr.state.az.us/Parks/parkhtml/catalina/html

Getting there: Located 9 miles north of Tucson on State Highway 77 (Oracle Road) at mile marker 81

Fees/permits: Admission is $6 per vehicle

Horse rentals: Available locally

Horse camping: Available in the park

Trail conditions/level of difficulty: Easy to difficult

GRAND CANYON NATIONAL PARK

Substitute the *grand* in Grand Canyon for *magnificent, monumental,* or even *imposing,* and the new name would still be an apt one to describe this majestic location. Look up at the limestone canyon walls soaring from the canyon floor, and you'll see towering walls striated in bands of oranges and reds. Looking down, you'll see plunging vistas that will awe you with the unstoppable power of nature. Carved over millions of years by the relentless Colorado River, the canyon, one of the world's largest, extends for 277 miles through northern Arizona. The canyon averages 10 miles wide and measures 18 miles at its widest point, more than 6,000 feet at its deepest.

Grand Canyon overlook

The canyon has been the home of native peoples who traversed its harsh and beautiful landscape for thousands of years, including early prehistoric peoples who hunted ground sloths, and later the Anasazi, Zuni, Hopi, Navajo, and Havasupai, among others. Today, Native Americans still call the canyon home; the Havasupai live in the canyon bottom, and the Hualapai in the western Grand Canyon. In addition to Native Americans, visitors flock here in large numbers, making Grand Canyon one of the ten most visited national parks in the country. And those who visit often leave with a feeling of wonder about the grand and magnificent canyon the river has so beautifully carved.

Most visitors to the Grand Canyon enter the park at its popular South Rim, which is open year-round. Grand Canyon Village is located there, offering visitors lodging, dining, and a variety of other services and amenities. Shuttle buses provide park transportation, which is important because parking at the village is very competitive during peak times. The buses offer canyon overviews and transportation to scenic overlooks. The North Rim, only 10 miles from the South Rim as the crow flies but hundreds of miles away via automobile, offers a quieter, less crowded getaway.

You can take mule rides from both the South and North rims and access the trails for riding your own horse into the canyon. Trails open to horses include the Bright Angel Trail, the River Trail (between the South Kaibab and Bright Angel trails), the South Kaibab Trail, the North Kaibab Trail, the Tonto Trail (between the South

The Grand Canyon

Kaibab and Bright Angel trails; register with the ranger at Indian Gardens when using this trail), and the Plateau Point Trail from Indian Gardens. Backcountry permits are required for riders planning to camp in the park. There are two campgrounds in the canyon that allow horses by prior arrangement, as the campgrounds allow only one equine group each. Permits are not required for day rides.

Grand Canyon mule train

Arriving to ride

At the North Rim, parking for day rides is available at the North Kaibab Trailhead, the main corridor route down into the canyon to the river. Overnight camping at the trailhead can also be arranged by calling 928-638-7870. At the South Rim, day-use parking is available across from the El Tovar Hotel in the dirt parking lot. The trailhead campground is being relocated. To make arrangements to camp at the South Rim trailhead, contact Ronnie Gibson at 928-638-7809.

SnapShot - Grand Canyon National Park

Description: Grand Canyon National Park offers an exciting adventure for riders, whether on their own horses or on one of the famous Grand Canyon mules. Multiple trails from the North Rim and South Rim are open to horse use. If you aren't bringing a horse, you can sign up for the canyon mule rides, including the overnight trip to Phantom Ranch at the bottom of the canyon, by contacting Xanterra Parks & Resorts (14001 E. Illiff, Ste. 600, Aurora, CO 80014; 303-297-2757/888-297-2757; http://www.grandcanyonlodges.com). The mule rides fill up quickly and may be booked up to two years in advance, so plan before you go. For mule ride waiting-list information, call 928-638-2631. You can also take day rides on the mules from the North Rim. Contact Canyon Trail Rides for information (PO Box 128, Tropic, UT 84776; 435-679-8665; http://www.canyonrides.com).

Open: The South Rim and its facilities and services are open year-round; North Rim facilities and services are open mid-May to mid-October; weather permitting, the North Rim is open for day use following the close of facilities and services in October. Note that the road from Jacob Lake to the North Rim (Highway 67) is subject to closure with little or no notice during this time and then remains closed until mid-May

Address: PO Box 129, Grand Canyon, AZ 86023

Phone: Park information: 928-638-7888/Stock use information: 928-638-7809

Web site: http://www.nps.gov/grca

Getting there: Grand Canyon Village (South Rim): 60 miles north of Interstate 40 at Williams via Highway 64, and 80 miles northwest of Flagstaff via Highway 180; North Rim: 44 miles south of Jacob Lake via Highway 67

Fees/permits: Admission is $20 per vehicle for a seven-day pass; Backcountry Use Permit required for overnight camping

Horse rentals: Mule rentals available in the park at both North Rim and South Rim

Horse camping: Available in the park

Trail conditions/level of difficulty: Vary, depending on weather; high heat in summer

One note when riding your own horse at the Grand Canyon: the park's mules have the right-of-way on the trails, so should you encounter a mule string, you'll need to find a safe place to get as far off the trail as possible. If there is no such place, you'll be required to backtrack to a suitable location so the mules can pass.

NEW MEXICO

GILA NATIONAL FOREST

When planning a trip to the Gila National Forest, the first thing that will impress you is the forest's sheer size. At 3.3 million acres, Gila is the sixth largest forest in the continental United States and contains more federal land than any national forest outside of Alaska. It lies in southwestern New Mexico, where the Chihuahuan and Sonoran deserts, the Rocky Mountains, the Great Plains, the Great Basin, the Mexican Plateau, and Mexico's Sierra Madre converge. Elevations range from 4,200 to 10,900 feet, and the diverse forest encompasses semiarid desert, grassy meadows, deep canyons, and rugged mountains.

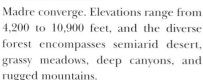

Gila Cliff Dwellings National Monument

The Gila National Forest contains more wilderness land than any of the Southwest's other national forests. Within its vast acreage are three designated wilderness areas: the Gila Wilderness, which was the first official wilderness area in the country and is the largest wilderness area in the Southwest at 558,056 acres; the Aldo Leopold Wilderness, named for the conservationist, ecologist, and author who helped establish the Gila Wilderness in 1924; and the Blue Range

Endurance riders stop to drink.

Wilderness, which meets Arizona's Blue Range Primitive Area to the west. As there are no roads or development allowed in wilderness areas, the only access to them is by foot or by horse, making these isolated areas ideal for riders seeking the peaceful tranquility of packing in the backcountry.

Of special note about Gila National Forest is its native history. Arriving in the 1200s and staying until around 1300, the peaceful Mogollon people flourished here. No one knows exactly when they left or why, but it is known by the legacy they left behind that they were impressive builders. Several sandstone caves with forty-six rooms have been identified as homes to the Mogollon. The cliff dwellings can be seen today by visitors of the Gila Cliff Dwellings National Monument.

Bordering Gila National Forest are several small towns, some of which originated as mining towns in the 1800s. The towns, where supplies, food, and lodging can be found, include Glenwood, Mimbres, Quemado, Reserve, Truth or Conse-

Gila Wilderness

quences, and Silver City. Other mining towns now stand as ghost towns or semi–ghost towns in the forest area. Silver, copper, and occasionally gold came out of the area, and some early mining of these precious metals can be traced back to Native Americans in the sixteenth century. Silver City, where silver was found (hence the name), was the center of mining and ore processing in the region. El Chino (or just Chino) Mine still operates outside of Silver City today.

SNAPSHOT - GILA NATIONAL FOREST

Description: Gila National Forest celebrated its one hundred–year anniversary in 2005. Nearly 1,500 miles of trails for horseback riding can be found within its six ranger districts, including trails in the Gila Wilderness area. Horseless riders can contact area outfitters for guided trail rides. Three outfitters are: Gila Wilderness Ventures (PO Box 280, Glenwood, NM 88039; 866-677-2008/505-539-2800; http://www.gilawildernessventures.com), U-Trail Gila Wilderness Horseback Vacations (Wild Horse Road, PO Box 66, Glenwood, NM 88039; 800-887-2453/505-539-2426; http://www.utrail.com), and WolfHorse Outfitters (PO Box 837, Santa Clara, NM 88026; 505-534-1379/505-538-3414; http://www.wolfhorseoutfitters.com). Check with the ranger districts for more.

Open: Trails are open year-round

Address: 3005 E. Camino del Bosque, Silver City, NM 88061

Phone: 505-388-8201

Web site: http://www2.srs.fs.fed.us/r3/gila

Getting there: Located in southwestern New Mexico, north of I-10, west of I-25, and south of US Highway 60

Fees/permits: No fees for trail use; parking fees may be charged in some locations; admission to Gila Cliff Dwellings National Monument is $3 per person

Horse rentals: Available locally

Horse camping: Available in the forest

Trail conditions/level of difficulty: Easy to challenging in the wilderness areas

GILA NATIONAL FOREST RANGER DISTRICTS

Black Range Ranger District
1804 North Date Street
Truth or Consequences, NM 87901
505-894-6677
This 552,615-acre district, located in the easternmost part of the forest, is best known for its access to the Aldo Leopold Wilderness. The majority of the district's 263 miles of trails are in the wilderness.

Glenwood Ranger District
PO Box 8
Glenwood, NM 88039
505-539-2481
The Glenwood Ranger District manages more than 523,000 acres of the forest for multi-use purposes. It includes the western portion of the Gila Wilderness and the Blue Range Wilderness. The Catwalk National Recreation area is in this district.

Quemado Ranger District
PO Box 159
Quemado, NM 87829
505-773-4678
The Quemado District is in the northernmost portion of the forest. Elevations in its 660,000 acres range from 6,600 feet to 9,700 feet. Popular activities here, in addition to horseback riding, include camping, hiking, and rockhounding.

Reserve Ranger District
PO Box 170
Reserve, NM 87830
505-533-6232
The Reserve Ranger District encompasses 573,537 acres in the northern portion of the forest. It features 155 miles of trails, including 55 miles on the Continental Divide. The district borders the Gila Wilderness to the south.

Silver City Ranger District
2005 E. Camino del Bosque
Silver City, NM 88061
505-388-8201
Silver City is the southernmost district of the forest. It comprises three areas—the Burro Mountain region, the area around Silver City, and a portion of the Black Range—which make up its 402,972 acres of forestland, and the district provides a variety of recreational opportunities. The Gila National Forest supervisor's office is at this address.

Wilderness Ranger District
HC68 Box 50
Mimbres, NM 88049
505-536-2250
As its name implies, the 900,000-acre Wilderness Ranger District, in the heart of the forest, is composed mainly of wilderness land. The Gila and Aldo Leopold wilderness areas make up the majority of this district's acreage. The Gila Cliff Dwellings are located in this district.

Gila National Forest is managed by six different ranger districts that can provide information on specific riding trails in their areas. Overall, the forest contains almost 1,500 miles of trails suitable for horseback riding. All the trails either follow or crisscross the river; some places are rocky, and some places are steep. Camping is allowed in several campgrounds on a first-come, first-served basis. In nonwilderness areas, you'll find corrals and trailheads with trailer parking. Other campgrounds also allow horses but do not have any horse facilities, so pickets or portable corrals may be used. Check with the ranger district you are visiting, or go to the Gila National Forest Web site (http://www2.srs.fs.fed.us/r3/gila) for detailed information on campgrounds. And for riders and horses venturing farther into the wilderness, there is also backcountry camping.

OKLAHOMA

ROBBERS CAVE STATE PARK
Robbers Cave State Park, located in the woodlands of the San Bois Mountains of southeastern Oklahoma, earned its

Riding in Robbers Cave

Robbers Cave

name honestly. The namesake cave within the park allegedly was the hideout of infamous outlaws Jesse James and his gang, Frank James, Belle Starr, and others. It was probably a convenient place to stash loot, since it's close to the Texas and California roads and the Butterfield Stage Line, which were preyed on by many an outlaw. Prior to these outlaws' use of the cave, Civil War deserters from both the Union and the Confederacy are said to have hidden here in the rugged terrain. The cave's secluded location in rocky hills and cliffs up to 1,500 feet in height would certainly offer an attractive sanctuary for people not wishing to be found.

Long before desperados and deserters used the cave, it was the home of early native peoples. A spring ran through the cave, so water was plentiful, and it offered strong shelter from the elements. Later Native American tribes also lived here, and they traded with French fur trappers, who were the first nonnatives to pass through the area.

Robbers Cave State Park itself consists of 8,246 acres, including 189 acres of lakes. The lakes include Carlton,

Across the expanse at Robbers Cave

Wayne, Wallace, and Coon Creek. The adjoining wildlife management area adds another 3,800 acres for recreational enjoyment. Predictably, with its natural amenities, it is favored for rock climbing and rappelling from its sandstone cliffs, as well as for fishing, swimming, and boating its bodies of water. Bass, crappie, sunfish, rainbow trout, and catfish can be caught. In addition to the lakes, there is an outdoor swimming pool. Hikers will enjoy the 12-mile trail system, offering nature walks near the notorious Robbers Cave. If you're feeling adventurous, you can take the stone trail, built by the Civilian Conservation Corp, which leads to the cave and above it for a scenic view of the surrounding mountains and valleys. There is also a nature center that was also built by the corp out of natural stone.

Just as the outlaws who hid here long ago rode into the area on horseback, so can you. Equestrians will find more than 60 miles of marked horse trails in the park and in the adjoining wildlife management area (note that some of the management area trails

SNAPSHOT - ROBBERS CAVE STATE PARK

Description: These days you can't hide out in Robbers Cave, but you can stay overnight in the park with your horse. There is an equestrian campground with facilities for horses, and the park also offers camping and other lodging options for visitors without horses. There is a small grocery store at the park that is open year-round; it is mainly convenient for purchasing snacks and some sundries. For groceries and fast-food restaurants, visit the nearby town of Wilburton. Starr D Outfitters and Riding Stables (918-564-5200), located inside the park, rents horses and provides other outings such as trail rides and chuck wagon trips.

Open: Year-round

Address: PO Box 9, Wilburton, OK 74578

Phone: 918-465-2565/800-654-8240

Web site: http://www.touroklahoma.com

Getting there: 5 miles north of Wilburton on Highway 2

Fees/permits: Admission is free

Horse rentals: Available in the park

Horse camping: Available in the park

Trail conditions/level of difficulty: Most are easy to moderate; a few difficult

A wide trail at Robbers Cave State Park

may be closed during hunting season). Some of the wide variety of wildlife you can marvel at as you ride through the pine-forest trails include white-tailed deer, foxes, opossums, and a variety of birds, including cardinals, blue jays, pileated woodpeckers, and turkey vultures.

TEXAS

GUADALUPE MOUNTAINS NATIONAL PARK

Ever wonder what the view from the top of Texas looks like? You can find out by visiting Guadalupe Mountains National

SNAPSHOT - GUADALUPE MOUNTAINS NATIONAL PARK

Description: Guadalupe Mountains National Park is located in West Texas near the Texas and New Mexico border. Horses are not allowed in the park overnight; riders and horses must return before nightfall to one of the two trailhead corral locations for overnight camping. There are no concessions in or near the park so you must bring your own food when riding at Guadalupe. There is water at the trailheads, but it's not available on the trails so be sure to take plenty for both you and your horse when riding. The closest dining and grocery facilities, as well as gas stations, to the park are 35 miles northeast in White's City.

Open: Year-round

Address: HC 60 Box 400, Salt Flat, TX 79847

Phone: 915-828-3251

Web site: http://www.nps.gov/gumo

Getting there: Located 55 miles southwest of Carlsbad and 110 miles east of El Paso; can be accessed via US Highway 62/180 between Carlsbad, New Mexico, and El Paso, Texas

Fees/permits: Admission is $3 per person for a seven-day pass; a backcountry permit is required for horse use

Horse rentals: None

Horse camping: Available at the trailheads only

Trail conditions/level of difficulty: Some flat and easy to moderate, most difficult (with rocks, high elevation); horses must be shod

Park. Opened as a national park in 1972, this rugged land rises starkly and dramatically out of the Chihuahuan Desert. Its elevations range from 3,600 to 8,749 feet. The land is difficult to classify because of its diversity; some scientists identify at least four general environmental habitats in its 86,000-plus

Guadalupe Mountains National Park

acres. Traveling upward, succulent and shrub deserts give way to semiarid grasslands, then to mixed woodlands, and, finally, to coniferous forests at its highest elevations.

The park's very tallest elevation, and the highest point in Texas, is the 8,749-foot Guadalupe Peak, a favorite destination for hikers. Another popular spot is the beautiful and ecologically diverse McKittrick Canyon, where many of the park's landscapes converge for a unique combination of plant and animal life. Perhaps, however, the park's most geologically well-known and striking feature is El Capitan, a solid cliff of limestone rising 1,000 feet straight up into

TRAILS OF GUADALUPE

To help riders determine the best rides for themselves and their horses, the trails at Guadalupe are classified by the National Park Service as easy, moderate, or difficult. Easy trails are easy to follow and have a gentle grade. Moderate trails are recommended for intermediate riders and horses who are conditioned to mountain trails. They have steeper grades, are rockier, and may require dismounts. Difficult trails require advanced trail riders and stock who can handle rugged mountain terrain. These trails have steep grades, have narrow sections, and can be hard to follow; they require specific knowledge of the trail or experience riding similarly difficult trails. Contact the Park Service for trail maps.

Guadalupe landscape

Easy: Foothills Trail, Williams Ranch Road, Frijole Trail

Moderate: Bush Mountain Trail: Dog Canyon to Marcus Trail, and Marcus Trail; Tejas Trail: Dog Canyon to Pine Top; McKittrick Canyon Trail: Tejas Trail to McKittrick Ridge Campground; El Capitan Trail: Pine Springs to Salt Basin Overlook, and the lower loop of Salt Basin Overlook Trail

Difficult: Tejas Trail: Pine Springs to Pine Top; Bush Mountain Trail: Pine Top to Bush Mountain Campground; Guadalupe Peak Trail; El Capitan Trail: Salt Basin Overlook to Williams Ranch

The majestic mountains

the air. The Guadalupe Mountains stretch northeast from the national park almost to Carlsbad, New Mexico. They are an uplifted portion of the Capitan marine fossil reef, built by sponges, algae, and other organisms, 250 million years ago. Geologists from around the globe visit the area to study the reef and to contemplate a time when this land was completely underwater, rather than the arid landscape it is today.

It was a geologist—although a petroleum geologist—who donated the initial land that became Guadalupe Mountains National Park. Wallace Pratt fell in love with McKittrick Canyon and purchased land there in the 1930s. In the late 1950s, he donated more than 5,600 acres to the National Park Service. Pratt's land, along with 70,000 acres purchased from J. C. Hunter Jr.'s Guadalupe Mountain Ranch, combined to form the park, which opened in 1972. Pratt died in 1981 at the age of ninety-six, and in accordance with his final wishes, his ashes were spread in the canyon.

Long before Wallace Pratt arrived in the area, humans had found sanctuary here. In fact, the human history of the park stretches back more than twelve thousand years to a prehistoric hunter-gatherer people, whose stone tools, bone fragments, and mescal pits have been used by archaeologists to reconstruct their lives in that long-ago time. Thousands of years later, the Apache lived in McKittrick Canyon, taking advantage of its wealth of food, water, and shelter. Over the years, set-

Riding solo

tlers, cattlemen, and stagecoach lines—including the original Butterfield Stage Line—moved in, and by the late 1800s all the Apache had been driven out. Helping the United States control the Apache in Guadalupe and in other areas of the country were the Buffalo Soldiers. These African-American regiments of soldiers were given their moniker by the Cheyenne for their appearance and fighting spirit.

You can almost feel the spirits of Guadalupe's previous inhabitants when you visit this quiet wilderness and ride its miles of trails. The only sounds you're likely to hear aside from the soft clip-clop of your horse's hooves are the call of the wind, the chirping of birds, and the quick rustle of animals in the brush. Of the park's 85 miles of trails, 50 percent are open to horses for day trips. Horses must be shod, as almost all

Beware of rattlesnakes.

Cattle once ruled in Hill Country SNA.

the trails are made of rocky material. Many of the park's trails are steep and narrow, so your horse must be in shape for rugged riding conditions. To prevent trail damage and to reduce conflicts with hikers, only one horse party (with no more than ten stock animals) is permitted on the same trail at the same time. (Bikes are not permitted on the trails.)

HILL COUNTRY STATE NATURAL AREA

When Louise Merrick, the final owner of the Bar O Ranch in the rugged Texas Hill Country, donated her ranch to the state, it was with the requirement that the land "be kept far removed and untouched by modern civilization, where everything is preserved intact, yet put to a useful purpose." The 5,370-acre Hill Country State Natural (SNA) Area, which opened to the public in 1984, is just such a place.

Located 45 miles northwest of San Antonio in Bandera and Medina counties, and near the city of Bandera (which bills itself as The Cowboy Capital of the World and offers many Old West activities, including twice a week rodeos in summer), Hill Country SNA is an undeveloped backcountry retreat for horse riders seeking their own Texas cowboy experience. As you ride its 40 miles of multiuse trails (hikers, mountain bikers, and wildlife watchers share the trails with equestrians), you might imagine that you hear the longhorns sounding in the distance.

With an elevation that climbs to 2,000 feet, the trails meander through verdant valleys, across flowing streams, through quiet canyons, and up limestone hills. The landscape includes oak groves and chaparrals, wildflowers, and

Hill Country trail

Hill Country at dusk

waterfalls. Armadillos, white-tailed deer, feral hogs, ringtail cats, jackrabbits, rattlesnakes, and various types of birds live in the park. Monarch butterflies migrate through the area in autumn, filling the sky with the fluttering of their delicate wings. Limited numbers of largemouth bass, catfish, and perch can be caught in the park's springs and swimming holes.

Bar O, the ranch that became the natural area, was a working cattle ranch from 1856 until the mid-1970s. After being given to the state, the land was allowed to revert to its natural and wild condition in keeping with its previous owner's wishes. The main ranch house, built in 1916, is still there and is now used by the park manager. Because it is a primitive area, park employees have a saying, "if you think you need it, we don't got it, you'll need to bring it." Riders will need to bring plenty of water for themselves, although the park's springs offer potable water for horses.

The park also offers horse facilities. There is a day-use facility called Bar O, situated on 6 shaded acres and located across from the park's headquarters, that is set up for equestrian use. It features a horse-washing area, water trough, and some pens and hitching posts. There are also fire rings and a chemical toilet. In addition to the day-use area, there are horse camps and a group lodge for equestrian or non-equestrian use.

SNAPSHOT - HILL COUNTRY STATE NATURAL AREA

Description: The park itself was once a working cattle ranch and is now a haven for riders seeking a quiet, undeveloped trail-riding locale. Horse campsites in the natural area as well as many dude ranches can accommodate both riders and their horses. For information on other lodging and dude ranches in the area, call the Bandera County Convention and Visitors Bureau at 800-364-3883 or go to http://www.banderacowboycapital.com. There are no horse rentals directly in the park, but you can rent horses for guided rides in the park from several dude ranches in the area, including the adjoining Running R Guest Ranch (see Where to Stay & Stable). If you are camping, you must bring in your own food and water, as there are no restaurants or grocery facilities at the park.

Open: Twenty-four hours a day, seven days a week February through November; 12:00 p.m. Friday through 10:30 p.m. Sunday in December and January

Address: 10600 Bandera Creek Road, Bandera, TX 78003

Phone: 830-796-4413

Web site: http://www.tpwd.state.tx.us/spdest/findadest/parks/hill_country

Getting there: From San Antonio: Take Highway 16 North to Bandera, then take State Highway 173 South, go approximately .25 mile to State Highway 1077, turn right, and go 10 miles to the park.

Fees/permits: Admission is $6 per day for people over twelve, no charge for children twelve and under, $3 for Texas residents who are sixty-five and older

Horse rentals: Available locally

Horse camping: Available in the park

Trail conditions/level of difficulty: Easy to difficult

UTAH

ZION NATIONAL PARK

In 1909, this park was originally established as Mukuntuweap National Monument. Then, in 1918, it became Zion National Monument and was expanded to a national park the following year to what is now the 146,597-acre Zion National Park. *Zion* is a Hebrew word for "a place of safety or refuge." The largest canyon in the park, which has a depth of 2,500 feet and is 6.5 miles long and up to .25 mile wide, was given the name Zion by Mormon settlers in the 1860s. The settlers came to the area from Salt Lake City in large numbers during the Civil War years. Because of the war, cotton was no longer available, so they came here to grow it. Today, the area of towns surrounding the park is still known as Utah's Dixie.

Located in three counties in southwestern Utah, Zion National Park encompasses dramatic canyon scenery that includes sheer vertical cliffs of Navajo sandstone, spectacular gorges, and colorful mesas. Massive monoliths such as The Temple of Sinawava, Weeping Point, and Angels Landing were carved over the millennia by the

Zion rock formations

relentless movement of the Virgin River and its tributaries, which transfer an average of 1 million tons of sediment per year. The park has 160 miles of rivers and streams. It rises in elevation to a towering 8,726 feet at Horse Ranch Mountain in its northern end, with low desert in its southern section.

Although you'll marvel at the park's incredible stone features, you'll also be amazed by the plant and animal life found here. With approximately 900 species of plants, Zion National Park is home to more diverse flora than any other area in Utah. There are also 78 species of mammals, 290 species of birds, 44 species of reptiles and

Zion National Park

amphibians, and 8 types of fish. Road-runners; Mexican spotted owls; pere-grine falcons; the endemic, and rare, Zion Snail; and many other interesting creatures are found here. Although rarely seen, there are a significant number of cougars in the park who survive by culling the mule deer population also found here.

Cougar on the prowl

Not all of these people are out on the trails, though. Many take the park's popular shuttle bus tour of the Zion Canyon Scenic Drive, which is worth the trip if you have the time. Only the buses, pedestrians, and bikers are allowed on this road.

Wildlife watching, hiking, biking, rock climbing, and, of course, horseback riding are popular activities at Zion. When visiting this park, it is wise to make lodging or camping arrangements far ahead of time since the park attracts many visitors. An average of 2.5 million people have come here each year for the past ten years, and during the peak months of July and August, eleven thousand people visited per day.

Happily for equestrians, the farther you go into the backcountry, the smaller the crowds. Trails that are open to horses include those in Hop Valley and Wildcat Canyon, the West and East Rim trails, and Sandbench, which is accessed through the main entrance and open November through February only. Riding parties are limited to a maximum of six horses. Contact the Kolob Canyons Visitor Center (435-586-9548) or park headquarters (435-772-3256) for overnight permits.

SNAPSHOT - ZION NATIONAL PARK

Description: Visitors to this dramatic and magical place enjoy hiking, backpacking, climbing, bird watching, and horseback riding. Backcountry camping is allowed, and you can bring your own horse or rent a horse for guided one-hour or half-day trips from the local livery: Canyon Trail Rides (PO Box 128, Tropic, UT 84776; 435-679-8665; http://www.canyon rides.com). Contact the Visitor Center for private stock use. Nearby Springdale, Mt. Carmel Junction, and Kanab offer restaurants as well as groceries and supplies.

Open: Year-round

Address: SR-9, Springdale, UT 84767

Phone: Park headquarters and Zion Canyon Visitor Center: 435-772-3256; Backcountry information: 435-772-0170; Kolob Canyons Visitor Center: 435-586-9548

Web site: http://www.nps.gov/zion

Getting there: Entrance is accessible via I-15, exit 40; I-15 passes west of the park and connects with UT-9 and UT-17 to the park; US-89 passes east and connects with UT-9 to the park; south entrance is off UT-9 adjacent to Springdale

Fees/permits: Admission is $20 per vehicle for a seven-day pass; $10 per vehicle for Kolob Canyons section only; no permits required to bring horses in for day use; $10 permit fee for overnight horse camping, limited to one night in any location

Horse rentals: Available from a local livery that operates in the park

Horse camping: Available in the park

Trail conditions/level of difficulty: Moderate

OTHER GREAT PLACES TO RIDE

Arizona

Petrified Forest National Park

1 Park Road, Petrified Forest, AZ 86028
928-524-6228
http://www.nps.gov/pefo
Petrified Forest National Park contains one of the world's most colorful and largest concentrations of petrified wood. The park more than doubled in size in 2004, when 125,000 acres were added, for a grand total of 218,522 acres. Riders can enjoy its beautiful wilderness area, and overnight backpacking is available with a free permit. There are no campgrounds or lodging in the park.

New Mexico

Carson National Forest

208 Cruz Alta Road, Taos, NM 87571
505-758-6200
http://www.fs.fed.us/r3/carson
You can ride seemingly forever in the 1.5-million-acre Carson National Forest and enjoy backcountry camping. The forest contains the highest point in New Mexico, the 13,161-foot Wheeler Peak.

Oklahoma

Great Salt Plains State Park

Route 1 Box 28, Jet, OK 73749
580-626-4731/800-654-8240
http://www.touroklahoma.com
One of the state's most intriguing natural wonders is the salt plains, or "sea of salt," in this state park. The park has horse camps, and its flat multiuse trails are great for beginning trail riders.

Ouachita National Forest

Box 1270, Hot Springs, AR 71902
501-321-5202
http://www.fs.fed.us/r8/ouachita
The Ouachita National Forest encompasses 1.8 million acres in the Ouachita Mountains of southeastern Oklahoma and central Arkansas. The Winding Stair Mountain National Recreation Area, with a network of outstanding equestrian trails with horse camping, is located in LeFlore County, Oklahoma, in the northern section of the forest.

Texas

Caprock Canyons State Park and Trailway

PO Box 204, Quitaque TX 79255
806-455-1492
http://www.tpwd.state.tx.us/spdest/findadest/parks/caprock_canyons

This historic park includes a Native American buffalo kill and butchering site that is ten thousand years old. Today, it has the largest herd of bison found in the state. Riders can enjoy 14 miles of trails, and there are campgrounds with horse facilities. Horse rentals are also available here.

Lake Somerville State Park and Trailway

Birch Creek Unit, 14222 Park Road 57, Somerville, TX 77879
979-535-7763
Nails Creek and Trailway Unit, 6280 FM 180 Ledbetter, TX 78946
979-289-2392
http://www.tpwd.state.tx.us/spdest/findadest/parks/lake_somerville
The two units of this horse-friendly park, located east of Austin, connect and offer miles of trails for equestrian use. Both units have designated equestrian campgrounds with corrals, water, and electricity.

Utah

Grand Staircase-Escalante National Monument

Bureau of Land Management, Kanab Resource Area Office, 318 North 100 East, Kanab, UT 84741
435-644-2672
http://www.ut.blm.gov/monument/
Visitor_Information/visitor_information.html
This 1.9-million-acre monument is located approximately 290 miles south of Salt Lake City in southwestern Utah. Riders will enjoy this wild and primitive area.

Portable pens

SOUTHWEST TRAVEL SECTION

IF YOU ARE TRAVELING WITHOUT YOUR HORSE, OR IF YOUR HORSE IS BOARDED SAFELY AT A STABLE, ENJOY THE SITES IN THE NEIGHBORING TOWNS. BELOW, YOU'LL FIND A MILEAGE CHART LISTING THE DISTANCES BETWEEN THE TRAILS AND ALL THE AREAS DISCUSSED IN THE FOLLOWING TRAVEL SECTION. THE AREAS CLOSEST TO THE TRAILS ARE INDICATED BY AN **X**. FOR AREAS WHERE NEITHER STABLING NOR HORSE RENTALS ARE AVAILABLE, NO SIGHTSEEING OPTIONS ARE LISTED.

COAST TO COAST	Grafton, Utah	Oracle, Ariz.	San Antonio, Tex.	Silver City, N.M.	Spiro, Okla.	Tucson, Ariz.	Williams, Ariz.
Catalina State Park (Ariz.)	505 miles	**X** 20 miles	885 miles	215 miles	1245 miles	**X** 20 miles	285 miles
Gila National Forest (N.Mex.)	545 miles	275 miles	815 miles	**X** 110 miles	945 miles	260 miles	335 miles
Grand Canyon National Park (Ariz.)	255 miles	345 miles	1230 miles	415 miles	1130 miles	340 miles	**X** 60 miles
Guadalupe Mountains National Park (Tex.)	945 miles	465 miles	500 miles	**X** 265 miles	775 miles	425 miles	735 miles
Hill Country State Natural Area (Tex.)	1365 miles	885 miles	**X** 70 miles	670 miles	600 miles	845 miles	1140 miles
Robbers Cave State Park (Okla.)	1275 miles	1140 miles	480 miles	945 miles	**X** 60 miles	1210 miles	1065 miles
Zion National Park (Utah)	**X** 20 miles	535 miles	1405 miles	590 miles	1305 miles	530 miles	305 miles

*The area to visit is the same as or is within 10 miles of the trails.

MUST SEE / MUST DO

ARIZONA

CATALINA STATE PARK AREA

Riders and other visitors to Catalina State Park can enjoy many other trails near Tucson. Other places to ride and hike include **Coronado National Forest** (300 W. Congress Street, Tucson, AZ 85701; 520-388-8300; http://www.fs.fed.us/r3/coronado),

A local prairie dog

Sagauro National Park (3693 South Old Spanish Trail, Tucson, AZ 85730; 520-733-5100; http://www.nps.gov/sagu), and **Oracle State Park** (3820 Wildlife Drive, Oracle, AZ 85623; 520-896-2425; http://www.pr.state.az.us/Parks/park html/oracle.html).

Coronado National Forest covers 1,780,000 acres in southeastern Arizona and southwestern New Mexico. It offers a variety of activities, including horseback riding, wildlife viewing, hiking, mountain biking, caving, and rock climbing. Saguaro National Park, open daily from 7:00 a.m. to sunset, has more than 150 miles of hiking trails. Or you can view the giant saguaro cacti by taking a leisurely drive on one of the park's scenic loops. Oracle State Park offers approximately 15 miles of hiking trails, tours of the historic Kannally Ranch House, and access to the Arizona Trail, open to horseback riders, bikers, and hikers. The park is open seven days a week, from 7:00 a.m. to 5:00 p.m. Entrance fees range from $2 to $6.

While in this area, you can also visit the **Arizona-Sonora Desert Museum** to learn more about the Sonoran desert ecosystem. It is located at 2021 North Kinney Road, Tucson, Arizona 85743; 520-883-2702; http://www.desertmuseum.org. From March through September, the museum is open from 7:30 a.m. to 5:00 p.m. (open until 10:00 p.m. on Saturday evenings June through August); from October through February, it's open from 8:30 a.m. to 5:00 p.m. Prices range from $9 to $12, depending on the season.

GRAND CANYON NATIONAL PARK

If you are visiting the area without a horse and want to arrive at the park in style, take the **Grand Canyon Railway**. The vintage train leaves from the town of Williams, Arizona, "The Gateway to the Grand Canyon," and heads to the Grand Canyon Village at the South Rim. Along the way, a mock train robbery and shootout occurs, and you'll also hear old-time melodies played by strolling musicians (233 N. Grand Canyon Blvd., Williams, AZ 86046; 800-84308724; http://www.thetrain.com). Rates for adults vary from $60 to $155 for a round-trip. The train departs daily at 10:00 a.m. for the Grand Canyon. It does not run on December 24 or 25. On your return to **Williams**, you can

Saguaro National Park

Along Route 66

explore that town and its historic district, including Route 66. Williams was the last town along the historic route to be bypassed by Interstate 40. In the town, you'll find hints of frontier days gone by, including restored saloons, bordellos, and shops from the town's colorful past. You can also visit the statue of trapper and mountain man Bill Williams, known as "Old Bill," for whom the town is named. For more information on the city of Williams, call 800-863-0546 or visit http://www.williamschamber.com.

At the canyon's South Rim, you can visit the **Tusayan Museum**, which is located 22 miles west of Grand Canyon Village. You'll learn what Pueblo Indian life was like at the canyon 800 years ago. The exhibit includes a self-guided walk through the adjacent ruins or a ranger-led tour. Ruin tours take place at 11:00 a.m. and 1:30 p.m. daily. The museum is open from 9:00 a.m. to 5:00 p.m.; admission is free (928-638-7888; http://www.nps.gov/grca/pphtml/facilities.html). Also at the South Rim, visit the **Yavapai Observation Station**, five miles north of the park's south entrance. The station contains temporary exhibits about fossils found in the canyon and also sells education materials related to the park and region. It is open all year, from 8:00 a.m. to 5:00 p.m.

Silver City

NEW MEXICO

GILA NATIONAL FOREST AREA

In addition to visiting Silver City for its historical value as a mining center, you can also enjoy Silver City's **Wild Wild West Pro Rodeo**, which takes place each June at the Southwest Horsemen's Park, located on US 180 East (505-388-5057; http://www.silvercity.org). Performances start at 7:00 p.m. Tickets are $10 in advance and $14 at the gate. In January each year is the **Red Paint PowWow**, a competition among Native Americans from across the continent held in recognition of the Chihene Apache of southwestern New Mexico. It is held in the Intramural Gym at Western New Mexico University (1000 West College Avenue, Silver City, NM 88061; 505-534-1379; http://www.silvercity.org). General admission is $5 per person per day.

OKLAHOMA

ROBBERS CAVE STATE PARK AREA

You can help kick off the fall season at Robbers Cave State Park. Each year, the **Robbers Cave Fall Festival and Car Show** is held in October. Activities include a car show, craft booths, a children's carnival, gospel and country-and-western music, and lots to eat. Contact the park for specific dates.

Northeast of Robbers Cave State Park is Oklahoma's only archaeological park, the 140-acre **Spiro Mounds**. The site contains twelve mounds with evidence of a Native American culture that occupied the site from 850 AD to 1450 AD. It is considered one of the most important prehistoric Indian sites east of the Rockies. Interpretive center hours are Tuesday through Saturday 9:00 a.m. to 5:00 p.m. and Sunday noon to 5:00 p.m. from May through October; Wednesday through

Saturday 9:00 a.m. to 5:00 p.m. and Sunday noon to 5:00 p.m. from November through April. Admission is free. For information, contact Spiro Mounds Archaeological Park, Route 2 Box 339A, Spiro, Oklahoma 74959; 918-962-2062; http://www.spiro.lib.ok.us/mounds.htm.

TEXAS

HILL COUNTRY STATE NATURAL AREA

When passing through San Antonio, be sure to visit **The Alamo** (300 Alamo Plaza, PO Box 2599, San Antonio, TX 78299; 210-225-1391; http://www.thealamo.org), where a small group of Texans, including Davy Crockett and Jim Bowie, held out for thirteen days against the army of General Antonio López de Santa Anna. Visitors can view the old mission where the Texans held out, walk through the Alamo gardens, and visit the Long Barrack Museum and the Gift Museum for exhibits on the Texas Revolution and the state's history. Admission is free, and The Alamo is open every day except Christmas and Christmas Eve, Monday through Saturday 9:00 a.m. to 5:30 p.m. and Sunday 10:00 a.m. to 5:30 p.m.; open until 7:00 p.m. Friday and Saturday in June, July, and August.

The Alamo

UTAH

ZION NATIONAL PARK AREA

In the shadow of Zion National Park is the ghost town of **Grafton**, established in 1859. Standing just south of the boundary of Zion, 1 mile from the approach road to the park, Grafton includes a combination schoolhouse and church, homes, and other buildings as well as a well-preserved cemetery with graves dating from the 1860s. Some of the gravestones tell the sad stories of Grafton residents, including a family of brothers all killed by Indians and several children from one family who all died before the age of nine years. Although Grafton is not easy to get to, it has been featured in several movies, including *Butch Cassidy and the*

Grafton ghost town

Sundance Kid (1969). To get there from nearby Rockville, cross the "historic bridge" on Bridge Street over the Virgin River, just south of Zion. Follow the road to the right for a couple of miles until it dead ends. Turn right at the No Outlet sign and drive 2 more miles to the ghost town. You'll pass the cemetery on your left. For more on Grafton and the move to preserve it, contact the Grafton Heritage Partnership Project, PO Box 630184, Rockville, Utah 83763; 435-635-2133; http://www.graftonheritage.org; http://www.americansouthwest.net/utah/zion/grafton_ghost_town.html.

WHERE TO STAY & STABLE

ARIZONA

CATALINA STATE PARK AREA

Horses and Riders:
Catalina State Park Equestrian Center
Located in the park
520-628-5798
http://www.pr.state.az.us/Parks/parkhtml/catalina/html
$15 per vehicle per night
The equestrian center campground includes picnic tables, barbecue grills, vault toilets, and water for people and horses. There are also pipe corrals and stalls. It is open year-round, seven days a week on a first-come, first-served basis.

Spirit Dog Ranch
13750 N. Bowman Road
Tucson, AZ 85739
520-237-4807
$20 per night, $5 for each additional horse; $115 per week, $30 for each additional horse; $350 per month, $100 for each additional horse
Spirit Dog Ranch, a private horse camp, is adjacent to Catalina State Park and has immediate access. It features sixteen RV sites with water, power, and sewer facilities as well as several with water and electric hookups only. There are two full bathhouses, two laundries, and a community room with a kitchen and Internet access. A group camp area accommodates approximately twenty rigs, with water and electric access scattered throughout the camp. The group camping area has a cooking tent with appliances, an eating area, two full bathrooms, and four tent-cabins with cots. For horses, forty-four large corrals with shade covers and automatic waterers, plus several open corrals are available. A hot-water horse wash rack is also available. Clean up after your horse, and bring your own hay and feed, although hay is available for purchase. Reservations are required.

Riders Only:
The Windmill Inn at St. Phillips Plaza
4250 North Campbell Avenue
Tucson, AZ 85718
866-613-9930
$99–$139 per night
The Windmill Inn offers 122 suites. You receive a complimentary morning newspaper, and there is a swimming pool to cool you off on those hot desert days as well as fully air-conditioned rooms. Pets are allowed.

GRAND CANYON NATIONAL PARK

Horses and Riders:
Bright Angel Campground
Bottom of Grand Canyon, .5 mile north of Colorado River along Bright Angel Creek
928-638-7875
http://www.nps.gov/grca/backcountry/campgrounds/bright_angel_cbg.htm
Backcountry Permit fee of $10 for the horseback group, plus $5 for each horse and $5 for each rider per night
Bright Angel Campground is accessible from the Bright Angel Trail and the South Kaibab Trail in the South Rim and from the North Kaibab Trail in the North Rim. The camp has running water and toilets and is shaded by cottonwood trees.

Cottonwood Campground
Seven miles below the North Rim, near the entrance to Manzanita Canyon
928-638-7875
http://www.nps.gov/grca/backcountry/campgrounds/bright_angel_cbg.htm
Backcountry Permit fee of $10 for the horseback group, plus $5 for each horse and $5 for each rider per night
Cottonwood Campground can be reached from the North Kaibab Trail in the North Rim. Drinking water is available from mid-May to mid-October. It is near Bright Angel Creek, and this water can be filtered and treated for drinking when potable water at the campground is not available.

Riders Only

El Tovar Hotel
South Rim of Grand Canyon
Xanterra Parks and Resorts
888-297-2757/Same-day reservations: 928-638-2631
http://www.grandcanyonlodges.com
$122–$299 per night
The most upscale lodging at the Grand Canyon, El Tovar has seventy-eight rooms and suites with cable television, air-conditioning, and other amenities. Opened in 1905 and renovated in 2005, the hotel has hosted many dignitaries throughout the years including Albert Einstein, Teddy Roosevelt, and author Zane Grey. In addition to El Tovar, the South Rim has several other lodgings, all managed through Xanterra Parks and Resorts. They include the Bright Angel Lodge, Thunderbird Lodge, Kachina Lodge, Maswick Lodge, and Yavapai Lodge. Rates vary from $55 to $132 depending on the lodge and room choice.

Grand Canyon Lodge
North Rim of Grand Canyon
Xanterra Parks and Resorts
918-638-2611
http://www.grandcanyonnorthrim.com
$90 and up per night
The Grand Canyon Lodge, on the canyon's quieter, less visited North Rim side, is listed as a National Historic Landmark. It is the only in-park lodging on the North Rim. It features both rooms and cabins as well as a sunroom, gift shop, and more. Open seasonally, mid-May through mid-October.

Phantom Ranch
Bottom of Grand Canyon, beside Bright Angel Creek
Xanterra Parks and Resorts
888-297-2757/Same-day reservations: 928-638-2631
http://www.grandcanyonlodges.com
$28 per night per person

Phantom Ranch is the only lodging available below the canyon's rim. It can be reached only by mule (see photo) or horseback, by hiking, or by raft via the Colorado River. Accommodations consist of dormitory beds and cabins, with separate dormitories for men and women. Cabins are available to riders on the overnight mule trips, and dormitory accommodations are available to hikers and others.

NEW MEXICO

GILA NATIONAL FOREST AREA

Horses and Riders:

Aeroplane Mesa Campgrounds
Located in the forest
Reserve Ranger District
505-533-6231
http://www2.srs.fs.fed.us/r3/gila
No fee
This campground features tent sites, vault toilets, grills, picnic tables, and fire rings. There are no RV hookups or designated RV sites. There are four horse corrals with ample trailer parking across the road. Open from May through November.

Bear Mountain Lodge
PO Box 1163
Silver City, NM 88062
877-620-BEAR/505-538-2538
http://www.bearmountainlodge.com
$115–$185 per night double occupancy, $95–$180 single occupancy; $15 per night for horse boarding, two-night minimum
Built in 1928 as the Rocky Mountain Ranch School, Bear Mountain Lodge became a dude ranch in 1938. Then in 1959, ownership passed on to Myra McCormick, an avid birder, and she donated it to The Nature Conservancy prior to her death in 1999. Renovated in 2000, the lodge features eleven guest rooms located in three buildings: the Lodge, Myra's Retreat, and the Wren's Nest. Hardwood floors run throughout the lodge, and all tables, chairs, headboards, and armoires are made from small-diameter trees cut as part of a forest restoration project. Rates include home-cooked breakfast and snacks of cookies and fruit; lunch and dinner are available for an extra fee and by prior arrangement. There is a $15 charge per night for each person over double occupancy, and no children under ten years are allowed.

Double T Homestead
PO Box 358
Glenwood, NM 88039
505-539-2812
http://www.doublethomestead.com
$20 per night for RV park; $60 per night for two people, $7 per night for each additional person for the cabin, sleeps five; $60–$75 per night for two people, $5–$10 per night each additional person for guest houses; $30 per stall for horses
Stay in an authentic homestead with various choices of lodging. An RV park accommodates travelers with rigs, or you can stay in the cabin or in one of the guesthouses, which come with kitchens and satellite television. There is a historic adobe house on site, and it can be rented for special occasions. Horses are welcome here and stay in covered or uncovered pipe stalls. Visitors with horses may use the round pen and the barn for storing tack and feed.

El Caso Throwdown
Located in the forest
Quemado Ranger District
505-773-4678
http://www2.srs.fs.fed.us/r3/gila
No fee
This partially developed campground outside Quemado Lake Recreation Area is primarily for equestrian use. Although it has no specific horse facilities such as corrals or stalls, the campground is a good base for people wishing to ride in the area. The

Quemado Lake Recreation Area itself does not allow horses. There are vault toilets and space available for parking self-contained rigs.

TJ and Woody's Corrals
Located in the forest approximately 1 mile from Gila Cliff Dwellings National Monument
505-536-9461 (the Cliff Dwellings National Monument)
http://www.nps.gov/gicl
No fee
These horse corrals, which are next to each other, are available on a first-come, first-served basis, and horse owners can camp at the corral sites. There are toilets and running water. Campers staying at area campgrounds may also use the corrals for their horses, but there is no oversight of the corrals.

Upper Scorpion
Located in the forest
Wilderness Ranger District
505-536-9461
http://www2.srs.fs.fed.us/r3/gila
No fee
Upper Scorpion is the campground nearest to the Gila Cliff Dwellings National Monument at .5 mile away. It offers tent camping, flush toilets, water, picnic tables, grills, and a horse corral.

Valle Tio Vinces
Located in the forest
Quemado Ranger District near Aragon
505-773-4678
http://www2.srs.fs.fed.us/r3/gila
No fee
There are picnic tables, vault toilets, tent camping, fire rings, and eight horse corrals. Water availability is dependent on current conditions in the area. There are no RV hookups, so RVs must be self-contained.

OKLAHOMA

ROBBERS CAVE STATE PARK AREA

Horses and Riders

Robbers Cave State Park Equestrian Camp
Located in the park
918-465-2565/Reservations: 800-654-8240
http://www.touroklahoma.com
$15 per night for standard site, $18 for preferred location
The horse camp features a limited number of electrical hookups as well as restrooms and hot showers. The grassy area features hitching posts, picnic tables, and shady trees. Reservations are highly recommended.

Riders Only

Belle Star View Lodge & Park Cabins
Located in the park
918-465-2562/Reservations: 800-654-8240
http://www.touroklahoma.com
$58–$78 per night
The Belle Star View Lodge features twenty rooms with views (see photo) and cozy comfort. Double and single king bedrooms are available.

There are twenty-six cabins with either one or two bedrooms. All cabins have fireplaces. Reservations are highly recommended.

Robbers Cave State Park Campsites
Located in the park
918-465-2565/Reservations: 800-654-8240
http://www.touroklahoma.com
$7 per night for a primitive site; $13–$16 for a site with water and electricity; $18 for a preferred location with water, sewer, and electricity
In addition to the equestrian camp, the park features two sites for RV and tent camping, and two group campsites. There are a total of 122 campsites. The campgrounds are open year-round; reservations are highly recommended.

TEXAS

GUADALUPE MOUNTAINS NATIONAL PARK AREA

Horses and Riders:
Dog Canyon
Dog Canyon Ranger Station, located on the north side of the park and accessed via New Mexico State Road 137
505-981-2418
$8 per night per site
Dog Canyon lies in a secluded forested canyon on the north side of the park. There are four corrals at Dog Canyon, accommodating a total of ten horses. Vehicles are parked in designated locations near the corrals, and horse owners are required to camp by the corrals to be near their animals. There are no RV hookups, but there are flush toilets. Water is available for horses. Reservations are required.

Frijole Ranch
Located near the park headquarters visitor center
915-828-3251, ext. 0
$8 per night per campsite
The Frijole Ranch corrals offer tent pads and RV camping with no hookups to visitors. Like Dog Canyon, it has four corrals and can hold ten horses. Stock owners must camp near the corrals and their animals. Reservations are preferred.

HILL COUNTRY STATE NATURAL AREA

Horses and Riders:
Bar O
Located in the park
830-796-4413
http://www.tpwd.state.tx./spdest/findadest/parks/hill_country
$10 per night
The 6-acre Bar O developed equestrian area is located near park headquarters. It is also used as the day-use staging area for horses and riders. There are fourteen portable stalls, fire rings, a water trough, a horse-wash area, and a primitive toilet. This site is available on a first-come, first-served basis and allows a combination of six people and horses per site.

Chapas Camp
Located in the park
830-796-4413/800-792-1112
http://www.tpwd.state.tx.us/spdest/findadest/parks/hill_country/fee.phtml
$100 per night

Chapas Camp offers a group site that is on two acres near a swimming hole. It can accommodate up to twenty trailers. The camp has a concrete-floor barn with stalls for nine horses, picket lines, electricity, water troughs, chemical toilets, fire rings, picnic tables, and shade trees.

Group Lodge
Located in the park
830-796-4413
http://www.tpwd.state.tx.us/spdest/findadest/parks/hill_country/
$250 per night
The group lodge sleeps twelve people and is available for both equestrian and non-equestrian use. It is a 1930s ranch house with four bedrooms, one bath, a kitchen, heating and air-conditioning, and more. The lodge can accommodate up to twelve horses in stalls and corrals. There is a cooking shack with a barbecue pit, a picnic table, and a fire ring. Tent camping is allowed outside the lodge.

Hill Country State Natural Area Trailhead Equestrian Camp
Located in the park
830-796-4413
http://www.tpwd.state.tx./spdest/findadest/parks/hill_country
$10 per night, combination of six people/horses per site
The trailhead equestrian camp has six sites, each with the capacity of a combined six people and six horses. It features picnic tables, fire rings, a chemical toilet, corrals, and water for horses. People must bring their own drinking water; water is available for horses.

Running R Guest Ranch
9059 Bandera Creek Road
Bandera, TX 78003
830-796-3984
http://www.rrranch.com
$105–$115 per night per person, double occupancy, includes two meals a day and two hours of horseback riding; call for current prices for horse accommodations
Enjoy the atmosphere of the Old West at the Running R Guest Ranch, which accommodates riders with and without horses. You can ride on the ranch and on the adjoining Hill Country State Natural Area. Guests stay in modernized rustic cabins or in the bunkhouse. In addition to riding, guests can swim, play Ping-Pong, pitch horseshoes, enjoy a country cookout, and more. Guest horses stay in outside pens or in covered stalls. Guided horse rentals are also available for visitors to the area who are not staying at the ranch.

UTAH

ZION NATIONAL PARK AREA

Horses and Riders

Hop Valley Camp (Camp A)
Located in the park, accessible through the Kolob Canyons entrance to the park or from Kolob Reservoir Road
435-586-9548, backcountry information
http://www.nps.gov/zion
Overnight permit fee of $10 for one to two people, $15 for three to six people, $20 for seven to twelve people; maximum of six horses per party
This is the only campground in the park that allows horses and has hitching posts. It is a primitive campground located in the Hop Valley.

Zion National Park Backcountry Camping
Located in the park
Kolob Canyons Visitor Center: 435-586-9548/ Park headquarters: 435-772-3256
http://www.nps.gov/zion
$10 overnight permit required (one-night only)
Off-trail areas open to stock animals include Coalpits Wash, Huber Wash, Scoggins
Wash, and Crater Hill. Riding parties are limited to six horses.

Riders Only:
Zion National Park Lodge
Located near the park's south entrance
Reservations: 888-297-2757 (Xanterra Parks & Resorts)/Same-day reservations: 435-772-7700
http://www.zionlodge.com/index.asp
$79–$148 per night, depending on the type of accommodation and the season
The lodge at Zion National Park is managed by Xanterra Parks & Resorts. Guests can
stay in comfortable historic cabins or in motel rooms. All cabins and rooms offer
porches or balconies as well as air-conditioning, hair dryers, and more.

WHERE TO WINE & DINE

ARIZONA

CATALINA STATE PARK AREA

Anthony's in the Catalinas
6440 N. Campbell Avenue
Tucson, AZ 85718
520-299-1771
http://www.anthonysinthecatalinas.com
$23.95 and up
If you are in the mood to splurge, try Anthony's in the Catalinas. This upscale restaurant in the foothills of the Catalina Mountains offers beautiful views and wonderful
cuisine, including duck, Kobe beef, and lobster fettuccine. The wine list includes
more than 1,700 entries ranging in price from $25 to $15,000 for a bottle.

Terra Cotta
3500 East Sunrise Drive
Tucson, AZ 85718
520-577-8100
http://www.dineterracotta.com
$8–$30

Terra Cotta offers an eclectic menu with a
southwestern flair. Interesting dishes such as
goat cheese–stuffed prawns and chipotle-
molasses-glazed chicken are sure to tempt
your taste buds. Accompany your dinner with
an icy margarita or a glass of wine. Lunch is
also served here, and although the portions
are smaller, the dishes are just as interesting
and tasty.

Ye Olde Lantern
1800 N. Oracle Road
Tucson, AZ 85705
520-622-6761

$16–$25
Founded in 1924, Ye Olde Lantern restaurant features American cuisine and specializes in prime rib. The restaurant also offers takeout. Live entertainment, including a piano player and monthly Dixieland and Hawaiian shows, rounds out the ambiance here.

GRAND CANYON NATIONAL PARK

Bright Angel Restaurant
South Rim of Grand Canyon
Xanterra Parks and Resorts
928-638-2631
http://www.grandcanyonlodges.com/Bright-Angel-419.html
$7.75 and up
This casual restaurant features a variety of meals, including burgers and sandwiches, steaks, pastas, and more. There is a wine list and full bar and Western and folk entertainment in the lounge. Seating is on a first-come, first-served basis. The restaurant is open year-round from 6:30 a.m. to 10:00 p.m.

El Tovar Dining Room and Lounge
South Rim of Grand Canyon
Xanterra Parks and Resorts
928-638-2631, ext. 6432
http://www.grandcanyonlodges.com/El-Tovar-421.html
$8.45 and up
A casual dress code and beautiful setting combined with fine food makes for an elegant yet relaxed atmosphere. The El Tovar Dining Room and Lounge offers a variety of delicious and unique dishes for breakfast, lunch, and dinner and features a wine list. Just some of the dinner entrées include wild Alaskan salmon tostada, broiled portobello Napoleon, and mesquite-smoked natural pork chop. Open daily 6:30 a.m. to 10:00 p.m. Reservations are highly recommended.

Grand Canyon Lodge & Dining Room
North Rim of Grand Canyon
Xanterra Parks and Resorts
918-638-2611, ext. 160
http://www.grandcanyonnorthrim.com/Grand-Canyon-Lodge-&-Dining-Room-838.html
$5–$28
The dining room offers fine dining and beautiful views overlooking the canyon. No need to dress up, though, as the dress code here is casual. Reservations are required for dinner and can be made up to two weeks prior to opening on May 10. Like the lodge, the restaurant is open seasonally, from mid-May to mid-October. During the season, it is recommended that reservations be made two months in advance. It is open daily, 6:30 a.m. to 9:45 p.m., though hours may vary. In addition to the lodge restaurant, you'll find light fare at the Deli in the Pines and the Rough Rider Saloon at the lodge.

Market Plaza
Grand Canyon Village (South Rim)
Prices vary
You can visit the Canyon Village Marketplace and the Delicatessen at the Marketplace for groceries and other supplies. They are open daily, year-round. Canyon Village Marketplace is open from 8:00 a.m. to 7:00 p.m. The Delicatessen is open from 8:00 a.m. until 6:00 p.m.

Phantom Ranch Canteen
Bottom of Grand Canyon, beside Bright Angel Creek
Xanterra Parks and Resorts

928-638-2631
http://www.grandcanyonlodges.com/Phantom-Ranch-Canteen-712.html
$9–$31
The Canteen serves breakfast and dinner at specific seating times. Steak, stew, and vegetarian options are available for dinner. Sack lunches are available anytime. Reservations for meals must be made well in advance of your descent into the canyon if you are traveling down on your own. Riders on the mule trips will have dinner reserved for them. Open April 1 through October 31 from 8:00 a.m. to 4:00 p.m. and 8:00 p.m. to 10:00 p.m.; opens November 1 through March 31 at 8:30 a.m.

NEW MEXICO

GILA NATIONAL FOREST AREA

The Daily Pie Café
Pie Town, north of the Gila National Forest off of Highway 60
505-772-2700
http://www.dailypie.com
$5–$18
For a slice of local ambiance, visit the Daily Pie Café in Pie Town for, you guessed it, a slice of delicious pie. Pie Town is said to have been established in the 1920s by a miner who also opened a general store that sold fresh-baked pies. The café also serves seafood, steaks, chicken, chops, and more to hungry visitors.

Doc Campbell's Post
Route 11, Box 80
Silver City, NM 88061
505-536-9551
Prices vary
If you're camping near the Cliff Dwellings National Monument, stop by Doc Campbell's Post, which was opened in the early 1960s by Dawson "Doc" Campbell, an influential inhabitant of the area since 1930, who died in 1998. The store, still family owned, sells groceries, gasoline, fishing and hunting licenses, and more. It also has a snack bar and offers homemade ice cream as well as gift items that reflect its southwestern locale.

OKLAHOMA

ROBBERS CAVE STATE PARK AREA

Kentucky Fried Chicken
413 West Main
Wilburton, OK 74578
918-465-3432
$4–$30
A national chain, Kentucky Fried Chicken serves up chicken and all the sides, to go.

Pizza Hut
805 Highway 2 North
Wilburton, OK 74578
918-465-2148
$3.25–$20.00
Another chain restaurant, this pizza place offers the usual pizzas and sides.

Roy's Cardinal Food Store
621 Highway 2 North
Wilburton, OK 74578
918-465-2452
Prices vary
You will find a full lineup of groceries and supplies at Roy's Cardinal Food Store.

Subway
209 West Main
Wilburton, OK 74578
918-465-2300
$2.50–$8.50
This international chain offers custom-made submarine sandwiches, salads, wraps, chips, beverages, and more.

TEXAS

HILL COUNTRY STATE NATURAL AREA

Fool Moon Café
204 Main Street
Bandera, TX 78003
830-460-8434
$6–$13 for lunch, $12–$30 for dinner
Fool Moon Café is a local favorite. The dinner menu changes every week, so call ahead. Choices include Mediterranean and local Texas fare. Also, if you enjoy wine with a nice meal, bring your own. Open for breakfast and lunch Tuesday through Saturday; dinner from 7:00 p.m. to 9:00 p.m. Friday and Saturday and brunch on Sunday. Reservations are required.

Old Spanish Trail
305 Main Street
Bandera, TX 78003
830-796-3836
$5–$18
The Old Spanish Trail restaurant, known as the O.S.T., is a local favorite. It opened in 1921 and features horse-saddle bar stools, a room of John Wayne photos, and plenty of hearty grub such as chicken fried steaks, burgers, and Mexican fare.

UTAH

ZION NATIONAL PARK AREA

Red Rock Grill
Located at the Zion Lodge, near the park's south entrance
435-772-7760
http://www.zionlodge.com
$3–$9 for breakfast; $6–$10 for lunch; $13–$21 for dinner
Located in the park, the Red Rock Grill serves pastas, seafood, steaks, and southwestern specialties. Box lunches are available, but you must order eight hours in advance. (Quick sandwiches and snacks can be purchased at the seasonal Castle Dome Café, also located at the lodge.) Reservations are required for dinner, but the dress is casual. The grill is open daily 6:30 a.m. to 9:00 p.m.; open until 10:00 p.m. in summer.

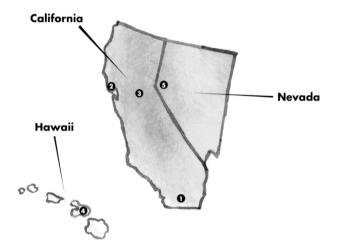

Far West Map Legend

California

❶ Anza-Borrego Desert State Park

❷ Point Reyes National Seashore

❸ Yosemite National Park

Hawaii

❹ Haleakala National Park, Maui

Nevada

❺ Washoe Lake State Park

THE FAR WEST

*y*ou'll find many trails for miles of happy riding in the diverse far western states of California, Hawaii, and Nevada.

Riding in California is like discovering a miniature world unto itself. You can trot among grand redwoods, giant sequoias, or towering palms; through fertile wine-country valleys or past golden pastures of grain; across sandy beaches and rocky shores; down winding mountain trails or flat desert roads. The list goes on and on. You'll find generally cooler, rainier weather in the northern part of the state and drier, sunnier weather in the south. And even though California has the largest population of any state in the country, it is still possible to escape on horseback and find solitude among its hundreds of state and national parks and national forests.

In Hawaii, the beauty of the tropics will enchant you. Its warm blue ocean, lush greenery, white sand beaches, and sunny weather, disturbed only by occasional warm rainstorms, will make you want to stay forever. You'll find many riding opportunities on the main islands of Hawaii, Oahu, Maui, and Kauai, and even on the less visited islands of Molokai and Lanai.

Aptly nicknamed the Silver State, Nevada is the country's largest producer of silver, gold, and mercury. However, the major contributor to Nevada's economy is tourism. And you'll know why once you visit. Although Nevada is well know for attracting people through its gambling towns such as Las Vegas (its largest city), Reno, and Lake Tahoe, it is also a land of beautiful recreational areas with many trails on which you can enjoy riding your horse.

CALIFORNIA

ANZA-BORREGO DESERT STATE PARK

At 600,000 acres, Southern California's Anza-Borrego Desert State Park is not only the largest of California's 278 state parks but also the largest state park in the Southwest. Located in eastern San Diego County, with portions extending into Riverside and Imperial counties, the park has more than 500 miles of dirt roads, miles of hiking trails, and twelve wilderness areas within its boundaries. It is truly an oasis, offering its visitors both solitude and the unusual and striking beauty of desert locales. And

Anza-Borrego Palms Oasis

although you may think of the desert as flat, the elevation of Anza-Borrego varies from 150 to 6,200 feet above sea level.

The park's name comes from two important elements of its past and present. *Anza* is from the Spanish explorer Juan Bautista de Anza, who passed through what is now the state park on his quest to open an overland route from Mexico to California's Pacific coast. He is credited with helping open up California to European colonists. In 1990, the United States Congress created the Juan Bautista de Anza National Historic Trail, which follows de Anza's colonizing expedition from Tubac, Arizona, to San Francisco, California. *Borrego* is the Spanish name for the desert bighorn sheep who live in the area. Although these endangered animals are rarely seen by park visitors, they are an important part of the desert's ecosystem.

Other wildlife living in the park include the roadrunner, the kit fox, the mule deer, the golden eagle, and, of course, the creatures who may most characterize the desert to some visitors: the reptiles. The park protects the largest concentration of lizards and snakes in the state, and there are more than fifty different reptile species here. A

Anza-Borrego desert

few of the reptilian inhabitants include the speedy zebra-tailed lizard, the country's fastest reptile, reaching speeds up to 18 miles per hour and the most often seen reptile at the park; the red diamond rattlesnake, which you'll want to see only from a safe distance; and the chuckwalla, a bulky, pear-shaped lizard. Wildflowers bloom from February through April, and cacti, palm groves, and hundreds of other desert plants characterize the park's vegetation.

Experiencing the wonders of the California desert is best done in the cooler seasons such as late fall, winter, and early spring. During the summer months, the temperature here often climbs over 120 degrees Fahrenheit, which can make physical activity dangerous; horseback riding is not recommended during this time. If you do visit during the summer, take it very slowly, and be sure to carry plenty of water, for both you and your horse. Even in springtime, you'll need to cover up and wear plenty of sunscreen as the daytime temperatures average 80–100 degrees Fahrenheit. In winter, daytime temper-

Cow skull and sand verbena

atures are comfortable, averaging around 70 degrees Fahrenheit, but nighttime temperatures can drop to freezing, so be prepared.

When traveling here with your horse, you'll find 110 miles of riding trails. Riders can use the equestrian trails in Coyote Canyon—the trailhead begins at the Vern Whitaker Horse Camp (these trails are closed in summer)—the 6-mile California Hiking and Riding Trail, the Pacific Crest Trail, and the primitive roads that wind

SNAPSHOT - ANZA-BORREGO DESERT STATE PARK

Description: Massive Anza-Borrego Desert State Park offers the chance to view the unusual beauty that is the desert on its miles of riding trails. There is a horse campground, and the ultimate horse for desert riding, the Arabian, can be rented for guided rides from Smoketree Arabian Horse Rental (302 Palm Canyon Drive, Borrego Springs, CA 92004; 760-767-5850; http://www.smoketreearabianranch.com). One note of caution: the temperature during the hot summer months can climb as high as 125 degrees Fahrenheit.

Open: Year-round, dawn until dusk

Address: 200 Palm Canyon Drive, Borrego Springs, CA 92004

Phone: 760-767-5311

Web site: http://www.parks.ca.gov

Getting there: About a two-hour drive from San Diego, Riverside, and Palm Springs: From the east or west, take Highways S22 and 78; Highway S2 enters the park from the south off of Interstate 8. (See the Web site for maps and directions.)

Fees/permits: Admission is $6 per vehicle

Horse rentals: Available locally

Horse camping: Available in the park

Trail conditions/level of difficulty: Easy to difficult

through the park. Horses are not allowed on hiking trails, and there is no cross-country riding. Coyote Canyon is closed each year during the hot summer, from June 1 through September 30, to allow the bighorn sheep to drink from the canyon's stream without being disturbed.

Waiting at the trailer

You can camp with your horse in the park. If you're planning to eat in camp, there is a small grocery store in Borrego Springs (The Center Market; 760-767-3311), and you can also pick up groceries and camping supplies at Julian Market and Deli, in Julian (2202 Main Street, Julian, CA 92036; 760-765-2606). Additionally, every Friday from November through May, 7:00 a.m. to 12:00 p.m., a farmers market is held in Borrego Springs (622 Palm Canyon Drive, Borrego Springs, CA 92004; 760-767-5555/800-559-5524). Horse supplies and feed can be found at Julian Feed and Supply (2902 Washington Street, Julian, CA 92036; 760-765-1212).

POINT REYES NATIONAL SEASHORE

Point Reyes National Seashore lies on California's coast less than one hour northwest of San Francisco. The more than 71,000-acre national seashore includes 80 miles of undeveloped coastline and 147 miles of trails. There are approximately 32,000 acres of wilderness land within its boundaries. White-sand beaches, coastal scrubland, grassy meadows, and coniferous forests provide habitat for more than twenty rare and endangered species and various rare and recovering species, including the red-legged frog, the tule elk, the northern elephant seal, and the western snowy plover. Found on the seashore are 65 species of mammals, 28 species of reptiles and amphibians, 125 species of fish, more than 120 tree species, and 900 flowering plant species. The American Bird Conservancy named the seashore as

Point Reyes ranger

one of one hundred "globally important bird areas" because nearly half of the bird species in North America have been spotted here.

In addition to being known for its abundant wildlife, Point Reyes is further distinguished as an excellent example of plate tectonics at work. Put

Wildflowers and lichens

Morgan Horse Ranch

simply, plate tectonics describes the constant movement of Earth's crust. The Point Reyes Peninsula lies on the Pacific plate, which has moved northwestward a couple of inches each year for millions of years. The mainland is part of the westward-creeping North American plate. Between these two plates is the infamous San Andreas Fault, responsible for the massive 1906 San Francisco earthquake, during which the peninsula actually moved 20 feet northwestward, and the 1989 Loma Prieta quake, otherwise known as the World Series earthquake. The differing plates account for the peninsula's distinct geology, which more closely resembles the land of its source region hundreds of miles to the south than anything found on the neighboring

SNAPSHOT - POINT REYES NATIONAL SEASHORE

Description: This national treasure on California's northern coast is very popular with riders. Horse camping is allowed in three established campgrounds as well as at a nearby private campground (Stewart's Horse Camp; .25 mile north of Five Brooks Trailhead, and 1 mile off of Highway 1 in Olema; Point Reyes National Seashore, Point Reyes Station, CA 94956; 415-663-1362). All the camps are backcountry sites with ride-in, hike-in, or bike-in access only. You can also stable your horse overnight at the park's riding concession and stay elsewhere. There is a dormitory-style hostel in the park for horseless riders, which has hot showers, a fully equipped kitchen, and outdoor barbecue and patio (415-663-8811). Horseless riders can also marvel at the seashore's diversity by renting horses at the park's riding concession, Five Brooks Stable (see Where to Stay & Stable), which also offers overnight boarding. This is a very popular area with horse people and others, so make reservations as far in advance as possible.

Open: Year-round, sunrise to sunset; overnight camping by permit

Address: 1 Bear Valley Road, Point Reyes Station, CA 94956

Phone: 415-464-5100

Web site: http://www.nps.gov/pore/index.htm

Getting there: Located approximately 22 miles north of San Francisco on Highway 1 along the west coast of California; approaching from Sir Francis Drake Boulevard is the better route for travelers pulling horse trailers

Fees/permits: Admission is free

Horse rentals: Available locally

Horse camping: Available in the park

Trail conditions/level of difficulty: Easy to difficult; some are steep and tiring

Toward the beach at Point Reyes

Marin County mainland. During your visit to the park, be sure to walk the short Earthquake Trail (horses are not allowed). It features exhibits of the 1906 earthquake and the San Andreas Fault zone.

While the history of the land dates back millions of years, the history of the area's people reaches back approximately 5,000 years. The Coast Miwok Indians were the first human inhabitants of the peninsula, and more than 120 known village sites exist within the park. You can visit Kule Loklo within the park, which is an authentic replica of a Coast Miwok village. Later years brought European explorers, one of whom may have been Sir Francis Drake; many experts believe the sixteenth-century seafarer visited here. Mexican ranchos dotted the land scape during the 1800s, and dairy farming later became a major use for the land. The Point Reyes National Seashore was established by President John F. Kennedy in 1962.

Riders can explore the seashore's unique beauty on more than 100 miles of trails as horses are allowed on many established trails and beaches. During the fall and spring, flocks of hundreds of migrating birds fill the sky, and if you're visiting anytime from January through April, you may be lucky enough to catch a glimpse of migrating gray whales. The park service provides a map with riding trails and can provide information on such popular trails as those leading to Wildcat Beach, the San Andreas Fault, Inverness Ridge, and others, including information on trail conditions and closures. Horse lovers will also enjoy visiting the Morgan Horse Ranch within the park. Morgan horses are bred and trained here for use by park rangers (415-464-5169).

Yosemite Valley

YOSEMITE NATIONAL PARK

Yosemite National Park stretches across the scenic western slopes of the Sierra Nevada mountain range, which lies along California's eastern border. The majority of the park's land is designated wilderness. Yosemite's elevations range from 2,000 feet to more than 13,000 feet, encompassing five major vegetation zones. There are thousands of lakes and ponds and 1,600 miles of

There are numerous areas in the park sure to delight and inspire visitors to Yosemite. They include the approximately 1-mile wide, 3,000-foot-deep Yosemite Valley, widely considered the centerpiece of the park. It is especially famous for its granite cliffs and soaring waterfalls. Half Dome, perhaps the most recognizable landmark in the park, stands at the elevation of 8,842 feet at the eastern end of the valley. It

Waterfall and rainbow

streams. Within its borders, grand waterfalls, steeply walled valleys, Alpine meadows, and giant sequoia groves come together to create a place of almost indescribable beauty. As naturalist and conservationist John Muir said about Yosemite, "It is by far the grandest of all the special temples of Nature I was ever permitted to enter."

Many decades after Muir's pronouncement, the state of California "officially" recognized Yosemite's grandness by featuring the park on the California state quarter. The quarter, released in 2005, became the thirty-first released as part of the United States Mint's 50 State Quarters Program. It depicts Muir admiring Yosemite Valley's Half Dome and also contains a soaring California condor. The coin bears the inscriptions *California, John Muir, Yosemite Valley,* and *1850.*

is composed of a type of granite, plutonic rock. Half Dome's missing half is presumed to have fallen off when the Ice Age glaciers passed through. El Capitan, standing 4,800 feet above the valley floor, is the largest granite monolith in the world, 3,593 feet from base to summit, and it is especially popular with rock climbers who seek the challenge of climbing up its sheer granite face.

Yosemite warning sign

Yosemite Falls, which flows from winter through early to mid-summer, combine with an intermediate cascade to create the highest waterfall in North America; they drop 2,425 feet. If you visit in the spring, you'll witness the full force as the water flow will be at its peak. Other popular waterfalls include the 620-foot Bridalveil Fall, which flows year-round; the 317-foot Vernal Fall, also flowing all year; the 1,612 foot Ribbon Fall, which is seen in spring only; Staircase Falls, which cascades 1,300 feet downward in the springtime; and the 1,000-foot Horsetail

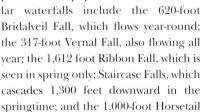

Everyone takes a break.

Fall, which falls off the east side of El Capitan in the winter and early spring.

Other major attractions in the park include Glacier Point, an overlook 30 miles east of the valley that offers a king's view of Yosemite Valley and the High Sierra. The Mariposa Grove of Giant Sequoias is near the park's south entrance, and it is the largest of three stands of giant sequoias in the park. Tuolumne Meadows in the high country offers peace and solitude in a large subalpine meadow graced by a winding river and surrounded by forest and soaring

SnapShot - Yosemite National Park

Description: Experience one of the most beautiful of our national parks. Bring your horse to the nearly 1,200 square-mile Yosemite National Park, approximately the size of Rhode Island, to ride and camp. If you don't have your own mount, you can rent a mule from one of the three rental stables in the park: Tuolumne Meadows (209-372-8427), Wawona (209-375-6502), and Yosemite Valley (209-372-8348). Rental rides are two hours, half a day, or a full day, and customized rides and pack drops are also offered. Overnight boarding facilities are available through the liveries located within the park; call 209-372-1000 for more information. The Bridalveil Creek Stock Camp has two sites, and each can accommodate six people and six head of stock. Two area outfitters that rent horses for hourly and overnight rides into the park include Yosemite Trails Pack Station (559-683-7611; http://www.yosemitetrails.com) and Minarets Pack Station (559-868-3405; http://www.highsierrapackers.org). While in the Yosemite area, you can also enjoy the nearby trails, horse camps, and horse rentals of Sierra National Forest (1600 Tollhouse Road, Clovis, CA 93611; 559-297-0706; http://www.fs.fed.us/r5/sierra/recreation.
Open: Year-round
Address: PO Box 577, Yosemite National Park, CA 95389
Phone: 209-372-0200
Web site: http://www.nps.gov/yose
Getting there: Yosemite can be accessed via Highway 41, Highway 140, and Highway 120. (Highway 120 is seasonal from the east, June through October.)
Fees/permits: Admission is $20 per vehicle for a seven-day pass
Horse rentals: Mule rentals available in the park
Horse camping: Available in the park
Trail conditions/level of difficulty: Easy to difficult; high elevation, mountain conditions; horses should be shod

WHO WAS JOHN MUIR?

The legacy of John Muir, naturalist, conservationist, and first president of the Sierra Club, is so closely intertwined with Yosemite that, in addition to being called the father of the national parks, he is often called the father of Yosemite.

Originally from Scotland, Muir immigrated with his family to the United States in 1849. (One year later, when Muir was twelve, California would become the nation's thirty-first state.) The family settled in Wisconsin, where Muir explored the woods and countryside near his home on the rare occasions he was allowed away from farm work. These forays into nature stoked the embers of what would become his lifelong love of the natural world.

Dwarfed by a giant sequoia

Muir attended college but dropped out after three years to study at the "university of the wilderness." He traveled through the northern United States and Canada, walked 1,000 miles from Indianapolis, Indiana, to the Gulf of Mexico, and ultimately ended up on a ship sailing to San Francisco, where he docked in 1868. Supported by a variety of odd jobs, including sheepherder, Muir settled in Yosemite. He would live in California for the rest of his life, eventually marrying and moving to his wife's ranch in Martinez.

The first time Muir entered the Sierra Nevada mountains, he called them the Range of Light and said they were the most "divinely beautiful of all the mountain chains I have ever seen." He became a student and a champion of the land there. He discovered living glaciers in Yosemite Valley and concluded that these huge glaciers had carved the valley. This theory, which is now generally accepted, was controversial in Muir's day, as most geologists of the time believed massive earthquakes and rockslides were responsible.

Over the ensuing years, Muir worked to protect Yosemite from the encroachments of grazing cattle and sheep as well as the logging industry. He wrote and spoke about the importance of experiencing and protecting the land, attracting the attentions of famous men of the day, including Ralph Waldo Emerson, with whom he became friends. He also spent the night in Yosemite with President Theodore Roosevelt and helped inspire Roosevelt's conservation programs, including establishing the first national monuments. His work led to the creation not only of Yosemite (which became a national park in 1890) but also of Sequoia, Mount Rainier, Petrified Forest, Grand Canyon, and ultimately the National Park Service itself. He founded the Sierra Club in 1892 to "do something for wildness and make the mountains glad" and became its first president, a post he held until his death twenty-two years later.

Although Muir's heart was strongly tied to Yosemite and California, he continued to travel throughout the world and write about his experiences. Some of his adventures would have been too harrowing for lesser mortals, such as sliding down glaciers and being caught all night in a blinding snowstorm; but Muir, who was so comfortable in the wild, took these things in stride.

One thing he didn't take in stride was the battle, which he eventually lost, to preserve the Hetch Hetchy Valley in Yosemite. Following the great San Francisco earthquake in 1906, politicians submitted a plan to Congress to dam up the Hetch Hetchy Valley to supply the San Francisco Bay area with a clean water source. Muir's battle to stop the damming and flooding of the valley lasted seven years. Muir lost the battle in 1913, and its loss, some speculate, led to his death a year later. It was the only fight Muir lost to protect his beloved Yosemite.

Although Muir lost that battle, he didn't lose the war. His legacy of conservation and contributions to environmental thinking will live forever. Every time someone visits Yosemite or another wild place that has been preserved and marvels at its beauty, it is another small victory for John Muir. In 1976, the California Historical Society named Muir the greatest Californian in the state's history. John Muir's birthday on April 21 (the day before Earth Day) is now celebrated each year as John Muir Day.

peaks. Hetch Hetchy Valley is also not to be missed. Hetch Hetchy was considered by Muir to be a smaller version of the Yosemite Valley because of its similar and equally incredible scenery. It contains the Hetch Hetchy Reservoir, a source of drinking water for San Francisco.

You'll find many areas in Yosemite to admire when visiting here with your own horse or by renting a mule or horse through the park concessionaire or a local outfitter. Be aware that much of the wilderness in Yosemite is more than 8,000 feet high, so animals must be acclimated to the elevation. Horses must stay on trails; no cross-country riding is allowed. All trails are open to stock use with the exception of the following: Mist Trail from Happy Isles to Nevada Falls, Snow Creek Trail from Mirror Lake, Lower Chilnualna Falls foot trail from the parking area in North Wawona,

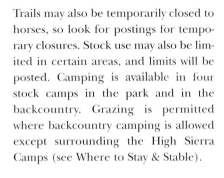

The trail at Haleakala

Mariposa Grove inner loop, Gaylor Lakes foot trail from Tioga Pass Entrance Station to Gaylor Lakes, Gaylor Lakes Basin above Lower Gaylor Lake, and the Muir Gorge Trail segment from Return Creek to Pate Valley. In addition, the Yosemite Falls Trail from Yosemite Valley to the top of upper Yosemite Falls is not recommended for horses.

Haleakala Crater

Trails may also be temporarily closed to horses, so look for postings for temporary closures. Stock use may also be limited in certain areas, and limits will be posted. Camping is available in four stock camps in the park and in the backcountry. Grazing is permitted where backcountry camping is allowed except surrounding the High Sierra Camps (see Where to Stay & Stable).

HAWAII

HALEAKALA NATIONAL PARK, MAUI

You're visiting Maui, which has been voted the best island in the world by readers of *Condé Nast Traveler* magazine for eleven years running. You think that nothing could be better than riding horseback across its lush and verdant lands, but the vast Pacific Ocean is standing between you and your horse. Don't despair. The 30,183-acre Haleakala National Park offers horseback riding opportunities from rental stables that ride into the park.

Haleakala, which means "house of the sun," is the world's largest dormant volcano. According to Hawaiian legend, it was here that the demigod Maui snared the sun, releasing it only after it promised to move more slowly across the sky. Haleakala was established as a national park in 1961 after originally being part of Hawaii Volcanoes National Park, which was established as Hawaii National Park in 1916. Haleakala was designated an International Biosphere Reserve in 1980. Of its vast acreage, 24,719 acres are designated wilderness.

The park extends from the 10,023-foot summit of Haleakala, down the southeast flank of the mountain, to the Kipahulu coast near the town of Hana. The two park sections, made up of the summit and coastal areas, are not directly connected by road, but both can be reached by driving from Kahului, where Maui's main airport is located, as well as from other island towns. The park preserves the outstanding features of the crater as well as the unique and fragile ecosystems and rare biotic species of the Kipahulu Valley,

Swimming at Haleakala

SnapShot - Haleakala National Park

Description: Even though your horse can't be with you, there are still lots of riding opportunities at Haleakala National Park. Contact one of the stables that takes riders into the park, which sits on the rim of the world's largest dormant volcano, for a beautiful horseback riding experience that you'll never forget. Pony Express Tours (808-667-2200; http://www.ponyexpresstours.com/index.htm) offers rides across Haleakala Ranch or to the Haleakala Crater. Maui Stables (PO Box 536, Kula, HI 96790; 808-248-7799; http://www.mauistables.com) takes riders on cultural heritage tours into the rain forest or to the crater's rim. Riders leave knowing a little more about Hawaiian culture than when they started.

Open: Year-round, twenty-four hours a day

Address: PO Box 369, Makawao, Maui, HI 96768

Phone: 808-572-4400

Web site: http://www.nps.gov/hale

Getting there: From Kahului: Take State Roads 37, 377, and 378, and follow the signs posted along the highway. The summit area of Haleakala is a three-hour round-trip drive from Kahului. From the Kipahulu area: Take Highway 36, a curvy, often wet road. Kipahulu is about 90 miles from the resort areas of Wailea or Ka'anapali and 60 miles from central Maui; driving time is about three to four hours each way. An extension of Highway 36, Highway 31, goes around the dry side of the island, past Kaupa, and on to Ulapalakua; it is only partially paved and can be hazardous or closed during periods of stormy weather.

Fees/permits: Admission is $5 for walk-in, $10 for vehicle; stables are outside the park

Horse rentals: Available locally

Horse camping: None

Trail conditions/level of difficulty: From Maui stables, easy to moderate; guided rides only

Haleakala flora

the scenic pools along 'Obe'o Gulch, and the coast.

The once active volcano has not erupted for more than two hundred years. About 1790, which is quite recent geologically, two minor flows at lower elevations along the southwest rift zone of Haleakala reached the sea, altering Maui's southwest. According to today's earthquake records, the earth's crust is still undergoing internal adjustments, but there is no volcanic activity visible in the crater. It is possible, however, that Haleakala could erupt again someday; scientists just don't know when or if the volcano will spew lava into the sky once more.

Horseback riding opportunities in the park can take you down into the dramatic crater, to the crater's rim; or you can choose to explore the beautiful Kipahulu area, with its rain forests and waterfalls. Other activities that will make your trip to Haleakala a full one include one of the most popular things

to do here: get up early and watch the spectacular colors of the sunrise from Haleakala. Good viewing locations are Leleiwi and Kalahaku overlooks, the summit, and the Haleakala Visitor Center. Get here early, as it gets crowded, and wear warm clothes. You can see the equally spectacular sunset at the Halemau'u Trail and at the summit.

In addition to watching the colors made by the sun's daily cycle, keep an eye on the sky for shifting formations in the clouds, rainbows, and moonbows (rainbows formed by light from the moon). The visual horizon in many spots in the park is up to 115 miles out to sea. You can rent binoculars at one of the island's dive shops and look at stars, planets, and even the moons of Jupiter after dark.

Wildlife viewing is another activity Haleakala has to offer. Keep an eye out for the nene (pronounced nay-nay), a Hawaiian goose and the official state bird; at night, look for the 'ope'ape'a, the Hawaiian hoary bat, in the treetops; in winter, watch for humpback whales from the porch of the Kipahulu Ranger Station. You can also go for a hike, swim in 'Ohe'o stream, or take a guided educational nature walk with park rangers.

NEVADA

WASHOE LAKE STATE PARK

Washoe Lake State Park is located in the Washoe Valley, between Carson City and Reno, and just a few miles east of Lake Tahoe. The park, which sits at an elevation of 5,029 feet, was established in 1977 to ensure preservation of part of the scenic valley in light of the rapidly expanding cities nearby. At its high altitude, it offers visitors majestic views of Sierra Nevada in the south and west and the Carson Range in the east. The lake itself is 7 miles long and

2 miles wide, much smaller than the more famous 12-mile-long, 22-mile wide Lake Tahoe.

The park's name comes from the Washoe Indians, original inhabitants of the area, who used cattails and willows from Washoe Lake's wetlands to weave elaborate baskets. The Washoe spent winters in the valley and summers at Lake Tahoe, which was the center of Washoe life for thousands of years. The name *Tahoe* is thought to have come from *da ow ga*, which is Washoe for "lake." At the height of their existence in the area, there were approximately 5,000 Washoe tribal members. Their population diminished—by the late nineteenth century, only 300 were left—and their way of life changed forever with the discovery of silver in the Comstock Lode of nearby Virginia City in 1859. Today, the Washoe tribe has about 1,500 tribal members.

The discovery of silver brought thousands of miners, traders, loggers, and others to the area. Mills were built to process the ore, and supply towns sprang up to support mining activity. The ruins of the New York Mill are still seen by Little Washoe Lake, and the

A peaceful ride

Ophir Mill, on Washoe Lake's west shore, can be seen from Highway 395. Less than fifteen years later, the Virginia and Truckee Railroad came to the valley, connecting Reno to Carson City. Twenty years after the silver boom began here, it was over. The towns began emptying, and the few who stayed turned to ranching and farming.

These days, with Reno and Lake Tahoe nearby, the area is heavily reliant on tourism, and there are many recreational activities for park visitors. It is a prime spot for bird watching, so be sure to bring your binoculars. Hundreds of resident and migratory birds can be found here, including hawks and eagles, red-winged blackbirds, magpies, mountain bluebirds, killdeers, rufous-sided towhees, pelicans, great blue herons, Canada geese, and white-faced ibis. There is also a wetlands area with a viewing tower and interpretive displays, a relatively new addition to the park's facilities. When you've finished watching and studying the natural

Washoe Lake

aspects of Washoe Lake State Park, you can enjoy a variety of lake activities such as water skiing, catamaran sailing, jet skiing, and fishing. Hiking and equestrian trails lead you through the park, and the park is also a trailhead for many other trails in the surrounding area.

Nighttime at camp

SnapShot - Washoe Lake State Park

Description: Nature lovers will enjoy the myriad species of birds found in the park and the wetlands viewing tower. Miles of trails in the sagebrush and thousands of acres of backcountry riding are sure to please equestrians, especially since off-road vehicles are not allowed. Riders share trails with hikers and bikers. There is even a 3-mile beach to ride on, and you can enjoy splashing or swimming with your horse in the shallow water. The park features a horse camp and a special equestrian area, the North Ramp facility, with ample parking for rigs, picnic tables, and water for day-use riders. Dining is scarce right around the lake, so plan to eat in camp or grab a meal in Carson City, where there are plenty of restaurants and casinos offering food.

Open: Year-round

Address: 4855 E. Lake Boulevard, Carson City, NV 89704

Phone: 775-687-4319

Web site: http://www.parks.nv.gov/wl.htm

Getting there: From Carson City: Take US 395 North to the East Lake Boulevard exit, then travel north on East Lake Boulevard approximately 3 miles. From Reno: Take 395 South to the East Lake Boulevard intersection, turn left, and head south on East Lake Boulevard for approximately 7 miles.

Fees/permits: Admission is $4

Horse rentals: None

Horse camping: Available in the park

Trail conditions/level of difficulty: Trails in the park: easy; Virginia Range trails on the BLM side of the park: range of easy, moderate, and difficult

OTHER GREAT PLACES TO RIDE

California

Jack London State Historic Park

2400 London Ranch Road, Glen Ellen, CA 95442
707-938-5216
http://www.parks.ca.gov
Located in California's Sonoma wine country, this 800-acre park contains the cottage where Jack London spent five years writing. Some of the trails permit horseback riding, and there is a horse rental facility in the park (Triple Creek Horse Outfit; 707-933-1600).

Joshua Tree National Park

74485 National Park Drive, Twentynine Palms,
CA 92277
760-367-5500
http://www.nps.gov/jotr
There are more than 250 miles of equestrian trails and trail corridors at Joshua Tree National Park, in Southern California. Ryan and Black Rock campgrounds have areas for horse camping, and backcountry camping is available by permit.

Lake Oroville State Recreation Area

400 Glen Drive, Oroville, CA 95966
530-538-2200
http://www.parks.ca.gov
This 28,450-acre human-made lake in north central California offers myriad recreational activities, including horseback riding on trails around the lake. There is a horse camp with fifteen sites, corrals, and a restroom with showers.

Lassen Volcanic National Park

PO Box 100, Mineral, CA 96063
530-595-4444
http://www.nps.gov.lavo/index.htm
You can ride and camp with your horse at this national park at the southern end of the Cascades mountain range in northeastern California. It has 150 miles of trails and a volcanic history that includes activity as recent as 1921. All four types of volcanoes found in the world are represented here.

Sequoia and Kings Canyon National Parks

47050 Generals Highway, Three Rivers,
CA, 93271
559-565-3341
http://www.nps.gov/seki
These two national parks, featuring giant sequoias, share a border and are managed as one park. You can bring your own horse for backcountry riding or rent a mount from Horse Corral (559-565-3404 in summer, 559-564-6429 off-season) in Sequoia National Forest, from Cedar Grove Pack Station (559-565-3404 in summer,

OTHER GREAT PLACES TO RIDE

559-564-6429 off-season) in Sequoia National Forest, and from Cedar Grove Pack Station (559-565-3464 in summer, 559-337-2314 off-season) and Grant Grove Stables (559-335-9292 in summer, 559-337-2314 off-season) in Kings Canyon.

Hawaii

Kalaupapa National Historical Park
PO Box 2222, Kalaupapa, HI 96742
808-567-6802
http://www.nps.gov/kala
For a beautiful and historically interesting ride, take a mule trip that winds down a 1,700-foot cliff to Kalaupapa Village on the island of Molokai. The village is where native Hawaiian peoples who had contracted leprosy were sent in the nineteenth century (Molokai Mule Ride, Inc.; 808-567-6088/800-567-7550; http://www.muleride.com).

Nevada

Great Basin National Park

100 Great Basin National Park, Baker, NV 89311
775-234-7331
http://www.nps.gov/grba
Located in east central Nevada, Great Basin features backcountry riding and camping. This more than 77,000-acre park features numerous limestone caves, Alpine plants, groves of ancient bristlecone pines, and plenty of wildlife.

Red   Rock   Canyon   National Conservation Area

1000 Scenic Loop Drive, Las Vegas, NV 89124
702-515-5350
http://www.redrockcanyonlv.org
Although located near Las Vegas, you won't find any slot machines or poker tables here. Instead, you'll find trails leading you through mountainside meadows and red sandy desert near the conservation area. Horse rentals are available at Bonnie Springs Ranch, a few miles from the Red Rock Canyon.

FAR WEST TRAVEL SECTION

IF YOU ARE TRAVELING WITHOUT YOUR HORSE, OR IF YOUR HORSE IS BOARDED SAFELY AT A STABLE, ENJOY THE SITES IN THE NEIGHBORING TOWNS. BELOW, YOU'LL FIND A MILEAGE CHART LISTING THE DISTANCES BETWEEN THE TRAILS AND ALL THE AREAS DISCUSSED IN THE FOLLOWING TRAVEL SECTION. THE AREAS CLOSEST TO THE TRAILS ARE INDICATED BY AN **X**. FOR AREAS WHERE NEITHER STABLING NOR HORSE RENTALS ARE AVAILABLE, NO SIGHTSEEING OPTIONS ARE LISTED.

COAST TO COAST	Borrego Springs, Calif.	Julian, Calif.	Kahului, Hawaii	Kihei, Hawaii	Kula, Hawaii	Lahaina, Hawaii	Makawao, Hawaii	N. Washoe Valley, Nev.	Point Reyes Station, Calif.	Wailukui, Hawaii
Anza–Borrego Desert State Park (Calif.)	**X** * miles	**X** 30 miles	–	–	–	–	–	700 miles	595 miles	–
Haleakala National Park, Maui (Hawaii)	–	–	**X** 45 miles	55 miles	**X** 40 miles	70 miles	**X** 40 miles	–	–	50 miles
Point Reyes National Seashore (Calif.)	575 miles	565 miles	–	–	–	–	–	260 miles	**X** * miles	–
Washoe Lake State Park (Nev.)	645 miles	690 miles	–	–	–	–	–	**X** * miles	255 miles	–
Yosemite National Park (Calif.)	490 miles	480 miles	–	–	–	–	–	160 miles	230 miles	–

*The area to visit is the same as or is within 10 miles of the trails.

MUST SEE / MUST DO

CALIFORNIA

ANZA-BORREGO DESERT STATE PARK AREA

When visiting Anza-Borrego Desert State Park, be sure to take a day trip to the historic mountain town of **Julian**, off Highway 78, west of the park. Founded in the 1870s as a gold rush town, you can still tour a **gold mine** there today (Eagle and High Peak Mine, End of C Street, Julian, CA 92036; 760-765-0036; call for current operating hours). You can also view historic sites on the **Julian Historic Walking Tour** (maps are available at the Chamber of Commerce office on 2129 Main Street, Julian, CA 92036; 760-765-1857) and see history remade live before your eyes by a local gunfight skit group, Julian Doves and Desperados. Skits take place in town at the group's stage area near the Julian Market and Deli every Sunday (weather permitting) at 1:00 p.m., 2:00 p.m., and 3:00 p.m. Call 760-765-1857 for more information. Admission is free. You can also rent horses to ride in the Julian area from **Julian Stables** (760-765-1598; http://www.julianactive .com/julian_stables .htm), just 1.5 miles from historic Julian. For even more interesting things to do in historic Julian, visit the town's Web site at http://www.julian ca.com.

Julian soda fountain

Doves and Desperados

Point Reyes shoreline

POINT REYES NATIONAL SEASHORE AREA

Housed in Point Reyes Station's old emporium building, the **Cabaline Country Emporium & Saddlery** (11313 Highway 1, Point Reyes Station, CA 94956; 415-663-8303; http://www.svn .net/cabaline) will surely delight horse lovers. It features English, western, Australian, and endurance tack and riding clothes, as well as unique gifts, books, jewelry, health and beauty supplies, and more. Need horse-themed toilet paper? It's here! The emporium is open weekdays from 10:00 a.m. to 6:00 p.m. and weekends from 9:00 a.m. to 6:30 p.m. in summer, and Monday through Saturday from 10:00 a.m. to 6:00 p.m. and Sunday from 10:00 a.m. to 5:00 p.m. in winter.

Opened in 1942, the family-run **Toby's Feed Barn** (11250 Highway 1, Point Reyes Station, CA 94956; 415-663-1223) is a must-see while in the area. It sells not only hay and other feed but also organic food, handmade children's clothing, garden supplies, and more. On site at Toby's are a yoga studio and an art gallery featuring local artists. On Saturdays in summer, Toby's hosts the Point Reyes Farmers Market.

Western saddles for sale

YOSEMITE NATIONAL PARK

If you'd like to see a different view of Yosemite than the one you gain from horseback, why not try a motorized tour? Knowledgeable guides will tell you about the park's geology, wildlife, and history, enriching your total Yosemite experience. Tour reservations may be made up to seven days ahead of time by calling 209-372-1240. While in the park, reservations may be made by dialing ext. 1240 from any house phone or by visiting the Tour and Activity desks at the Yosemite Lodge,

Checking out the picnic fare

at Curry Village, and at Yosemite Village. Following is just a sampling of the many tours offered.

The **Glacier Point** Tour is a four-hour tour from Yosemite Valley to Glacier Point, 3,200 feet above the valley floor. It departs daily from Yosemite Lodge, and you have the option of purchasing a one-way ticket and hiking down. The tour operates from late spring through early fall, weather permitting. The cost is $32.50 round-trip for adults and $26.00 for children five and older. Children under five are free.

On the **Moonlight Tour**, you'll enjoy the late-night sky and Yosemite landmarks such as Half Dome and El Capitan on this open-air tram tour. The two-hour tour takes place on full-moon nights from late spring through early

fall. It leaves from Yosemite Lodge, and departure times vary based on the moon rise. Fares are $22 for adults and $17 for children.

Big Trees Tram Tour is a seventy-five minute audio tour that takes you through the Mariposa Grove of Giant Sequoias. You'll meet the tour at the Mariposa Grove Gift Shop located just beyond Yosemite's south entrance. It runs from late spring through early fall and departs several times daily. For departure times for this tour only, call 209-375-1621. Prices are $16 for adults and $10 for children; children under five are admitted free.

In addition to or instead of taking a motorized tour, you can gain even more perspective on Yosemite by taking part in a park interpretive program. And Yosemite has numerous interesting programs and activities to offer. For example, the **Historic Ahwahnee Tour**, designed for adults and mature children, will take you back into the past as you explore the architecture, design, and background of this historic hotel. The tour is free and takes place year-round. Start times for the approximately one-hour tour vary, so check with the hotel. It leaves from the concierge desk at the Ahwahnee hotel.

Imagine you are Ansel Adams as you learn how to take great photos of Yosemite on the **Camera Walks**. Professional photographers from the Ansel Adams Gallery, Kodak, and others lead instructional walks designed for inexperienced through advanced photographers. These free walks are offered five to six times a week June through August and two to three times a week September through May. For more information, contact the Ansel Adams Gallery at 209-372-4413.

Or enjoy one of the **evening programs**: relax after dinner and learn more about Yosemite through a slideshow presentation. A wide range of topics cover the natural and cultural history of the park. These hour-long programs are held at the amphitheaters at Curry Village and Yosemite Lodge,

Loping along the beach

Lower Pines Campground, and the LeConte Memorial Lodge. In winter, programs are held indoors at Yosemite Lodge and the Ahwahnee hotel. Times vary, and the presentations are free.

HAWAII

HALEAKALA NATIONAL PARK AREA

Watch an exciting polo game put on by the **Maui Polo Club** (415 Dairy Road, Kahului, HI 96732; 808-877-7744; http://www.mauipoloclub.com) while you are visiting the island. Polo games are held every Sunday beginning at 1 p.m in April, May, and June at the Haleakala Ranch Polo Field, 1 mile above Pukalani Town off Highway 377 on the way to Haleakala National Park. Games are played every Sunday beginning at 1:30 p.m. at the Olinda Polo Field on Olinda Road at Kaonoulu

Bob Nooney and Puukolo

Ranch, 1 mile above Makawao town, from January to November. The cost for both the spring and fall season games is $5 at the gate. Call or e-mail the club at info@mauipoloclub.com for more information.

In addition to horseback stables that offer rides into Haleakala National Park, other stables throughout the island give you more horseback riding options while visiting Maui. Be sure to reserve your ride as far ahead as possible. This 729-square-mile island welcomes 2.2 million visitors each year, so recreational opportunities fill up fast. Ride in the West Maui mountains in the area near the popular Lahaina and Ka'anapali resort areas at **Lahaina Stables** (808-667-2222; http://www .maui.net/~ray/index.htm). Improve your understanding of horses by taking a half- or full-day program at **The Maui Horse Whisperer Experience/ Adventures on Horseback** (PO Box 1419, Makawao, HI 96768; 808-572-6211; http://www.mauihorsewhisper er.com). You can include a trail ride at additional cost. Half-day programs are $200, full-day programs are $300, and optional trail rides are an additional $50. Take a ride with Adventures on Horseback on privately maintained horses. Ride on a 20,000-acre ranch overlooking the water at **Makena Stables** (8299 South Makena Road, Kihei, HI 96753; 808-879-0244; http://www.make nastables.com/index.htm). Or visit **Mendes Ranch** (3530 Kahekili Highway, Wailukui, HI 96793; 808-871-5222; http://www.mendesranch.com/rides .htm), and take a trail ride through lush rain forest to the Eki Crater, where you will see some of Maui's largest waterfalls.

WHERE TO STAY & STABLE

CALIFORNIA

ANZA-BORREGO DESERT STATE PARK AREA

Horses and Riders:

Horseman's Inn
3298 Old Cuyamaca Road, PO Box 217
Julian, CA 92036
760-765-1034
http://www.horsemansinn.com
$150–$175 per night
This romantic bed-and-breakfast on a horse ranch caters to couples, although guests over twelve years old are welcome. Visitors with horses will find accommodations for their equine friends, and horseless visitors will enjoy the comforts found here.

Stagecoach Trails R.V., Equestrian and Wildlife Resort
7878 Great Southern Overland Stage Route of 1849
(off Highway S2 at mile marker 21 in Shelter Valley)
Julian, CA 92036
760-765-2197/877-TWO-CAMP
http://www.stagecoachtrails.com
$30 per night for full hookup; $25 per night for tent and primitive camping; $50–$150 per day for rental units; $5 per horse per night for corrals
Stagecoach Trails is located adjacent to the state park. It has 285 full hookup RV sites, a tent camping area, rental RV units, and seventy horse corrals. There is also a heated swimming pool, a shuffleboard and horseshoes area, a store, and movie rentals. Reservations are recommended.

Vern Whitaker Horse Camp
From the Visitor's Center, take Borrego Springs Road past Indian Head Ranch Road to horse camp signs
760-767-5311/Reservations: 800-444-7275
$16 per night
The Vern Whitaker Horse Camp, at the mouth of Coyote Canyon and the Coyote Canyon horse trails, is only for people camping with horses. There are ten sites and forty horse corrals, and each site holds up to eight people and four horses. The sites can accommodate vehicles up to 24 feet long. This is a developed campground with flush toilets, solar-heated showers, and other amenities. Reservations are recommended during high-season weekends.

Riders Only:

Borrego Valley Inn
405 Palm Canyon Drive
Borrego Springs, CA 92004
800-333-5810
http://www.borregovalleyinn.com
$140 and up per night, breakfast included
The Borrego Valley Inn has many amenities, including two swimming pools, one of which is designated clothing optional. All the rooms are decorated in Southwest/Mexican style with saltillo tile floors, private patios, and walk-in showers. Pets are welcome for an additional $25 fee. Children under fourteen are not allowed.

POINT REYES NATIONAL SEASHORE AREA

Horses and Riders:

Chanslor Guest Ranch
2660 Coast Hwy 1
PO Box 1510
Bodega Bay, CA 94923
707-875-2721
http://www.chanslor.com
$135–$220 per night;double occupancy; $20 per night per horse for paddock
Chanslor Ranch is a full-service, operating horse ranch that offers activities for the whole family and overnight accommodations for you and your equine companions. They are located one mile north of the fishing village of Bodega Bay and overlook the magnificent Salmon Creek Beaches and coastal wetlands. Stay in one of the six guest rooms at their charming Bed & Breakfast. Chanslor Ranch offers an array of services, including rental horses and guided trail rides. Their horse care services include grooming, custom feeding, exercise, and even training for additional fees; lessons are available as well. All board includes oat and alfalfa hay fed twice a day, daily mucking out of the stall or corral (with daily turnout if in a stall), and on-site personnel twenty-four hours a day to keep a eye on your horse. The tack room and sand arena are available for your use.

Point Reyes Country Inn and Stable
12050 Highway 1
Point Reyes Station, CA 94956
415-663-9696
http://www.ptreyescountryinn.com
$115–325 per night weekends and holidays,
$95–$260 weekdays; $10–$15 for horse stabling

The Point Reyes Country Inn and Stable combines charming rooms for you with a comfortable place for your horse. Stay in a private room or rent one of two apartments situated above the stables. Point Reyes National Seashore is only a short trailer trip away, or you can enjoy the trails at Tomales Bay by riding from the inn to the trailhead.

Sky, Coast, and Wildcat Campgrounds
Located in the park
Reservations: 415-663-8054, 9:00 a.m. to 2:00 p.m. Monday through Friday only, or by walk-in when the visitor center is open
$15 per night for up to six people, $30 per night for seven to fourteen people, $40 per night for fifteen to twenty-five people
Hitch rails, picnic tables, and potable water from faucets are available at the camps. The Sky and Wildcat campgrounds also have water troughs for horses. These are extremely popular spots, so reserve early. Reservations can be made up to three months in advance. Obtain a permit from Bear Valley Visitor Center (Park Headquarters) Monday through Friday from 9:00 a.m. to 5:00 p.m. and weekends from 8:00 a.m. to 5:00 p.m.

Riders Only:

Hostelling International-Point Reyes
Point Reyes National Seashore
1 Bear Valley Road, PO Box 247
Point Reyes Station, CA 94956
415-663-8811
http://www.norcalhostels.org/reyess

$16 and up per night for adults, $54 and up for a family room
The main lodging at the hostel is in the Ranch House, built in the late nineteenth century by area settlers and located just off Limantour Road in Zone 5 of Point Reyes National Seashore. It has a kitchen, a common area, hot showers, and an outdoor patio, but there is no food available; bring your own. There is also a bunkhouse for groups. Open all year; reservations are recommended.

Horses Only:
Five Brooks Stable
Point Reyes National Seashore
PO Box 99
Olema, CA 94950
415-663-1570
http://www.fivebrooks.com
$30 per night per horse for stall, includes bedding, cleaning, feed, and use of the arena; $20 per horse for paddock, includes cleaning, feed, and use of the arena
This national park concession provides overnight and long-term boarding, lessons, and guided trail rides on rental horses. Personnel are on site twenty-four hours a day to look after horses, and there is a sand arena for boarder use. Riding lessons are offered to riders renting horses and to boarders. Trail rides are from one to three hours, all day, or you can customize your own private ride; horse rental rates range from $35 to $220 per person. Call for information or to make reservations daily from 9:00 a.m. to 5:00 p.m.

YOSEMITE NATIONAL PARK AREA

Horses and Riders:
The Homestead Cottages
41110 Road 600
Ahwahnee, CA 93601
559-683-0495/800-483-0495
http://www.homesteadcottages.com
$145–$349 per night; $15 per horse per night
The Homestead Cottages, near Yosemite, offer six guest accommodations: four one-bedroom cottages, a loft room, and the two-bedroom Ranch House. All accommodations have fully equipped kitchens stocked with coffee, hot chocolate, muffins, and other goodies. Your horse will also find the living comfortable here in one of five pipe stalls. The hosts have mapped out many of the area trails in Yosemite and the Sierra National Forest and are happy to assist riders in planning their riding adventures. Area trailheads are between fifteen and fifty minutes away.

Stock Campgrounds
Yosemite National Park Public Information Office
PO Box 577
Yosemite, CA 95389
800-436-7275/800-436-PARK
http://www.reservations.nps.gov
$20 per night
Stock campgrounds are available in the park in Wawona, Tuolumne Meadows, Bridalveil Creek, and Hetch Hetchy. The Wawona, Bridalveil, and Hetch Hetchy stock camps have two sites, each accommodating six riders and six stock animals. The Tuolumne Meadows camp has four sites, each accommodating six people and six head of stock. Backcountry wilderness camping is also allowed. Wilderness permits are required for overnight backcountry trips. The permits are free; however, during the peak visitor months of May through September, reservations for permits are highly recommended as the park uses a quota system to regulate the number of people beginning overnight trips from each trailhead. There is a $5 processing fee for reservations.

Riders Only:
The Ahwahnee
Located in the park
559-253-5635 (DNC Parks and Resorts)
http://www.yosemitepark.com
$393–$964 per night
The Ahwahnee, completed in 1927, is striking for its massive stonework, soaring beamed ceilings, and elegant stained glass windows. The historic hotel offers 123 guest rooms consisting of standard hotel rooms, suites, parlors, and cottages. Guests enjoy concierge service, a heated outdoor swimming pool, tennis courts, a gift shop, and more. In addition to The Ahwahnee, DNC Parks and Resorts operates several other lodging properties within Yosemite with a variety of amenities. They include the Yosemite Lodge at the Falls ($100–$170 per night), the Wawona Hotel ($105–$183), Curry Village ($69–$113), Tuolumne Meadows Lodge ($83), and White Wolf ($82–$105).

High Sierra Camps
Located in the park
559-253-5674 (DNC Parks and Resorts)
http://www.yosemitepark.com
$126 per night per person includes lodging, dinner, and breakfast; $786 four-day saddle trip, $1,241 six-day saddle trip, $719.50 five-day guided hike, $1,027 seven-day guided hike; all saddle trips and guided hikes include lodging, meals, and guides and saddle trips include mules
Experience the thrill of Yosemite's high country by staying at the High Sierra Camps. The five High Sierra Camps are accessible only by foot or guided mule trip through Tuolumne Meadows Stables. The camps are spaced on a loop trail for trekking from camp to camp. Lodging is in canvas tent cabins with dormitory-style beds; guests must bring their own sheets or sleep sacks. Comforters, pillows, and blankets are provided. Warm showers and restroom facilities are subject to water availability. As this is a highly popular way to experience Yosemite's majesty, there is a lottery system for reservations. Open late June through early September.

Housekeeping Camp
DNC Parks and Resorts
559-252-4848
http://www.yosemitepark.com
$72 per night, one to four people, $5 each additional person
At Housekeeping Camp, you can camp without the work of setting up a tent. Located along the Merced River in the Yosemite Valley and featuring views of Half Dome and Yosemite Falls, the camp has 266 units that sleep up to six people each. The units consist of concrete floors, three concrete walls with a fourth curtain wall, and a double canvas roof. Sleeping areas have bunk beds and a double bed with tables, chairs, mirror, lights, and electrical outlets. There are central restrooms and showers. The camp has sandy beaches for swimmers and sunbathers. You can also cook your own meals, and each camping unit has an outdoor firepit and grill.

HAWAII

Haleakala National Park Area

Riders Only:
The Banyan Tree House
3265 Baldwin Avenue
Makawao, HI 96768
808-572-9021
http://www.banyantreehouse.com

$110–140 per night, $20 surcharge for one-night stay, $10 surcharge for two-night stay
The Banyan Tree House offers peaceful and spacious grounds featuring large banyan and monkeypod trees. Located on the slopes of Haleakala, The Banyan Tree House is a fifteen-minute drive from the beach and only a short walk from the historic cowboy town of Makawao, where you can find many fine restaurants and shops. The hotel also boasts a pool and jacuzzi. The surrounding area offers the finest hiking, biking, and horseback riding on the island. There are two golf courses in the area, and telephone, fax, wireless Internet, and laundry facilities are on the premises.

Kula Lodge
Haleakala Highway, Route 377
Kula, HI 96790
808-878-1535/In Hawaii: 800-233-1535
http://www.kulalodge.com
$115–$175
Stay in a "chalet" in the rustic Kula Lodge, at 3,200 feet up the mountain toward Haleakala. Rooms offer views and fireplaces. There is also a restaurant on the premises that serves breakfast, lunch, and dinner. (See Where to Wine & Dine.)

Lahaina Inn
127 Lahainaluna Road
Lahaina, HI 96761
800-669-3444
http://www.lahainainn.com
$130 per night
The Lahaina Inn bed-and-breakfast has been rated one of the world's best places to stay by *Condé Nast Traveler*. It offers twelve comfortable rooms with all the charm and romance of an intimate turn-of-the-century inn, located within walking distance of Ka'anapali Beach, shopping, and restaurants. Standard rooms, ocean-view rooms, and parlor suites are available. For larger groups or families, the inn also offers two cottages in Ka'anapali located on lush, tropical grounds with two swimming pools: a two-bedroom cottage that accommodates up to six people, and a three-bedroom cottage for up to eight. Each is individually furnished with full kitchens, a living room, bedrooms, bathrooms, and a laundry room.

Royal Mauian Resort
2430 S. Kihei Road
Kihei, HI 96753
808-879-1263
$195–$245 per night, five night minimum stay
Located on a beautiful stretch of beach on Maui's South Shore, this condominium hotel offers an excellent location, resort amenities, and very comfortable lodgings at reasonable rates. Shopping and dining are nearby, and the hotel is happy to help facilitate day trips and outdoor activities. One-, two- and three-bedroom units are available, all with private lanais overlooking the ocean. The spacious, bright units are decorated with rattan furniture and ceiling fans.

NEVADA

WASHOE LAKE STATE PARK AREA

Horses and Riders:

Washoe Lake State Park Main Area Equestrian Camp
Located in the park
775-687-4319
http://www.parks.nv.gov/wl.htm

$12 per night

The campground features restrooms, water troughs, tie racks, and a covered barbecue area with tables, grill, sink, power, water, and lighting. It offers tent and RV camping with easy horse trailer access. All campsites are available on a first-come, first-served basis.

WHERE TO WINE & DINE

CALIFORNIA

ANZA-BORREGO DESERT STATE PARK AREA

Bailey Woodpit Barbecue
2307 Main Street
Julian, CA 92036
760-765-3757
$8–$12

The Bailey Woodpit Barbecue offers Texas-style barbecue, wood-smoked meats, homemade salads, pie, and more. Beer, wine, and cocktails are available. Listen to live music on Friday and Saturday nights.

Bighorn Restaurant & Saloon
221 Palm Canyon Drive
Borrego Springs, CA 92004
760-767-5341
$25 and under

Located at the Palm Canyon Resort Hotel, Bighorn Restaurant offers patio and indoor seating. Menu items include steaks, chicken, lamb, seafood, barbecue, and more. There is a full bar.

POINT REYES NATIONAL SEASHORE AREA

Busy Bee Bakery
PO Box 447
12301 Sir Francis Drake Boulevard
Inverness Park, CA 94937
415-663-9496
busybeebakery@hotmail.com
$1.25–$4.50

Located in nearby Inverness park, the bakery offers old-fashion organic baked goods and espresso. The bakery also takes custom orders. Open weekdays from 7:30 a.m. to 4:00 p.m. and weekends from 8:00 a.m. to 5:00 p.m.

Drake's Beach Café
641 Drake's Beach Road
Point Reyes National Seashore
Point Reyes Station, CA 94937
415-669-1297
$5.50–$13.00

Loved by both locals and visitors, Drake's Beach Café is not your typical beach concession. It features oysters prepared fried, smoked, or in a stew; thick, juicy hamburgers; and delicious sandwiches. You get great food and a topnotch ocean view as you sit and eat outdoors not far from the beach's curling breakers.

Sand Dollar Restaurant
3458 Shoreline Highway

Stinson Beach, CA 94970
415-868-0434
$9–$32
The Sand Dollar in nearby Stinson Beach is the town's longest running restaurant and bar. The establishment has been serving classic American cuisine and seafood since 1921. They offer a fully heated outdoor patio and live music on the weekends. Open seven days a week for lunch and dinner.

Station House Café
11180 State Route 1
Point Reyes Station, CA 94956
415-663-1515
http://www.stationhousecafe.com
$15–$20
Station House Café offers California cuisine with many ethnic styles of cooking including American, Spanish, Mexican, and Italian. Organic meat is served in a beautiful patio in a garden setting, and a live band plays on Friday and Saturday nights. Dress is casual. Open for breakfast, lunch, and dinner; closed Wednesdays. Reservations are accepted.

YOSEMITE NATIONAL PARK

Ahwahnee Dining Room
Located in the park
DNC Parks and Resorts: 209-372-1489
http://www.yosemitepark.com
$24–$39
The dining room at The Ahwahnee offers an imaginative menu based on traditional American cuisine. Sample dinner meals, which change seasonally, include ginger poached salmon, slow-roasted certified Hereford prime rib, mustard crusted sea bass, and more. There is also an extensive wine list. The restaurant is open for breakfast, lunch, and dinner. Casual dress (T-shirts, jeans, shorts) is fine for breakfast and lunch; however, requested dinner attire is long pants and collared shirt for men and long pants, dresses, or skirts for women. Wearing blue jeans, athletic wear, and sneakers is not appropriate here for dinner.

Degnan's Deli, Loft, and Café; and Village Grill
Yosemite Village
DNC Parks and Resorts: 559-253-5635
http://www.yosemitepark.com
Prices vary; reasonable
Degnan's Deli, in the heart of Yosemite Village in the Yosemite Valley, offers sandwiches, salads, vegetarian fare, espresso, lattes, and other beverages year-round. Above the Deli is Degnan's Loft, a family-style restaurant serving pizzas, salads, soups; it is open spring to fall from noon to 9 p.m. Wine and beer are also served. Degnan's Café, next door to Degnan's Deli, serves coffee, pastries, and ice cream. The Village Grill offers hamburgers, fries, chicken strips, and more for lunch and early dinner; it is open spring to fall from 11:00 a.m. to 5:00 p.m.

The Mountain Room
Yosemite Lodge at the Falls
DNC Parks and Resorts: 559-253-5365
http://www.yosemitepark.com
Call for current prices
The Mountain Room, featuring views of Yosemite Falls, serves dinner daily. Dinner entrées include pastas, steaks, seafood, and more. A children's menu offers cheeseburgers, macaroni and cheese, and other delectable items sure to tempt the kids.

There is also a food court at the Yosemite Lodge with hot breakfast stations, sandwiches and salads, and dinner choices. For on-the-go eating or picnicking, you can pick up prewrapped sandwiches and other items.

Wawona Dining Room
Located in the park
DNC Parks and Resorts: 209-375-1425
http://www.yosemitepark.com
Call for current prices
The dining room at the Wawona Hotel is decorated in Victorian style but with a rustic flair. This restaurant is open for breakfast, lunch, and dinner every day during spring, summer, and fall. In winter, it is open weekends and holidays only. The restaurant serves steaks, seafood, poultry, pasta, and more for dinner; soups, salads, sandwiches, quesadillas, pastas, and more for lunch; and standard American breakfast fare. Additionally, during the summer season, a lawn barbecue takes center stage on Saturdays, complete with checkered tablecloths.

HAWAII

HALEAKALA NATIONAL PARK AREA

Kula Lodge and Restaurant
Haleakala Highway, Route 377
Kula, HI 96790
800-233-1535/In Hawaii: 808-878-1535
http://www.kulalodge.com
$8–15 for breakfast; $11–18 for lunch; $14–30 for dinner entrées
The restaurant offers breakfast, lunch, and dinner and is one of the last places to eat on your way to Haleakala's summit. Dinner entrées include fish, pastas, and meat dishes.

Makawao Steak House
3612 Baldwin Avenue
Makawao, HI 96768
808-572-8711
$19–$60
This small, family-run upcountry restaurant is popular with the locals. Dishes include great prime rib, steaks grilled over local kiawe wood, rack of lamb, poultry, and fresh fish. Entrées are accompanied by fresh baked bread and your choice of soup or salad and potatoes or rice. There is also a salad bar. Set in a restored 1927 house on the slopes of Haleakala, the building boasts three fireplaces and an intimate lounge.

Roy's Kahana Bar and Grill
4405 Honoapi'ilani Highway
Lahaina, HI 96761
808-669-6999
http://www.roysrestaurant.com
Entrées $27–$32
Roy's is an upscale eatery that serves Euro-Asian fusion cuisine by renowned chef Roy Yamaguchi. Roy's dishes blend fresh local ingredients with European sauces and Asian spices, with a focus on seafood. Here you'll find a tantalizing range of appetizers, entrées, fresh fish dishes, and desserts, along with a wide selection of award-winning wines and alcoholic beverages. Carryout is also available. Reservations are advised.

NEVADA

WASHOE LAKE STATE PARK AREA

Cattlemen's Restaurant & Lounge
555 Highway 395
N. Washoe Valley, NV 89704
775-849-1500
$16–$50
Cattlemen's is a family restaurant with the comfortable Western atmosphere you'd expect in a place with a name that heralds the ranching life. Cattleman's serves seafood and meat dishes, and it has a wine list and a full bar. Dress is casual, and there is a children's menu. The restaurant includes banquet facilities for special parties. Reservations are not required.

Mel's Diner
3225 Eastlake Boulevard
Washoe Valley, NV 89704
775-849-1949
$2–$7
Mel's Diner is noted for its American dishes and is a popular spot in the area for burgers and pizza.

Near the end of the trail

CONCLUSION

ow that you've gotten a taste of some of the best trails in the fifty states, it's time to head out and experience some of the most beautiful lands that America has to offer. Before you go, though, be sure to read the tips for happy trail riding in appendix 1. It provides valuable information for the safety and comfort of both you and your horse as well as tips for rental horse riders. Once you've done your homework and packed the necessary supplies for your particular riding trip, it's time to head for the trails and the many benefits that trail riding offers to both you and your horse.

If you've always wanted to see the country, trail riding is a great way to do it. You can go places that a car cannot take you and experience the land much as our forefathers did. You can camp with your horse and fall asleep looking at the starry sky above or stay in a snug bed-and-breakfast or other lodging with your horse safely in his own paddock or stall. Your mind and body will relax and unwind as you're loping across that sandy beach or trotting along a forest trail. Instead of traffic noise, you'll hear only the sounds of bird song, the wind whispering through the trees, and the gentle clip-clop of your horse's hooves.

Trail riding offers a chance for you and your horse to bond, and it is also a great way to become closer to family and friends. Sharing time together in some of the country's most beautiful places is something that you will never forget, and you will reminisce with your riding buddies about the places you've visited for many years to come. Horseless riders can experience the same thrill by visiting the many rental stables listed in the book.

So saddle up and enjoy the ride. Here's wishing you happy trails!

Happy trails

Appendix 1: Camping, Renting, and Riding Tips

by Cindy Hale

Note: The following offers general tips and information. For the contact information for the types of service providers and products mentioned, see the Service Providers and Vendors section at the end of this appendix.

Not every horse is suitable for horse camping. Just as some people prefer four-star accommodations, some horses don't seem to appreciate the rustic conditions associated with sleeping outdoors in the wilderness. You must determine whether your horse is both mentally and physically up to the excursion.

IS YOUR HORSE A HAPPY CAMPER?

The ideal horse for camping has a sociable nature who gets along well with other horses, especially unfamiliar ones he might meet on the trails. Yet he cannot be so herd-bound as to become neurotic when away from his stablemates. Such a horse begins to paw when tethered or corralled and often refuses to eat, traits that signify he is not a happy camper. You can determine if your horse has the right temperament for horse camping by trying some day trips as dress rehearsals. Haul to a new setting and go for a trail ride. Ride both with other equestrians and solo. If your horse is relaxed and obedient in the new surroundings and patiently ties to the trailer, he's mentally fit as a traveling companion.

Assess your horse's physical condition to ensure he's prepared to negotiate a variety of terrain. Proper hoof-care maintenance is vital because a lame horse puts a hasty end to a trail ride. If you'll be horse camping at high elevations, bear in mind that an abrupt change in altitude will sap your horse's stamina until he acclimates. Ride slowly the first couple of days, and give your horse plenty of breaks to catch his breath.

To help evaluate your horse's overall fitness, have your veterinarian give him a health check before the camping trip. This is also an opportunity to keep your horse up to date on vaccines. The stress of travel makes horses more prone to respiratory diseases, so boosters for equine influenza and rhinopneumonitis are in order. A booster for West Nile virus is good insurance as well, especially if you'll be riding near waterways that could harbor mosquitoes, which transmit the deadly disease. Another potentially fatal illness in horses is equine infectious anemia (EIA). To check your horse's blood for EIA antibodies, your vet will perform a Coggins test. An official health certificate, complete with a negative Coggins test and signed by your vet, is necessary for crossing virtually all state lines. If you'll be camping out of your home state, consult the official regulations posted by the state veterinarian of your destination. Even if you're traveling within your state's borders, the health certificate is a wise document to carry. It aids in the treatment of your horse on the road, plus it can validate that your horse is not a current carrier of communicable diseases.

Finally, even if your horse checks out mentally and physically, consider his training. The soundest horse in the world is worthless for horse camping and trail riding if he isn't prepared for the adventure's unique challenges. Think about the particular trails you'll be riding. Is your horse up to the task, or will you be mounted on the one horse who holds up the rest of the group? For example, if the trail includes crossing water or riding over bridges, work on those skills at home. You can simulate trail obstacles with a little imagination. Don't wait until your horse balks on the bank of a stream or panics in the middle of a noisy wooden bridge to discover that you need to do more homework. Basic ground manners are also important. Horse camping by definition means that your horse will spend a great deal of time doing nothing, usually while tethered to a tree, hitching post, picket line, or horse trailer. Make sure your horse agrees to stand quietly while tied. A vice such as sitting back or pulling back while tied eliminates a horse from the camping corps.

HOW TO PACK YOUR HORSE'S LUGGAGE

Hauling your horse along for an adventure in the great outdoors requires some forethought and planning. Your horse camping trip can become a calamity if you neglect to pack some necessary items.

Reserve a lot of room for feed. Horses do indeed have their favorite foods, and it's unwise to suddenly switch feeds. Be aware, however, that some riding locales require that visiting horses are fed only certified weed-free hay. That's because nonnative plants propagated from seeds found in various hays can invade the natural ecosystem. Consult with the park or forest ranger at the area you'll be visiting to determine if weed-free hay is necessary. If so, there should be a dealer near the park that caters to horse campers. An alternative to feeding hay is to feed your horse a pelleted ration using a canvas nose bag. Pellets contain feed mixtures that are ground and extruded through a machine, which ruins the viability of any grain kernels or seeds. Most horses readily accept eating from a nose bag, as it's not much different from sticking their heads into a feed bucket. Just make sure you practice at home so that you know how often you have to fill the nose bag for your horse to get his proper meal. The added benefit of a nose bag is that very few stray bits of pellets or grain hit the ground. That leaves less for you to sweep up. You will be sweeping, raking, and shoveling manure, however, so pack a mucking utensil or two. Most horse campgrounds provide a dumpster for manure. If poop happens away from camp, it's common etiquette to scoot the pile of manure off the path and scatter it.

If it seems as if you're packing up your entire tack room, focus on the essentials. What's necessary for your horse's welfare? Besides the feed, add a water bucket because you can't always depend on there being a reliable water source at the horse camp. You may be toting a bucket a number of yards, as horses generally are required to camp 100 feet or more from any water source, so select a bucket you feel comfortable carrying. An equine first aid kit is also imperative. Although there are resources for locating an equine practitioner away from home, you have to be prepared to treat lacerations, strains, and serious insect bites until help arrives. Topical wound dressings, leg quilts, and wraps are standard components in your first aid kit. Two other items to keep on hand are equine ice packs and temporary horseshoes. The ice packs are made with a special polymer that is kept easily frozen in your own cooler. They can help alleviate pain and swelling following a leg strain or a bruise. If your horse has the bad luck of losing a shoe, you can get him back to camp without damaging his unshod hoof, and perhaps even finish your trail ride, with a slip-on horseshoe boot. The heavy-duty hoof-wear includes a treaded sole and fits snugly over your horse's foot. And since your horse's welfare includes creature comforts, don't forget his pajamas. How cold are the nighttime temperatures at your destination? Unless your horse is hearty and used to living outdoors in inclement weather, he'll need at least a lightweight, waterproof turnout sheet if the temperature dips below 50 degrees Fahrenheit.

Once you've packed your horse's luggage, do your equine traveling companion a favor, and chart your trip to the trails on a map. Do you have any preplanned rest stops? It's not natural for a horse to remain stationary for hours at a time, especially with his head elevated as it is in a trailer. Ideally, you should stop every six to eight hours, unload your horse, and allow him to eat and drink. Those actions will permit him to lower his head and drain accumulated secretions, which will reduce the chance of developing a respiratory infection.

Highway rest stops may look inviting, but not many are equipped to permit the unloading of a horse. Instead, your long-distance travel plans should include so-called horse motels. They are boarding stables and private ranches that offer the traveling trail horse a brief respite from the road.

But before you hitch up the trailer, do a maintenance check to ensure that the brake and signal lights work and that the trailer tires—including the spare—are inflated properly. Added peace of mind may come from subscribing to a roadside assistance service offered to horse owners. That way, if your trailer gets a flat or your truck falters, attendants will arrive who know how to deal with equestrians and their rigs. Then the breakdown will be just a bump in the road to your horse-camping adventure.

CAMPGROUND CONSIDERATIONS

Chances are that the last time you booked a hotel room you made some inquiries first. You should take the same precautions with your horse. It would be unfortunate to arrive thinking your horse will be sleeping in his version of a king-size bed, such as an indoor stall, only to discover his accommodations amount to a hitching post.

Established horse campgrounds generally offer only basic amenities, and they're set up with the notion that riders are fully acquainted with how to manage their animals. That means you need to obtain clear rules from the park or forest ranger or on-site manager regarding available water sources, how far your horse must be kept from nonequestrian campers, the expected methods for disposing of manure, and regulations regarding allowing your horse to graze and applying a picket line. There is no consensus from one area to another in regard to these rules. It often depends on the types of trails (designated for general use or equine only) and the fragility of the ecosystem (horses can potentially trample sensitive plants). By conscientiously adhering to the rules, you'll help ensure that other recreational riders will continue to enjoy the pleasures of trail riding in the area.

If it turns out that corrals are not offered at the campground, you have two potential options: bring along your own portable corral, or become well-versed in setting up a picket line. Each has pros and cons.

Portable corrals are manufactured in several sections, with some designs offering panels that both expand and contract, allowing you to adjust the shape of the corral to fit the environment. Some styles must be hauled atop the cargo rack of your horse trailer, but those created from adjustable panels shrink down to fit in the bed of a standard pickup truck. Portable corrals create a small pen about the size of a box stall (10 x 12 feet in diameter). Since they're constructed of lightweight tubular metal or engineering grade resin with interlocking pins holding the sections together, they can be unloaded and set up in a few minutes. These qualities make them convenient, as they're no more difficult to configure than a tent. But they're a bad choice for clever or brawny horses who quickly learn to push against the framework and scoot the corral whichever direction they desire.

Picket lines are sturdier, but they require some practice in knot tying. Basically, a line is stretched tautly from one solid anchor to another, and each individual horse is then tied to a ring or immovable loop in the line. Horses must be kept spaced safely apart so that they cannot kick or annoy each other. Once trained to a picket line, horses accept the device willingly; it's the human who often struggles with it. First, if trees are used to anchor the picket line, something must be wrapped under the rope to prevent damage to the bark. Next, the rope must not be made of nylon because nylon stretches under stress and becomes slack. Instead, use ½-inch-diameter cotton rope, which holds its tension and remains pliable after multiple uses. You can purchase it at most hardware stores. The picket line must be above the horse's eye level. Any lower, and he could get his head hung in the line. Finally, a tie rope about 8 feet long tethers the horse from his halter to the picket line to allow the horse some freedom of movement. Although there are products on the market that make picket lines more user friendly, they're not a task for the uninitiated. Keep in mind that horses are herd animals: if one horse suddenly spooks and bolts in the middle of the night, a sloppy picket line may come crashing down if his equine friends should decide to join him.

An added ounce of security when placing a horse on a picket line can be obtained by using hobbles. As the word infers, hobbles prevent the horse from wandering away by dramatically restricting his movement. Strong leather straps (preferably lined with fleece) are placed around the horse's ankles and then coupled together. This is yet another exercise not to be tried for the first time at the campground. Horses must be trained to accept hobbles lest they panic and injure their legs. Another use for hobbles is to confine your horse's movement while he's grazing. Venues that permit open grazing give your horse a chance to experience the life that perhaps his ancestors enjoyed: munching away on the tender grasses of an open meadow.

While you're contemplating the amenities of your horse's home away from home, think about the campground's security as well. Rarely does a horse camper leave a horse unattended. When you're sleeping, snap a lock on the corral gate. If you're using a picket line or hobbles, hang a bell around the lead horse's neck, or attach it to his halter. Although the chance of someone absconding with your horse for a joy ride is remote, you can't rule out misguided pranksters or a mischievous horse. Loose horse lips can play with a snap or a knotted rope, and suddenly your horse is trotting off into the wild. Enjoy sleeping with your horse in the great outdoors, but make sure he's going to be there when you wake up.

MAKING THE RENTAL RIDE MEMORABLE

If you're horseless, or if you opt to leave your horse at home, you can still enjoy the experience of riding through many locales, thanks to concessionaires who have rental agreements with the park and forest services. One of the major benefits of renting a horse is that you can dismount, walk away, and enjoy sightseeing without worrying about leaving your horse behind. Yet, to help guarantee that your rental ride memories will be pleasant ones, there are a few tips to follow.

First, keep in mind that riding is a physical sport. If you're not in shape for riding, a trail ride may leave your knees and thighs so sore that you forego any nature hikes for the rest of your trip. If you've been out of the saddle for a while, a few riding lessons at a local stable will help you regain your riding muscles. There's no denying that riding is more enjoyable if you're physically fit; that includes maintaining a proper weight. Although a person's weight is a touchy subject, it must be considered when it comes to how it might impact a horse. A horse can develop a sore back and be unable to work if he carries an oversize rider for long distances. The general rule throughout the guest ranch industry is that a horse should not carry more than 20 percent of his weight. The average saddle horse weighs about 1,000 pounds, so 20 percent equates to a 200-pound rider. There are some ways to accommodate a heavier rider, however. For example, stable managers can arrange for the use of a larger-framed horse, providing they're made aware of that need when reservations are made.

Next, when the wrangler, guide, or stable manager inquires about your riding skills, be honest. If you're timid, say so. Being overmounted will cause you anxiety and ruin the pleasure of the ride. And if you'll be frustrated aboard a dull, lazy horse, offer to ride one who is more responsive, but don't expect to be galloping off on your own under most circumstances. Due to liability concerns, the majority of rental strings cater to the beginner or novice rider. Hence the rides are slow-paced, guided tours that are ridden head-to-tail. If you're more adventurous and really want an opportunity to bond with your rental horse while you commune with nature, seek out the sites that allow trail riders to be more independent. You may still be accompanied by a wrangler or a guide, but he or she will take you places off the beaten bridle path and treat you more like a horseman or horsewoman than like the typical tourist.

Regardless of the rental stable's protocol, use your horse sense when you're presented with your assigned mount. A horse who appears overworked, ill, or lame should not be ridden. Check the hooves for major cracks. Is a shoe loose or missing? If your horse health radar goes off, be assertive and bring your concerns to the attention of the stable manager. Since revenue depends on healthy horses and return customers, the manager will appreciate your interest.

Finally, follow one of the wise rules of the Old West: always saddle your own horse. Although the horse may already be tacked up, you're the one about to hop aboard. A broken latigo strap, a frayed cinch, or a cracked rein can spell disaster for you out on the trail. A quick inspection of your tack, including a check to make sure the cinch is properly adjusted, will demonstrate your knowledge of horsemanship and help guarantee a merry ride.

WHAT NOT TO WEAR: A GUIDE TO GEAR FOR YOU AND YOUR HORSE

Although the fashion police aren't patrolling the bridle trails, your riding adventure will go more smoothly if you and your horse are properly outfitted. Even if you're renting a horse, you need to be dressed as if you're ready to ride. Nothing alerts a rental string wrangler to your greenhorn dude status like a pair of skintight designer jeans and inappropriate footwear.

So what's the avid trail rider wearing these days? Western saddles are the norm on rental strings, and most recreational riders—even those who ride English at home—opt for the roomy, supportive seat of a western stock saddle on the trail. In keeping with tradition, a nice-fitting pair of denim jeans is standard attire. Select jeans several inches longer than necessary for street wear. That's because once you're mounted, the legs of your jeans will hike up, revealing bare ankles and short socks. Not only is that visually unappealing, but it can lead to painful rubs and skin blisters. An alternative is a pair of stretchy riding tights. If you choose to trail ride in an English saddle or simply desire the ultimate in comfort, riding tights are a good choice. They offer mild support to leg muscles yet they're still cut for an active equestrian. Will your trails take you through a lot of scratchy brush? If so, a pair of leather chaps (which cover the entire leg) or chinks (coverage is from thigh to just over the knee) will further protect your legs.

Well-made boots protect your feet, but you don't have to sacrifice comfort anymore. You shouldn't feel as if you have to kick off your boots the moment you dismount. Technology and comfort have become standard features in riding footwear, so investigate the latest styles. Originally designed for endurance riders who periodically lead their horses over rough terrain, these new age riding shoes let you go from bridle path to hiking path. If they don't meet your tastes, at least make sure you're wearing hard-soled boots that are cut high enough to offer ankle support. They must also have at least a 1-inch heel to prevent the risk of your foot slipping through a stirrup if your horse suddenly bolts forward.

Owing to the instinctive nature of the horse, sometimes even the most docile horse will spook, buck, or bolt. There's always the potential for falling off, and it's increased on a trail ride because you're either riding your own horse in foreign territory or riding an unfamiliar rental horse. You can help prevent a head injury by wearing a safety helmet that's tagged with ASTM-SEI certification for equestrian use. Although associated with English riders, there are helmets with a more workmanlike appearance than the traditional black velvet. Choose a helmet that appeals to your tastes and that fits snugly on your head without causing a headache. That way you'll be safe and comfortable.

Of course, the safety and comfort of the horse is imperative. Although you don't have much control over the tack used on a rental horse, your own horse should be outfitted in gear that is designed for trail use. Lightweight materials such as neoprene and nylon have replaced heavier leather in the construction of many accessories such as saddlebags and canteen holders. Less weight means your horse will have more stamina. An added bonus of these alternative materials is that they're water resistant, which means your lunch won't get soggy if you splash across a river.

The saddle, however, is the most important piece of tack. It must feature a comfortable seat since you'll be sitting in it for a long while. Special gel-cushioned seats are available on some models of trail saddles, but you can also purchase easy-to-pack gel and fleece pads that strap onto the seat of your saddle. For the sake of both you and your horse, your trail saddle should also be of a moderate weight. Rather than a 45-pound roping saddle, consider a lighter saddle designed for avid trail riders and their horses. Then, to cushion your horse's back, add an orthopedic gel or fleece pad. A proper saddle pad conforms to your horse's back, thereby preventing sores. But it also must allow air to circulate so that your horse doesn't develop painful hot spots under the saddle.

Although you ride in the saddle, you steer with the bridle, and that piece of tack has also undergone some changes for trail riding fans. There are combination bridles that quickly transform into halters by unsnapping the bits from the cheekpieces, theoretically allowing horses to graze or to be tied to a tree during a rest stop. But there will be some fumbling with snaps while you're trying to place a bit back in your horse's mouth. A conservative choice is to leave a thin rope halter on your horse and place the bridle over it so he's wearing both. Carry your lead rope tied to your saddle with a latigo strap. Another handy item is a get-down rope. It's a loop of braided rope placed around your horse's neck with the attached lead tethered to your saddle. This is not meant to be used to tie up your horse but rather as a convenient lead if you need to "get down" and escort your horse over difficult terrain.

A rocky, uneven, or soggy trail can lead to leg injuries for your horse. To help prevent him from nicking a tendon or bruising a heel, wrap his legs with protective boots. Splint boots for the front legs and bell boots for the front feet have saved many a trail ride from an abrupt end. Again, neoprene and nylon—along with hook-and-loop closures—make these horse care products lightweight, easy to apply, and resistant to water damage.

Thanks to the growing popularity of recreational riding, there is an abundant supply of tack, equipment, and apparel available. Do a little browsing, and you might be surprised by how much you can find to make your camping trip or rental ride a grand adventure!

SERVICE PROVIDERS AND VENDORS

Below are a few references that all horse campers and avid trail riders should keep handy. They are by no means all-inclusive but rather a sampling of the information and services available.

American Association of Equine Practitioners (AAEP)

The toll-free number provides listings of member equine vets throughout the United States. Links on its Web site also take you to informative articles related to traveling with horses written by AAEP veterinarians.
800-GET-A-DVM
http://www.myhorsematters.com

Carrilite Corrals

This is one of several companies that manufacture and distribute portable horse corrals.
888-337-SPUR
http://www.carrilitecorrals.com

Health Certificate Requirements for Transporting Horses

This government service Web site has links to horse health requirements for intrastate transport throughout the United States. The recorded, computerized phone system allows callers to access information through touch-tone prompts.
800-545-8732
http://www.aphis.usda.gov/vs/sregs

Horse Motel Locator

These Web sites offer prepaid listings of private and public stables that will provide overnight stays for horses on the road.
http://www.horsetrip.com
http://www.horsemotel.com

Jeffers Equine

Jeffers offers horse health care products and common tack items at discount prices.
800-533-3377
http://www.jeffersequine.com

Montana Mountain Horse

This vendor sells a wide range of practical horse camping gear for the truly dedicated trail rider.
866-781-4465
http://www.montanamountainhorse.com

State Line Tack

This popular catalog and Web site offers a wide selection of footwear, ASTM-SEI safety helmets, tack, chaps, and accessories appropriate for trail riders, all at discount prices.
800-228-9208
http://www.statelinetack.com

Tucker Trail Saddles

This company sells a distinctive style of lightweight trail saddle made with a patented gel-cushioned seat.
800-882-5375
http://www.tuckersaddles.com

U.S. Rider

For an annual fee, members subscribe to an equestrian motor plan that includes roadside assistance when hauling horses.
800-844-1409
http://www.usrider.org

Valley Vet Supply

This vendor sells discounted horse health care items such as ice packs and temporary horseshoe boots, and recreational riding equipment such as picket line kits.
800-356-1005
http://www.valleyvet.com

Looking to the trails

*F*ollowing are some national organizations that can provide information on trail riding and other trail riding locales. You can find information on state parks that allow horses by contacting the state park office for the state you are visiting. To find state parks online, type the name of the state you want to search for and the words *state parks, parks and recreation, parks and tourism*, or something similar. You can also contact the local horse council or trail organization for your state for leads on trail information. Visit the American Horse Council Web site at http://www.horsecouncil.org/sites.htm for links to state horse councils and trail organizations.

NATIONAL ORGANIZATIONS

Back Country Horsemen of America
PO Box 1367
Graham, WA 98338
888-893-5161
http://www.backcountryhorse.com

Bureau of Land Management
1849 C Street, Room 406-LS
Washington, DC 20240
202-452-5125
http://www.blm.gov

National Park Service
U.S. Department of the Interior
1849 C Street NW
Washington, DC 20240
202-208-6843
http://www.nps.gov

North American Trail Ride Conference
PO Box 224
Sedalila, CO 80135
303-688-1677
http://www.natrc.org

Rails-to-Trails Conservancy
1100 17th Street, NW, 10th Floor
Washington, DC 20036
202-331-9696
http://www.railstotrails.org
(organization website) or
http://www.traillink.com (trail search page)

USDA Forest Service
1400 Independence Avenue, SW
Washington, DC 20250
202-205-8333
http://www.fs.fed.us

PHOTO CREDITS

The images in this book are provided courtesy of the following:

COVER

Front cover: Sharon P. Fibelkorn. Back cover **(far left):** © Bonnie Sue; **(middle left):** Cherie Langlois; **(middle right and bottom):** © CLiX/Shawn Hamilton; **(far right):** National Park Service. **Inside back flap:** Kathleen Zechmeister-Bishop.

FRONT MATTER

2, 6, 8: © CLiX/Shawn Hamilton.

THE NORTHEAST

11 (far left), 14 (right), 15, 29 (center), 33 (bottom), 38 (bottom): L. Diane Lackie. **11 (center left), 17 (top right):** Greater Boston Convention & Visitors Bureau. **11 (center right), 21:** Jennifer Hammell/www.butterflyink designs.com. **11 (right), 32:** New York Railroads. **14 (top), 16 (left):** © Bonnie Sue. **12 (bottom), 19, 33 (top):** Fred Mastele. **13 (left), 18 (bottom), 24, 25 (top), 27 (bottom), 37 (top), 41:** © CLiX/Shawn Hamilton. **13 (right):** Connecticut Commission on Culture & Tourism. **16 (right), 20, 30 (right):** National Park Service. **17 (bottom), 22 (right), 29 (top):** Heidi Nyland. **12 (top), 18 (top):** Bev McMullen. **22 (left), 26 (center), 27 (top):** © Donald T. Kelly. **23:** Nancy M. McCallum. **25 (bottom):** Ron and Diane Salmon. **26 (top):** Jessica Fredyma, JAF Equine Photography. **26 (bottom):** USDA Forest Service, Allegheny National Forest. **27 (center):** Rhode Island Tourism Division. **29 (bottom):** Melissa Devine, Rhode Island Tourism Division. **30 (left):** Peter Travers. **31:** Walden Pond State Reservation, the Massachusetts Department of Conservation and Recreation (DCR), © Kindra Clineff for the DCR. **34:** Eochaidh Stables. **36:** White Lilac Inn. **37 (bottom):** Jim Somers. **38 (top):** Atlantic Brewing Company. **39:** Union Oyster House.

THE SOUTHEAST

43 (far left), 48, 55 (left and top right), 57, 62 (bottom): © CLiX/Shawn Hamilton. **43 (center left), 46 (bottom), 47, 58, 62 (top):** Ron and Diane Salmon. **43 (center right), 49:** Jane Faircloth/TRANSPARENCIES, Inc. **43 (far right), 51, 52 (top):** Robert Clark/TRANSPARENCIES, Inc. **44, 45, 46 (top), 53, 59 (top), 61 (bottom), 64:** National Park Service. **50 (left), 59 (bottom):** Kim and Kari Baker. **50 (right), 52 (bottom), 56 (top):** Heidi Nyland. **54:** Bev McMullen. **55 (bottom right):** Aaron Stevenson/TRANS-PARENCIES, Inc. **56 (bottom):** Harold Street/Wilburn Ridge Pony Association. **61 (top):** Gary Berdeaux/National Park Service. **62 (center):** Rich Thompson, Town Creek Indian Mound. **63:** Aiken Thoroughbred Racing Hall of Fame & Museum. **66:** Hoof Prints in the Sand. **68:** Uwharrie Stables.

THE SOUTH:

77 (far left), 78, 79 (top), 80: Arkansas Dept. of Parks & Tourism. **77 (center**

left), 81 (top), 93: Kennedy Space Center Visitor Complex. 77 (center right), 79 (bottom), 82 (left), 89 (bottom), 103: © CLiX/Shawn Hamilton. 77 (far right), 81 (bottom), 83 (top), 95: National Park Service. 82 (right), 94: NASA. 83 (bottom), 85 (bottom), 88 (bottom left): Bev McMullen. 84, 87: **Heidi Nyland**. 85 (top): Jessica Fredyma, JAF Equine Photography. 86, 88 (top and center), 89 (top), 91: Kim and Kari Baker.

THE MIDWEST:

105 (far left), 107, 108 (top): Wendy Daugherty. 105 (center left), 111 (bottom), 112: Larry Ulrich. 105 (center right), 108 (bottom), 121 (bottom), 130: Brown County Convention & Visitors Bureau. 105 (far right), 113 (center), 123, 131: Ohio Division of Travel and Tourism. 106 (top): Nancy M. McCallum. 106 (bottom), 121 (top): Illinois Bureau of Tourism. 109 (right): © CLiX/Shawn Hamilton. 109 (left), 114: Heidi Nyland. 110: Marji Silk/Travel Michigan. 111 (top): Thomas A. Schneider/Travel Michigan. 113 (top), 119 (bottom): Courtesy of the National Park Service, photos by Tom Jones. 113 (bottom): Pamela Burton, Photojournalist. 115 (top): © Bonnie Sue. 115 (bottom): Bonnie Gruber, Wisconsin Department of Natural Resources. 116: A.B. Sheldon. 117: Wildcat Mountain State Park. 118: ©Linda Sherrill. 119 (top): http://www.travelwisconsin.com. 122 (left): Vito Palmisano/Travel Michigan. 122 (right): Travel Michigan. 133: Bev McMullen.

THE GREAT PLAINS

135 (far left), 136 (center and bottom), 154 (top): Brushy Creek Recreation Area. 135 (center left), 152 (bottom): VisitBemidji. 135 (center right), 140 (bottom), 141 (top), 147: Bev McMullen. 135 (far right), 153: Black Hills Wild Horse Sanctuary. 136 (top), 140 (top), 161. © CLiX/Shawn Hamilton. 137, 138 (top), 154 (bottom): Bryan Pulliam. 138 (bottom), 139: Wendy Bowles. 141 (bottom), 143 (center and bottom): U.S. Army Corp of Engineers. 142: Pamela Burton, Photojournalist. 143 (top): Heidi Nyland. 144: © 2002 Erik Stenbakken/stenbakken.com. 145, 152 (top): Nebraska Division of Travel and Tourism, part of Nebraska Department of Economic Development. 145 (center), 146 (top), 149 (center): National Park Service. 146 (bottom): Kim and Kari Baker. 148, 149 (top): Elwin Trump. 149 (bottom): L. Diane Lackie. 151 (left top and bottom): International Horse Archery Festival, Inc. 151 (center): Chris Newton. 160: Wall Drug Store.

THE WEST

163 (far left), 164 (bottom), 180: © Donald T. Kelly. 163 (center left), 184 (bottom): Idaho Department of Parks and Recreation. 163 (center right), 166, 168 (left), 169, 172, 174 (bottom), 175 (center), 176, 181, 184 (center), 185 (top and bottom): National Park Service. 163 (far right), 185 (center): Jackson Hole Chamber of Commerce. 164 (top), 175 (bottom): Londie G. Padelsky. 165 (top), 183: L. Diane Lackie. 165 (bottom), 168 (right), 171 (bottom), 175 (top): © CLiX/Shawn Hamilton. 167 (top): Elwin Trump. 167 (bottom), 179: Nancy M. McCallum. 170: Idaho Travel Council. 171 (top), 173, 174 (top), 178 (top): Kim and Kari Baker. 177 (top): **Cherie Langlois**. 177 (bottom), 178 (bottom), 193: Jim Peaco, National Park Service. 184 (top): Estes Park Museum. 186 (top): J. Tyers,

National Park Service. **186 (bottom):** Ed Bovy, National Park Service. **197:** Jo Suderman, National Park Service.

THE PACIFIC NORTHWEST

199 (far left), 200, 202 (bottom), 215, 217 (bottom): Bev McMullen. **199 (center left), 204 (left), 216:** © Tom Till. **199 (middle right), 201, 205, 207 (bottom), 208, 209 (bottom), 210 (right, bottom left), 211, 213 (bottom):** National Park Service. **199 (far right), 206, 217 (top):** Cherie Langlois. **202 (top), 203 (top), 207 (top), 210 (top left), 227:** © CLiX/Shawn Hamilton. **203 (bottom), 204 (right):** Kim and Kari Baker. **209 (top):** L. Diane Lackie. **213 (top):** Pamela Burton, Photojournalist.

THE SOUTHWEST

229 (far left and middle left), 232 (bottom), 233 (right), 234 (bottom), 240, 241 (left), 244, 249 (bottom left), 253: National Park Service. **229 (middle right), 250:** Courtesy of the New Mexico Tourism Dept., photo by Dan Monaghan. **229 (far right), 250:** PhotoDisc, Inc. **230, 231 (top), 246 (top), 249 (top):** Cherie Langlois. **231 (bottom), 245:** Bev McMullen. **232 (top):** Ron and Diane Salmon. **233 (left), 241 (top right), 247 (bottom):** © CLiX/Shawn Hamilton. **234 (top):** © Linda Sherrill. **235:** New Mexico Tourism Dept., photo by Jim Orr. **237, 238, 239, 255:** Oklahoma Tourism & Recreation Department. **241 (bottom):** Nancy M. McCallum. **242 (top), 249 (bottom right):** Londie G. Padelsky. **242 (bottom), 243:** Texas Parks and Wildlife Department. **246 (bottom):** Elwin Trump. **247 (top):** © Donald T. Kelly. **251 (right):** © Tom Till. **258:** Rick Maehle, Tucson Convention & Visitors Bureau.

THE FAR WEST

263 (far left), 264, 265, 277 (bottom), 282 (top): Londie G. Padelsky. **263 (center left), 280 (top and center):** Julian Chamber of Commerce. **263 (center right), 266 (center), 268, 269, 271, 272 (bottom), 273, 274, 277 (center bottom), 278 (top), 280 (bottom):** National Park Service. **263 (far right), 272 (top), 282 (bottom):** © Ron Dahlquist. **266 (top), 270, 275 (top), 276:** © CLiX/Shawn Hamilton. **266 (bottom), 267, 277 (top):** L. Diane Lackie. **275 (bottom):** Washoe Lake State Recreation Area. **277 (center top):** Cherie Langlois. **278 (bottom):** Ron and Diane Salmon. **281:** Bev McMullen. **284:** Pamela Burton, Photojournalist.

BACK MATTER

292: © CLiX/Shawn Hamilton. **294:** Heidi Nyland. **304:** Kim and Kari Baker

INDEX